THE MEXICAN FOOD DIET™ 2ND EDITION

HEALTHY EATING THAT FEELS LIKE CHEATING™

Maru Dávila

Healthy, Beautiful and Happy!

THE MEXICAN FOOD DIET™
Healthy Eating That Feels Like Cheating™

Get Healthy, Lose Weight and Improve your Mood with Delicious Food!

Want the recipes in full color? Sign up today to get a pdf file with all the recipes from this book in full color. You will also get exclusive access to book updates, special bonuses, and free useful information and training on health, wellness, healthy cooking, and many other topics to support your journey to get healthy, lose weight, and feel happy.

Register now at www.flacaforever.com/TheMexicanFoodDiet

Your Best Self Ever, Inc.
7514 Girard Avenue, 1-337
La Jolla, CA 92037

Info@flacaforever.com

www.TheMexicanFoodDiet.com

www.FlacaForever.com

FOR BOOKING, PRESS & SPEAKING INQUIRIES:

info@flacaforever.com

CONTENTS

BONUSES

As a thank you for buying this book, I want to give you some free bonuses!

Simply register your book at:
www.flacaforever.com/TheMexicanFoodDiet.

YOU WILL RECEIVE:

- Receive all the recipes from this book in PDF format, so you can print them if you'd like.
- Free updates to your Kindle version of this book. We will be continuously adding and improving the content (like more recipes, videos for the recipes), and you can get all the updates for free!
- A variety of tips, training, recipes, and tools to stay on track with your health, your weight, and your healthy cooking.
- A 15% discount on the print version of this book, coming out soon.
- A $20 coupon to be used for any of my Flaca Forever® products like the Flaca Detox™ Reset and Renew Program, Flaca Get Lean™ Weight Los Program, Flaca Stay Lean™ All-in-One Shake, or Flaca Choco-Coconut™ Healthy Snack Bars. You can find the products at the shop at www.FlacaForever.com.
- The opportunity to apply for a complimentary Health and Weight Loss Breakthrough Session, where we will identify YOUR best next steps to creating your best self ever. This is a $497 value (limited availability).

Like us on Facebook!   Follow us on Instagram!
Flacaforever1   Flacaforever1

DEDICATION

To my daughter, Charlotte, and all the amazing kids around the world. May you learn soon enough that your future depends on the type of food you eat today and every day for the rest of your lives.

May you learn soon enough how to choose food that makes you healthier, more beautiful, smarter, and happier—and NOT food that can do the opposite.

FOREWORD-BY JJ VIRGIN

In September 2012, the importance of self-care became brutally apparent during the worst time of my life.

A few weeks before *The Virgin Diet* launched, my then-16-year-old son Grant crossed the street one night and became the victim of a hit-and-run and was basically left for dead.

Despite this horrendous tragedy, I couldn't stop this crucial book launch. After all, I'm a single mom and sole financial support for my two sons. I invested everything in that book, and if that launch didn't happen correctly, I would go bankrupt.

Grant ended up being in the hospital for four and a half months. I stayed beside him the entire time and literally launched my first *New York Times* bestselling book from the hospital.

Few experiences prove more stressful than launching a book while someone you love is in the hospital. People asked me how I juggled such a herculean responsibility while being my son's primary caregiver.

While I want to say you can't prepare yourself for such trauma, to some extent you absolutely can when you focus on your own health and wellbeing.

Perhaps that might sound selfish, but it's anything but: I've seen too many women put their health on the back burner to care for their family or loved ones, and have that neglect seriously backfire later.

Realistically, I couldn't have functioned (much less thrived) or maintained strength and focus during that nightmarish time without eight hours of sleep, burst training, eating well, controlling stress, and relying on friends and colleagues.

When you're not at the top of your game, you can't help those around them. You can't be your personal best to someone who desperately needs and deserves that attention when you don't prioritize your own health.

Maru Dávila understands that, and self-care becomes the basis of *The Mexican Food Diet*. She knows you need to be lean and healthy, yet you don't have hours to spend in the kitchen or at the gym.

Maru learned self-care's importance when she overcame her own depression to care for her daughter's asthma and help her mom reverse her autoimmune disease.

Eliminating food intolerances, particularly dairy and gluten, became the key in that last situation. I've seen this numerous times working with my own clients who reversed chronic illnesses, lost weight, and created optimal health by removing highly reactive foods, or as Maru calls them, "stupid foods."

These foods sabotage your health and weight, trigger inflammation, undermine your immune system, create hormonal imbalances, spike toxicity, and damage gut health.

You can do everything correctly, but if you're eating stupid foods (heads up: some you might even consider healthy), your fat loss crashes to a grinding halt, you'll feel terrible, and you'll lack the energy or focus to serve others.

Fortunately, following the right course doesn't demand superwoman effort. Rather than become an impossible-to-maintain diet, Maru's plan radically simplifies things and takes the guesswork out about what to eat. Flavorful, delicious foods, not deprivation and hunger, become this plan's foundation.

Through her book, Maru provides you the tools to detoxify, reduce cravings, lower inflammation, and create hormonal balance that will leave you feeling lean and sexy.

These fundamentals can change your life, helping you get off the yo-yo diet roller coaster and paving the path towards becoming vitality and happiness.

Maru calls them "smart foods," those that support fat loss, minimize toxicity, improve your mood and emotions, reduce inflammation, and help maintain hormonal balance.

Around these foods Maru designs a sensible, easy-to-apply "smart" plan that incorporates things like optimized sleep, stress control, smart supplementing, and exercise that effortlessly fit into the busiest lifestyle.

Within these pages, you have the tools to ditch that refuse-to-vacate belly fat, cultivate vital health, and transform your life.

You only get one life, and every day becomes an opportunity to shine. Self-care ultimately becomes crucial for you to be your best for yourself and others. You deserve it, but you also have an obligation to be that brilliant, amazing, sexy person you were destined to be.

"*The Mexican Food Diet* is for you if you don't want to go through your life without knowing what absolute wellness feels like," writes Maru. "Believe me, you may think you know it, but you will find out you don't and will be glad you did what it took to discover and enjoy absolute wellness."

Here's to your health, happiness, and absolute wellness.

JJ Virgin

SUCCESS STORIES

Very soon after starting Maru's Mexican Food Diet™ I got rid of the bloating and gas I always had following meals. I had been struggling with stomach pains for years and thought they were something I would have to live with forever, so just by getting rid of this, I was already sold on this nutritional plan. As I continued with Maru's diet, I felt happier, and less irritable with my family, and more patient with my children. I could make it through the day without needing caffeine or wishing I could take a nap mid-day, and I was excited about every aspect of my life.

Seeing the great results I got with The Mexican Food Diet™, I felt motivated to accelerate my journey and the weight loss. So, I started the Get Clean, Get Lean, Stay Lean™ Program, and through it all, I managed to lose 16 pounds and 5 sizes over several months. I started at size 9 and got down to a size 3. I am excited to go out with my husband because I feel sexy and excited to show off my new shape. I have never felt more confident in my own skin, which by the way, is clear from this diet. I don't have to wear as much makeup, and I love all of the compliments I receive from people telling me that I look younger and that I am glowing.

The reason all my past diets failed was because I was not educated in nutrition. You don't need to be an expert. You just need someone like Maru leading you down the right path. She knows exactly what steps to take to lose weight and keep it off, and to find happiness along the way! Through the Mexican Food Diet™, I have gained the tools I needed to change my lifestyle, and it has also affected my family in amazing ways. I now cook healthier food for my kids and husband, and they are happier, healthier, and more energized as a result. I loved Maru's Flaca Detox™ which cleansed more of my body toxins, and while I thought it wasn't possible, it gave me even more energy! I love my lean body and my life!

~ Laura, 30, Mom of 3 kids

Maru's book is the missing link between starving yourself to look good and micromanaging your eating habits. I could never complete a full day without eating something unhealthy with bad carbs or too much sugar. Even though, I'm thin and in relatively good health, I've always struggled with slight phlegm down my throat, a spongy look on my thin body, and a periodic bloated belly. I always tried to eat healthy . . . (until around 5 o'clock when my sugar cravings would start), so after I read Maru's book, everything started to make sense! Sugar, dairy products, and wheat do not make my body happy!!!! I started to buy and eat the foods in Maru's Mexican Food Diet™ Plan and in only two weeks, my phlegm was gone!!! I don't have a swollen belly, **and I lost fat by eating more!!!**

Fancy dinners, trips, or parties can break my healthy eating, and I immediately notice a swollen or achy belly and stiff joints. The minute I am back home I start eating in a detoxing way, and in a couple of days I feel great again. It only took fifteen days to convince myself of how to eat for the rest of my life!!!

I plan to give this book to my mom and my friends who have a lot of extra weight and are full of aches and pains. Gracias, Maru!

~ Marianela, 48, Mom and Business Owner

Thank you very much for writing this book that has interested me so much. I realize that you have studied very well the whole nutrition issue that has to do with staying in your ideal weight but above all in a healthy way.

The tips and the recipes have been very useful for me to feel energized and lose the weight that had been bothering me. We believe that we know everything that makes us fat, but thanks to all the information in your book, I have realized the mistakes that we make when wanting to lose weight in an incorrect way. Hopefully soon we can have your book in Spanish and in a print-version in Mexico. I would like very much to be able to easily consult it and make annotations that would be very useful to me. Thanks, Maru.

~ Maria Antonieta, 71, Mom and Investor

I just finished reading Maru's book, *The Mexican Food Diet*, and strongly encourage you to read it. 2017 has been a year seeking alternative modalities to better manage my existing condition. This book has reiterated many things I have learned during my healthier path. Maru effectively captured valuable information in this book, and I can't wait to try the yummy recipes. I am so proud of you, Maru, "y soy muy afortunada de conocerte".

~ Venus, 48

Hi Maru, My daughter and I went on the 7-day diet, and we loved it, I truly loved cooking all the food, and it was so delicious! The whole family loved these 7 days because it was so tasty for them (and healthy). My mom always made the chile/salsa when growing up, and sadly I never followed this tradition until now, so a BIG THANKS to Maru for showing me!

~ Lorraine S.

A wonderful diet book targeted towards a Hispanic-American audience, who as a group wrestle with obesity, based mainly on their traditional diet. The book offers an educated take on Western nutrition issues many people have today, such as too much gluten, oils, and other fats. Mexican food, at least in the United States, is thought of as a heavy meal, but Maru Davila presents 21+ meals (breakfast/lunch/dinner, plus snacks and dessert), which are low carbohydrate, gluten-free, sugar-free, and cholesterol friendly.

The 7 days are a "kick-start" diet that will lead a person into a longer plan to lose weight and maintain a new level. In that sense it is similar to the cabbage soup diet, previously known as the Dolly Parton diet, seven days with a similar weight loss predicted. After 7 days she believes the reader will lose 7 pounds.

Maru Davila's own accomplished journey was plagued with digestive issues as well as fatigue, which she eventually traced to gluten and sugar-based foods. Overcoming these problems and regaining her energy led to the writing of this book as well as a nutrition consulting business and several related products.

~ Robert, 62, Investor

Nice yummy recipes for those of us who love Mexican food. It is a great addition to any cooking library. I have never been on a "diet." I just love to eat good healthy food. Maru, the author, is a delight if you get the good fortune to see her on TV.

~ Paul

I've seen author and chef Maru Davila on television more than once, and the food she makes is fun and easy. I expect to eat happy saying, "Adios, extra pounds. Thanks but, no thank you, fat gut."

~ Thomas

WELCOME-HOW CHANGING MY DIET SAVED MY LIFE

I learned the hard way that food can either empower me to be my best self, or it can take away my power and rob me of my life. Most people are like me: they wait until sickness strikes before they realize this truth. I have gone through hundreds of challenges in my life, positioning me as an expert to guide you, so you do not struggle for thirty years as I did or lose everything as I almost did—my health, my business, and my relationship. I expended incredible amounts of energy to be thin, so I could feel good about myself, losing sight of what truly mattered in my life—health and happiness. It was when I gained up to 60 pounds that the transformation happened. I wanted to fully understand what was strongly affecting my physical and mental health.

I feel blessed that I learned the SMART way of eating and living that allowed me to lose the weight and keep it off without starving myself or needing excessive exercise (which never worked). Today I enjoy eating abundantly, but the right kind of foods. I have also recovered my health, my happiness, and joy, as well as my focus and drive. It sounds like a miracle, but it is not. With these experiences in hand, I have created a simple but effective diet and plan that can guide you to get healthier, lose the weight you want, and get a life you love.

BEFORE AFTER

My struggle to gain control of my weight began at age fifteen. Like many teens (and adults) of this generation, I was obsessed with the existing craze for low-fat foods and counting calories. As a type A personality, I went all the way. I stopped eating all fat and became a "fat detective." Simultaneously, I was hooked on the aerobics fad, on top of training for a swim team that involved exercising for several hours a day. Soon, I became extremely thin, and I lost my period. Not aware of how thin I was, I still worried about putting any fat in my mouth and counted every calorie I consumed. I received hormones to regain my period. The treatment made me gain quite a bit of weight. From there began a very painful and dangerous journey of eating disorders and yo-yo dieting. As high achievers, our norm is to keep moving and reach our goals, and not be concerned with the status of our health or how we treat our bodies until we reach a physical and mental bottom.

Maru at 15

My breakdown included multiple physical and emotional health issues, food addictions, and punishing myself by malnourishment or excessive exercising. My journey could have been fatal had it not been for my accidental stumbling into nutrition in my early forties. I did not find nutrition. Nutrition found me.

THE START OF MY JOURNEY

I was born in Mexico City and lived there for twenty-six years before moving to the United States where I happily reside today with my family. I am Mexican-American, and the first woman in my family to not only go to college and graduate school but to attend an Ivy League school: the prestigious Harvard Business School. I was also the first woman in the family to work at a Fortune 500 company (Procter & Gamble) as a brand manager while I was still going to college. I am also the first woman in my family to have a baby after forty. A lot of firsts!

I do not state my firsts to brag but to tell you that with all this drive to achieve, I had a very busy and stressful life as a young adult. My focus was on achieving as much as possible, both in a very demanding college and a very competitive corporation. My days started with college classes at 7am, then work from 9 to 6 or later, then school from 7 to 9 at night. I also managed to keep a quite active social life. You may be wondering how did I do all this. I did it by sleeping very little, skipping lots of meals, and then binging on sugar and junk in the afternoons or evenings to be able to complete my day and to deal with the stress. When I was not binging, I was eating almost nothing, trying to compensate for the poor food choices I had made. My health started to show the first signs of deterioration during this phase of my early 20s. I began to faint at work and while going out. I was diagnosed with hypoglycemia, which is a condition that occurs when the sugar levels in your blood are too low either because your body is unable to keep sugar levels stable or you produce too much insulin. In my case, it was mainly an inability to keep blood sugar stable because I had no regular eating schedule, was skipping meals too often, and my food choices involved lots of sugar or carbs. I started a medical treatment and eventually bounced back. It is amazing what a young person's body can tolerate. I cannot believe the amount of abuse my body was able to put up with for so many years.

MY HARVARD DIET

HARVARD BUSINESS SCHOOL

As I look back at my life, I can see that when I was accepted at Harvard Business School, I did not have the tools to handle the pressure that came along with such a commitment. When you combine the lack of tools, immaturity, anxiety, the compulsion to eat away stress, and the hard work to survive the workload and expectations at Harvard, you have a very dangerous combination.

I began a long journey of simultaneously using food as a friend and an enemy, and suffered from eating disorders. To be specific, the foods I ate to relieve my stress were junk foods: lots of sweets and refined carbs, like cakes, cookies, ice cream, bread, etc. After my frequent night binges, I would always feel awful the following day and would punish myself by not eating or by over-exercising. I did not know at the time how dangerous and addictive sugar and junk foods were, and how much they were going to impact me later in all areas of my life. The sugar and carbs I was consuming were affecting my brain and my overall health. I also did not know how malnourished I was getting by trying to eat very little when I was not binging. I was barely managing to get by at Harvard, and after the first year, it was clear that I had to take a year off to get myself back together and finish the second year. This was devastating, but I am not a quitter, so I committed to come back and finish. And I did.

All through my life and even more at that time, I had done everything without any kind of support system. I had no one to talk to and was completely on my own to navigate nutrition, challenges, stress, and expectations.

DEPRESSION MAKES AN APPEARANCE

By the time I graduated from Harvard Business School, my emotional and digestive health were at an all-time low. I was insecure and unsure of who I was or where I wanted to go next. I had been putting junk in my body for too long, and now, parts of my future were starting to look like junk too. Although I began to sense that something was wrong, I did not have the nutritional education or guidance to figure out what was wrong. Little did I know, more negative changes, both physically and emotionally, were in store for me.

More problems with digestion developed, as well as depression and emotional anxiety. I learned to live with the on-and-off depression for almost two decades, seeing psychiatrists or psychologists, and taking antidepressants from time to time. Then the issue became very serious. I was busy running several businesses in male-dominated industries and co-founding a public bank. The medications I was taking for some of the digestive problems were worsening my condition even further.

Life went by, and I was suddenly 42, and finally a mother to a beautiful little girl. This was the happiest moment of my life, but it was short-lived. Although I seemed to be a happy and optimistic person all the time, I could never shake off the increasingly severe case of depression building up inside of me.

Even more, health problems developed. Some of them included chronic sinus and yeast infections that no medicine could resolve, asthma, joint pains, severe indigestion, anxiety, and depression. Over time, they got worse. I was frequently going to doctors and getting tests, living on expensive antibiotics, which only gave me relief for a short while. My life had become a complete disaster. Not only did my physical and mental state continue to deteriorate, but my finances had been compromised due to my inability to focus on my business and career.

I had no idea that my eating choices and problems would be causing such drastic conditions in my family and robbing me of my health, focus, money, and peace of mind.

SUPPORT BECOMES THE SAVIOR

While depression brought up a lot of problems in my life, it led me to the discovery of the importance of healthy eating.

Throughout my life, I was frequently traveling new paths where no one in my social or familial circle had been before. As a result, I never had role models or support groups to follow, so I created solutions by myself. One day I had the opportunity to join a women's support group, and I am grateful I decided to join. The group was part of an organization whose mission is to empower leaders to engage, learn, and grow, and it provided us with invaluable tools, resources, and learning opportunities. My decision to join was life-changing. It would be the first time in my life to be part of a group like this. The group's objective was to provide support and accountability, so that we, participants, could improve our lives.

One day, in a group discussion, I revealed that everything in my life was getting worse, and I was getting hopeless. The group suggested I find an item in my bucket list that could give me a new hope and focus. I had always dreamed about doing a triathlon, but I saw it as something that was unreachable and just a nice dream. My group motivated me to register for one and even committed to doing it with me even though most of the members were not the athletic type. So now, I had to do it. Little did I know that indirectly, this decision was going to save my life and my relationship, and would lead me to start the business of my dreams!

I began to train for the upcoming triathlon, but as always, I did it on my own. The race included a swim in the ocean, and on the day of the race, a storm created huge waves. I had not trained adequately for a challenge like that, so I had to be rescued and was disqualified from my first race. While I was disappointed, the failure opened my eyes to how much guidance and support I needed instead of trying to do everything on my own as I had done in so many areas of my life previously. As a result, I sought out the best coaches and training groups for each of the sports: swimming, biking, and running. I surrounded myself with successful people.

When I started, it was hard to be the worst in the training groups, but I committed to religiously following the plans that my coaches created for me. There would be no shortcuts. No reinventing the wheel. They knew how to succeed, and I didn't. So, I would do what they said because I didn't want to fail again. On my second race, I came in eighth, which inspired me to do another one. In my third race, I came in first!

At this point, I was asked to join a women's racing team, and of course, I accepted because I already knew the power of being surrounded and supported by strong, like-minded women.

It was extremely fortunate that the head of our team, Andi, a beautiful, strong, and successful triathlete herself, offered us a nutritional program to help improve our performance. I decided to take the opportunity, and this started the whole progression to where I am today—offering you a solution through **The Mexican Food Diet**™ Plan and my other programs at FlacaForever.com.

AN EPIPHANY: THE STRONG CONNECTION BETWEEN HEALTH AND FOOD

I followed the nutrition plan of the women's group religiously because I was motivated to continue winning in my races. I already knew the power of doing what the experts recommend. To my surprise, several more positive changes began to arise from the changes in my diet. Apart from the significant weight loss that I had not been able to achieve solely through my intensive trainings, which some days included up to 6 hours a day, I noticed that my digestive problems, chronic yeast and sinus infections, joint pain, and asthma were no longer a problem, and my emotional status had also been further uplifted. For the first time in my life I felt the strong connection between my health and my eating. It was a huge epiphany—a cure for my diseased life—and I felt so liberated.

HELPING MILLIONS LOSE WEIGHT AND TRANSFORM

I was inspired and curious about learning more, so I switched careers and joined the Institute of Integrative Nutrition to become an integrative nutrition health and wellness coach. As I increased my knowledge in the field, I focused on developing a system to make nutrition one of my strongest allies. Soon I created a customized nutrition plan for myself, which not only helped me look younger than ever—even after the age of forty—

but also helped me regain the confidence I had lost from all those unhealthy and unproductive years.

How would you like to look younger than your age from simply eating what is right for YOUR body and have confidence and purpose?

While I was going through my studies of integrative nutrition, I learned most of my issues were related to certain foods I was eating that my body could not process. I ran a food sensitivity test. I tested "highly sensitive" to gluten and dairy, specifically to whey and casein, the two proteins in dairy (which are discussed extensively in the book). Having these undiagnosed sensitivities had kept my body in a chronic state of inflammation and toxicity that had kept me fat, sick, and sad for many years.

This inflammation and toxicity had been building up for many years, but I had not been aware of it until it finally started to show up in many ways—an inability to lose weight, easy weight gain, frequent sinus and yeast infections, asthma, joint pain, migraines, depression, anxiety, brain fog, loss of drive and motivation, etc. I frequently see similar things happening to people as they approach their 40s or are in their early 40s.

I realized that my team's diet had excluded the consumption of dairy and gluten, and this had allowed my body to heal, resulting in the disappearance of my health issues. As a result, my better self emerged with a stronger and more determined drive. (Toxicity is covered in detail in the book.)

After I saw the great results in my body, my health, and my brain, I suspected that my daughter's severe respiratory and skin issues could also be related to food. So, I changed my daughter's diet, suspending milk and all other dairy products. This was a hard decision at the time, for I still believed milk was indispensable for children's growth. The irony is that milk was creating major respiratory problems for her, which required frequent use of antibiotics and treatments that compromised her growth and her future health. After a few months of eliminating dairy, her colds began to get more spread out and respiratory complications became minor. After a few more months, her asthma disappeared. Later, I did a food sensitivity blood test on her that confirmed that she is also extremely sensitive to dairy and a couple other things that I removed from her diet.

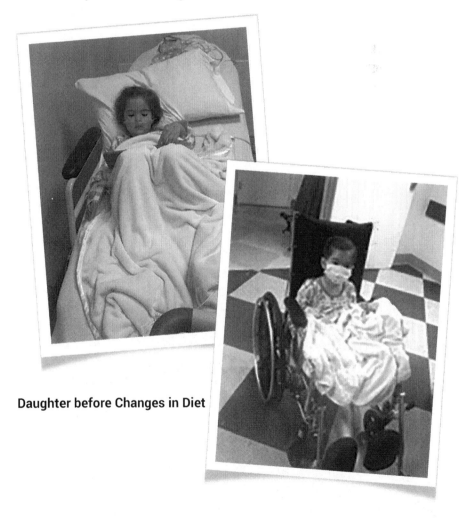

Daughter before Changes in Diet

On her next annual checkup, my daughter's doctor was surprised about her strong growth and intrigued about our lack of visits during the past year. Until this point, we had been coming to the doctor's office or a hospital almost every month and sometimes more frequently. When I explained to the doctor about the changes in her diet and her sensitivities, he was surprised. I could not believe that I had been the one to know how to cure my daughter's problems. I feel blessed for having the opportunity to impact her future in such an important way. Today, she is not only tall and healthy, but she is super smart, happy, and positive, which I know is a result of a fully-nourished brain and body.

In my case also, none of my doctors ever suspected that my food sensitivities could be at the root of my health issues. They had just kept on giving me antibiotics and steroids. Now I know that traditional doctors are trained to treat illnesses and symptoms, and not to find the causes of the illnesses.

Mom and Daughter after Changing Their Diets

These direct experiences shaped my core mission:

"I want to be at the front line of the new movement to educate people on how much food can affect their health, their weight, and their brain".

~ Maru Dávila

After I graduated from the Institute of Integrative Nutrition, laden with valuable knowledge in the field of integrative nutrition, I pursued an in-depth study in a variety of health and weight-loss fields. My objective was to further strengthen my customized plans so that I could help millions of people transform their lives as I'd done.

DISCOVERY OF THE MEXICAN FOOD DIET™

During the 30 years of struggling with my weight, I stayed away from Mexican food because, just like many people, I thought it was unhealthy and caused weight gain. Once I concluded my studies as an Integrative Nutrition Health Coach and became experienced and confident in my knowledge, I experimented with new foods and diets. I was determined to find an easy, nutrition-packed, and delicious way to reach my weight, health, and wellness goals in a sustainable way. No more short-term gains. I was ready for permanent progress. I was ready to share my findings with my clients.

It was not completely about the number on the scale anymore but about how I looked and felt in my clothes and throughout my days. Good nutrition not only helps with the weight and beauty of a person, but it also glorifies everything else in a person's life. Whether it's emotional issues, strained relationships, or poor health, it is my duty to help you remove such barriers to achieve in life what you would not have thought possible. Some of you may be like me, driven entrepreneurs who can't find time for their own health. Others may be stay-at-home moms or dads who put everyone else's needs before their own. Good nutrition is for everyone. We all deserve the best life.

My own tough life has taught me the love of nutrition in the most unique and surprising way. I have survived to the point where food almost ruined me, but I fought and turned nutrition from my enemy into my biggest power. The outcome? I am now healthier, happier, and I feel utterly empowered by my self-created healthy-eating regime. As the title of the book says, I make sure that I have "healthy eating that feels like cheating," which is a lot of fun, and I am now on a mission to share this with you.

I am not alone. Thousands of families wage the same war against the havoc that their health, weight, and food problems are wreaking in their lives. I am thankful for what my own journey has taught me and am even more determined to help others through this rewarding process of nutrition, health, and wellbeing.

Yours truly,

Maru

INTRODUCTION-GET HEALTHY, LOSE WEIGHT & IMPROVE YOUR MOOD WITH DELICIOUS MEXICAN FOOD!

I magine that you are throwing a big party or taking a trip to the beach in two weeks, and are not stressing about needing to diet or perform a strenuous exercise routine to like the way you look. The reason for not needing to diet would be because you have been at your optimal healthy weight for a long time. In fact, you cannot remember the last time you had to restrict yourself to be able to look and feel good in your clothes. For a long time, you have enjoyed going shopping because you lost several sizes and clothes look great on you. You are also not worried about how you will look in your bikini because you are confident and know you will look good. And, if you are in a relationship, you have never felt sexier.

How would it feel to be the woman I just described?

Now, imagine what it would be like to wake up each day with so much energy and mental clarity that you can do anything you set your mind to and face any challenge that comes your way. You no longer have periods of low energy or brain fog in the afternoon, so there is no need for that 3 or 4 PM caffeine or sugar-fix to survive your day. As the day goes by, you have a consistent feeling of energy and total wellness. You have participated in a wide variety of physical activities and can even keep up with your young and energized kids.

If you doubt this can be you, with the right support and guidance, you can change your life completely, just like I did, and not wait thirty years to do it.

Continue imagining: Everybody around you asks what you have been doing because you look amazing. And the great part is you do feel confident and amazing. You agree that you have never looked and felt younger, better, happier, sexier, or more beautiful. Your skin, your hair, and your body look better than ever.

Are you enjoying this feeling of beauty and happiness?

Continue to imagine *not* suffering from most of the health issues or concerns you've experienced. What would you do with all the money and time you save if you did *not* have to go to the doctor so often or buy so many medications? You *no longer* feel bloated after eating, your joint pain and headaches are gone, and your depression is a thing of the past. You are also confident that you have been taking the necessary steps to prevent many of the common health problems that people get when they grow old, such as Alzheimer's and dementia.

Now, imagine that the way you look, feel, and act has been possible thanks to eating Mexican food—yes, delicious Mexican food! You must be asking, "How can that be, right?" You love Mexican food, but you also consider it to be fattening and unhealthy.

I am here to tell you that all you imagined can become a reality for you . . . and all on **The Mexican Food Diet**™.

After I became certified in Integrative Nutrition, I wanted to be Flaca Forever. "Flaca" is a Spanish word that means "lean," "thin," or "skinny." I was ready to lose the weight and keep it off as opposed to always being on the next diet to try to lose my extra weight.

It is important to clarify that the way I understand "thin" is in the healthiest way possible. I can be thin, but healthy first. "Flaca" also represents energy, health, and young-looking skin and hair. From my own experience, I knew that if I became too thin and poorly nourished, I would not be able to achieve these healthy goals nor would I be able to be a role model or inspiration for other people who may be having similar struggles. Most importantly, I wanted to be my best self for my young and adorable daughter who needs me to be healthy and strong for a lifetime.

After several years of researching and testing many, many diets and foods, I finally found the missing link. I discovered that if I want to have lasting weight loss and get back to being healthy and feeling great, I needed address the toxicity and chronic inflammation inside my body.

The world has become increasingly toxic and your body cannot process the amount of toxins entering it daily. Unprocessed toxins accumulate inside your body, and over time, they can keep you fat, sick, and sad, which is exactly what had happened to me.

With this information in hand, I focused my research and testing to find the best products and foods to help my body get rid of the accumulated toxins. In my work, I kept coming up with ingredients and spices that were very common in the food I ate while growing up in Mexico, such as cilantro, onions, garlic, hot peppers, lemons and limes, avocados, cauliflower, cabbage, olive oil, cinnamon, cumin, apples, and others.

Very soon, I realized that Mexican food is not only delicious and exciting; it is also excellent for detoxifying, reducing inflammation, and getting healthier and leaner. Of course, not all Mexican food is this way; otherwise, we would not be having the major obesity crisis we are currently seeing in Mexicans, living both in Mexico and the US.

The Mexican food that I use in my recipes is absolutely yummy and healthy. It is vibrant, full of life, and very delicious, which makes it very easy to stay on plan. What a relief it would be to eat this way and at the same time lose weight, after having many years of deprivations and hunger. As soon as I realized this, I knew I was onto something big.

This further defined my mission: to empower women to transform their whole lives through the power of "**Healthy Eating That Feels Like Cheating**" nutrition. My diet plan can help both men and women. However, I am aware that women are more frequently responsible for selecting the food for the families. I am hopeful that as I change women's health, lives, and futures, I will be also having an impact on their husbands, their children, their extended families, their friends, and their communities.

THIS BOOK HAS THE DIET YOU HAVE BEEN WAITING FOR

While this book offers delicious recipes and great photos, it also offers an effective diet plan to get healthy, lose weight, and improve your mood with delicious food. Most of all, you will have a lot of fun! I act as a guide in your journey towards absolute wellness and an empowered and fulfilling life. This diet will allow you to experience a new way of thinking about eating and living. Most diets have a beginning and an end, but the journey I want to lead you on is an ongoing path. When you diet, you do it for a short-term goal, and in between diets you settle for not looking and feeling your best. With my guidelines and recipes in this book, you will look and feel your best, always and forever. I always tell my clients that my goal is to get them addicted to looking and feeling better than ever.

The Mexican Food Diet™ is the first step of the journey. It is a jumpstart that will enable you to enjoy delicious Mexican food that will make you feel like you are cheating. Plus, if you follow the plan as recommended, you will be able to lose up to 7 pounds in just 7 days and begin the transformation of your health and your life.

This Diet WILL NOT ask you to

- Count calories or points
- Be hungry or feel deprived
- Exercise a lot
- Eat bland and boring meals
- Make your life more hectic with complicated meal plans

This DIET will help you to

- Lose weight
- Reduce toxicity and internal inflammation
- Have more stable energy throughout the day
- Get better sleep
- Improve your digestion
- Feel good after eating and in between meals

In part 1, I will cover the reasons why you need to care about reaching and staying at a healthy weight. I hope you will conclude that being at a healthy weight is not only about vanity—you know, fitting in those skinny jeans or looking good in your bikini. What you eat today will determine how and if you live tomorrow. I will share all the many ways you may be sabotaging your weight, health, and life.

In part 2, I dive into **The Mexican Food Diet**™. It is based on the philosophy of **Healthy Eating That Feels Like Cheating**™. It focuses on S.M.A.R.T. ingredients and meals, and excluding the S.T.U.P.I.D ingredients that can cause damage to your health and weight.

In part 3, I provide all the tools necessary to begin your journey toward becoming your best self ever with absolute wellness and, of course, healthy weight loss.

If you have kids like I do, I will tell you how you can adapt some of the spicy recipes to feed your kids too. You will be cooking only one recipe and separating a portion for your kids before you incorporate the hot stuff.

You can do this diet for longer than seven days by cooking double quantities for each meal and reusing the food in different ways. I will show you how. You will be amazed at the impact this healthy eating will have on your health, wellness, and, of course, your weight. You may be shocked that some of the weight and fat you have been fighting with for the longest time will begin to melt.

Although you will be dropping pounds and clothing sizes, which feels amazing, there will be other very positive benefits that may not be part of your objectives now. However, once you get them, you will be happy you did. I'm talking about things such as when you regain your energy (or get even more energy), when you notice how much sharper your mind is, how your sleep and mood dramatically improve, and how your existing chronic problems go away. Yes, when you notice all this, you will be glad you began this path.

In part 4, I will share with you how you can take your health, your weight, and your life to the next level with **Flaca Forever®️ Programs** and my proprietary process "Get Clean, Get Lean, Stay Lean™️". It is a 3-step program designed to make it simple and fun for you to take control of your health, your weight, and your life, so you can get in the best shape of your life: physically, mentally, and emotionally.

I am VERY excited to share this new way of eating and living that has absolutely transformed my life in so many ways, and the lives of so many of my clients. I am confident that if you follow the plan, it will have a positive impact on your life and the life of your families. I would love to hear from you regarding your challenges in health, weight, and wellness, as well as any comments you have regarding this book. Please write me at maru@flacaforever.com

Remember—Rest if You Must . . . But Don't You Quit!

PART 1

LOSING WEIGHT IS NECESSARY TO FIT INTO SKINNY JEANS BUT ALSO TO STAY ALIVE

Chapter 1

OBESITY: THE UPCOMING HEALTH BOMB

As I shared earlier, until a few years ago, I used to think about eating healthier or losing weight only for vanity reasons, like fitting into skinny jeans or looking good for a party. If it was not for something related to these two reasons, I always thought in terms of tomorrow—tomorrow was the day I would no longer eat X or tomorrow was the day I would start eating healthier. Many times, "tomorrow" became Monday, which meant I had several more days of doing and eating whatever I wanted, particularly during the weekend.

Looking back, I can see this kind of procrastination and self-sabotage kept me in the same habits that caused weight gain and affected my health.

It was a dangerous way to live—always setting a time in the future when I would start a healthier life. It was a comforting system, looking to poor food to relieve my stress as I dealt with challenges or frustrations in my life. Little did I know at the time that the comfort food was doing the exact opposite. It was aggravating my stress and anxiety, and making me feel horrible very soon after eating it. Thank God I no longer think or feel this way. Through my own transformation, I learned that eating better is no longer about those skinny jeans or bikinis. Eating healthier is indispensable for staying healthy—physically, mentally, and emotionally.

To change one's life: start immediately.
Do it flamboyantly. No exceptions.

~ William James

Your life is yours to live. You can choose to live it any way you want. Ask yourself, "Is it wise to put your health on the line while you live your life?"

You are beautiful and deserve to be appreciated for who you are, any way you are. Being overweight takes that away from you. The way you eat and your lifestyle have more profound effects on your health than just on your waist or in affecting the way you look. Your food choices can either create health and wellness, or destroy them, creating disease and unhappiness. You may choose to neglect this fact and decide to eat whatever tastes good or is easily available to you. You may also pretend that putting on weight does not matter to you.

After all, you can always go on one more diet or see a doctor when some health issue arises, right? However, is this really how you want to spend your time and money—taking care of frequent health issues and taking a variety of prescriptions that carry with them so many negative side effects? I hope not! Just think about how many hours, days, and months you can lose if you add up all the time spent on medical things, even the non-threatening ones. Forget about the serious ones because those can take control of your whole life and your finances.

WHAT YOU EAT TODAY WILL DETERMINE THE ANSWER TO THE FOLLOWING QUESTIONS:

- Will you get up every day energetic and ready to take on all the challenges of life head-on—or will you drag yourself out of bed to deal with one more day while feeling tired?
- Will you be happy and calm—or sad and anxious?
- Will you experience absolute wellness—or be frequently sick?
- Will you enjoy your life and money—or spend your time and money on doctors, medications, and hospitals?
- Will you be independent—or will you struggle with dementia?
- Will you be a source of joy and support to your family—or will you put them through major stress while you and they try to take care of you?
- Will you be confident enough to pursue your dreams—or will you just watch your dreams pass by?
- Will you be a role model to your family and friends—or will you be ashamed of who you have become?

The choice is yours! You need to decide today. How do you want to live the rest of your life? Every day and every piece of food or drink you ingest has an impact on the type of life you will live.

OBESITY: THE UPCOMING HEALTH BOMB

The World Health Organization (WHO) recently defined obesity as follows:

"Obesity is one of today's most blatantly visible—yet most neglected—public health problem. An escalating global epidemic of overweight and obesity—"globesity"—is taking over many parts of the world. If immediate action is not taken, millions will suffer from an array of serious health disorders."

The obesity growth rate has doubled since 1980. Today, 7 out of 10 people are overweight or obese. Researchers have estimated a 33% increase in obesity by 2030. These stats are alarming!

Although the obesity crisis is global, America's waistline has continued to rapidly expand. It now tops the list of industrialized countries where a significant proportion of the population is either overweight or obese. When you look at obesity among different ethnicities in the US, the rates are quite different, making certain groups stand out, like Hispanics and African Americans. You can also notice that Hispanic and African-American women suffer from above-average obesity levels. A big reason behind these differences is believed to be genetics, so if you are among these groups, it is even more important that you follow a healthy diet and lifestyle because your weight and health will be more rapidly affected by unhealthy choices.

HOW MUCH DOES OBESITY COST YOU?

You may not even realize how much being overweight costs. It is A LOT—both as direct and indirect expenses. Why is that? Let me explain.

Although obesity is not a disease on its own, according to some researchers, it is the source for countless other medical conditions. Medical conditions take a lot of time and joy out of your life, and are also expensive to treat, so getting sick could cause great financial strain for you and your family. Obesity and its related complications can cost you directly by increasing your medical expenses, hospital stays, and so on. It can also cost you indirectly by increasing your job absentee rate, decreasing your productivity at work, and compromising your motivation and, as a result of all these indirect, compromising your future.

Here is a fact on how much money it could be costing you, your family, your company, and your country if you are overweight:

If you're overweight, you're more than twice as likely as a person with normal weight to be prescribed medications. In one research study, it was estimated that if you're obese, you're likely to spend 42% more on your health-care expenditures compared to others. This is approximately $1,429 per year, at least.

THE FAT IN YOUR BELLY IS NOT JUST UGLY-IT IS A TICKING BOMB WAITING TO EXPLODE!

Your body fat is not just some extra weight you're dragging around. It is an explosive tied around your waist. You may hate it because it affects the way you look. You may even consider it just a part of "getting old." Some of you may even have accepted to live like this for the rest of your lives, thinking that losing weight and having a flat belly is something that only younger people can have. Or you may also be extremely busy with your life and may not consider losing weight worth your time or money.

Let me tell you one thing, right here, right now—**Your belly fat is the greatest threat to your health, wellness, and future.** In fact, **I call belly fat the "silent killer."** Let me explain why I say this.

Putting on weight is a gradual process. It takes some time before you qualify to be labeled "overweight" or "obese." You don't even realize the situation is getting worse because it is so gradual. Suddenly you start seeing the visible features of obesity around your waist and hips, and by this time, there may have already been some internal damage.

Obesity is more dangerous than any other known disease because of its propensity to affect almost all body functions and systems. If you have a heart disease, it means only your heart is sick. It is very different when it comes to obesity. If you are overweight, it means none of your body systems are working at their peak and you probably have high levels of toxicity and internal inflammation throughout your body. Inflammation is the leading cause of most diseases like cancer, diabetes, dementia, and others. According to some estimates, obesity contributes to more than one hundred different diseases in a direct or indirect way.

It is never too late or too soon to start reversing this damage. I want you to commit to starting now, and I am providing you the easy way to do it. Just take this first step of following The Mexican Food Diet™, and you will be on your way to better health and a smaller waist.

THE OBESITY BOMB

Obesity affects your health and life in 3 ways, and when they happen together, they create what I call the "obesity bomb."

As described below, the obesity bomb is composed of (1) increased inflammation, (2) metabolic imbalance, and (3) hormonal imbalance. These 3 things are happening simultaneously in some overweight people and most obese people, and are making everything more difficult: losing weight, staying healthy, and feeling happy.

And more importantly, being exposed to the obesity bomb puts your future at risk in every way. I was never obese, but I was affected by the obesity bomb because it affected my health, sabotaged my efforts to lose weight, and stopped me from reaching my full potential.

The obesity bomb leads to numerous diseases that you can read about in the Reference Section in the back of the book. Some of the diseases include type 2 diabetes, cancers, brain disorders, like Alzheimer's and Parkinson's, and heart diseases, like coronary artery syndrome and angina, to name a few.

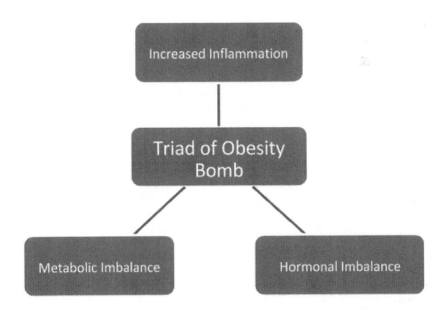

Below is a summary of the 3 conditions that make up the obesity bomb and how each can affect you.

1. INCREASED INFLAMMATION

The one thing I want you to remember about chronic internal inflammation is that it is the leading cause of almost all diseases including the terrible ones like diabetes, cancer, and dementia.

Under normal conditions, internal inflammation is good for you. It protects you from infections and invaders like bacteria and viruses. It also helps heal wounds. But, things take an ugly turn when inflammation gets out of hand. When that happens, your body cells start to die and body systems start to work in an abnormal fashion. Uncontrolled chronic inflammation makes you prone to diseases like diabetes, cancer, cardiovascular disorders, joint disorders, and so on.

Until recently, researchers didn't know much about the link between inflammation and obesity. Now, they believe that increased body inflammation is one of the ways through which obesity inflicts irreparable damage to your body. You can read more about inflammation and obesity in the Reference Section of the book.

START REDUCING INFLAMMATION TODAY BEFORE IT GETS TOO FAR

The 7-Day Mexican Food Diet™ outlined in this book is the first step to decrease the inflammation in your body that can lead to horrible diseases. You will reduce inflammation in 2 different ways.

The first way is by eating meals that do NOT include any of the ingredients that are known to increase inflammation, ingredients like sugar, refined carbs, processed foods, or unhealthy fats.

The second way is a result of the meal plan and recipes that use a lot of ingredients that reduce chronic inflammation. You will learn about these anti-inflammatory ingredients in the S.M.A.R.T. Ingredients Section in part 2.

Follow my guidelines and you will experience relief from the many health and weight issues that are caused by chronic inflammation, including an inability to lose weight, bloating, puffiness, water retention, fatigue, joint pain or stiffness, bloating, asthma, sinus problems, allergies, and red or itchy skin. If you are struggling with more severe issues or are already dealing with a chronic disease, you will also notice some improvements. Feeling and looking better will motivate you to take your health and your weight to the next level just like it happened to me. Doing this will require that you radically reduce chronic inflammation and keep it as low as possible. Through my own personal experience and by studying and working with some of the most advanced doctors, I discovered a very simple but effective method to achieve this.

In part 4, I will invite you to look at my revolutionary Flaca Detox™ Reset and Renew Program. It has been by far the easiest and most effective way to reduce inflammation, radically reduce accumulated toxins, and get your body fully nourished.

To learn more, turn to part 4 or go to www.flacadetox.com

In only 14 days you can see BIG improvements in how you look and how you feel. I use it regularly to keep toxins and inflammation as low as possible, so I can look and feel my best. My clients who have used it have also been happily surprised about how great they look and feel after only 14 days: leaner, reenergized, happier, and super motivated to continue a healthy path. Some have also seen their health issues go away, issues like weight loss resistance, asthma, constipation, depression, mood swings, or severe PMS symptoms, among many others.

2. METABOLIC IMBALANCE

Your fat cells are not just meant to store fat. They perform a lot other functions too. They secrete many hormones and have profound effects on your body's metabolism. Certain types of fat cells (adipocytes) release lots of chemicals. Each one of these chemicals has its own unique effect on your metabolism. The two components that are affected the most by these chemicals are sugar metabolism and fat metabolism.

Your fat cells and the chemicals they release can produce a condition called "insulin resistance." Insulin is the hormone responsible for storing fat and for keeping your blood sugar at healthy levels because high levels of blood sugar will damage your cells and organs. The more insulin your body produces, the faster you will accumulate fat. If your body is having to produce more and more insulin, at some point, your cells become resistant to insulin, and you could end up with type 2 diabetes. We will discuss this in more detail later in the Reference Section in the back of the book.

Having metabolic imbalance also leads to having higher levels of LDL (the bad cholesterol) and lower levels of HDL (the good cholesterol). This combination affects your heart and blood vessels putting you at risk of cardiovascular disease.

One more problem from metabolic imbalance is non-alcoholic fatty liver disease. When your body's fat exceeds the storage capacity of your normal fat reservoirs, like your belly and hips, it starts to infiltrate other parts of your body too. The part of your body that receives the hardest blow is your liver. High levels of fat act as a toxin to your liver and start to destroy it. You can't afford to damage your liver because the liver is the main organ responsible for getting rid of toxins and chemicals that enter your body daily and can keep you fat, sick, and sad.

3. HORMONAL IMBALANCE

Your body releases a lot of hormones, which are critical for the normal functioning of your body and each one of these processes your body relies on to keep you alive. You can think of hormones as chemical messengers that your body parts use to communicate with each other. If this messaging system is not functioning properly, you can face a lot of health complications that can include different forms of cancers, diabetes, infertility, and so on.

Having a hormonal imbalance will also affect the way you feel and deal with the challenges in your life. When you are out of balance, you will not feel as happy, and you may even fall victim to depression, irritability, anxiety, or radical mood swings. This is not fun. I suffered from all of this for many years, and it affected and compromised my future.

Hormonal imbalance will also make it harder for you to lose weight or keep it off. You can experience situations like the following:

- Unexplainable weight gain or inability to lose weight, no matter what you do
- Strong cravings for sugar and unhealthy foods
- Excessive hunger, no matter how much you eat
- Inability to feel full even when you eat a lot

Having your hormones out of balance can keep you feeling very stressed, which will make you store more fat, particularly in the belly, and will increase the toxicity and inflammation inside your body. High stress will also make you feel hungrier, crave junk foods, and keep you struggling with your mood, like with depression and anxiety.

By reading this section and reviewing the book's Reference Section, you are now aware of a few of the many diseases that are linked to obesity. But, the ill effects of obesity on your health go on and on. There is truly no limit to the damage obesity does to your health.

YOU NEED TO FIGHT BACK! START RIGHT NOW! TOMORROW MAY BE TOO LATE!

Every bit of food you put in your mouth today will affect your life tomorrow in many ways, not only in your weight. Every lifestyle choice you make is a deciding factor in your future health status. This is your only life. Don't wait to take on the challenge of overcoming excess weight until it may be too late or too expensive. With each day that you let weight overpower you, you're helping your enemy. It transforms your body subtly and ultimately comes a point where it will be impossible to reverse those changes.

I am so happy for you because you already took the first step, which is buying this book and reading it. Now I want you to act. You can start as small or as big as you want, just start moving. Gradual changes are the best way to achieve lasting results. So, let's JUST DO IT! I am committed to your success!

Chapter 2

THE SECRET FOR LASTING WEIGHT LOSS AND MAXIMUM HEALTH: DETOXING!

For many years, whenever I was having more and more problems concentrating or was exhausted every afternoon around 4pm, I blamed this on my hectic life and "getting older." I was trying to combine managing a household of five, being a mother of a baby, and a businesswoman. I was used to grabbing a coffee, a sugar-free Red Bull, or a Coke Zero to get me through the afternoon. Other times it was a scone, a muffin, or some sugary thing. At some point, early afternoon became too late. I started needing that pick-me-up stimulant around 11am, and of course, another one at 4pm. When I began lacking motivation and drive, I just got used to it and assumed that having recently become a mother was tough and I needed to adapt (hopefully sooner than later). When I started to feel joint pain in the morning, I attributed it to being over 40.

What I did not know was that the health and wellness issues that I was experiencing were ways that my body was sending me messages that it needed my help. Why?

It was because my body had become toxic and chronically inflamed.

How did I get toxic? The biggest reason was all those late-night binges on donuts, scones, frappuccinos, ice cream, or pizza, as well as frequent drinking, little sleep, excessive stress, and toxic environment. That toxic combination kept my liver working overtime for too long. On top of this, I would restrict calories to compensate for my binges. This deprived my body from the nutrients it needed to effectively deal with the toxins in my daily life.

And the chronic inflammation? It was a result from being unaware that I was intolerant of gluten and dairy, specifically whey and casein (the proteins in milk). Every time I ate something with dairy, gluten, or any of the other foods my body did not like, it would have a strong internal reaction provoking inflammation to protect itself. Inflammation is accompanied by water retention, which explains why I was always puffy on certain areas in my body. Up to this point, I had been drinking milk and eating gluten several times a day, every day, triggering this chronic internal inflammation that eventually made me very sick. While this was happening, I was unaware of it. This was my normal way of being and feeling. My body and I were used to our "normal." Today I can see that my "normal" was not that great. I was overweight, depressed, bloated, and lacking self-confidence.

Once I turned 40, my body started sending stronger signals, which soon became very noticeable health and weight issues. These symptoms were red flags that my body was not functioning at its peak—not because of aging but because of the accumulated and ongoing damage my body had been and was receiving.

Here is a list of red flags that you want to keep an eye out for because they may be signals that it is time for you to detox too:

- Difficulty losing weight or unexplained weight gain
- Persistent cravings for sweets or carbohydrates (like pasta, rice, bread, tortillas, or potatoes)

- Water retention and puffiness
- Increased cellulite
- Fatigue or loss of energy (particularly in the afternoon)
- Digestive issues (like bloating, gas, or constipation)
- Skin that is not clear, lacks a healthy glow, or makes you look older than you are
- Brain fog (lack of mental clarity) or difficulty concentrating
- Mood swings
- Anxiety
- Depression
- Irritability or short-temperedness
- Lack of restful sleep
- Achy joints or muscle pain
- Frequent colds and congestion
- Strong PMS (like cramps)
- Strong post-menopausal symptoms (like hot flashes or night sweats)

If you begin experiencing some of these red flags, pay attention. I will show you all the easy ways to reset and renew your body, so you can get back to a healthy path, start losing weight, and feel GREAT!

A periodic detox program, as outlined in part 4, at least once every three months, can lower the toxic burden in your body while also encouraging your natural ability to continuously detoxify effectively. Doing this should help you address most of your existing symptoms while boosting your immune system, so you can get healthy or stay that way. A good detox program also helps you jump-start your weight loss by getting rid of toxins that are keeping you fat. **Most toxins are stored inside your fat cells, and while they are there, you will not be able to lose that fat.** So, when you do an effective detox, your body releases toxins, and this allows you to lose that stubborn fat. When this happens, you will see a reduction in inches around your body, and your cellulite will diminish too.

An effective detox will also help you overcome those nasty cravings for sugar and unhealthy carbs or foods.

Getting accumulated toxins down will allow you to feel more energized throughout the days, to have a clearer mind, to reduce cellulite, to achieve skin that looks brighter and younger, to sleep better, and to experience maximize feelings of wellness and happiness.

It is magical when you start to experience this sense of absolute wellness and health. It permeates all parts of your life and brings you so many new opportunities.

The Mexican Food Diet™ may be your introduction to detoxing and resetting your body. You will not believe you are in a detox because the food is delicious and satisfying. Every meal in the diet plan is approved for a detox.

I am so happy you have decided to try this way of eating because you will get so many benefits.

I feel sad when I see women settling once they reach a certain age. They stop caring or investing time, money, and effort in where they are (personally, professionally, educationally) and how they look and feel. On the outside, they appear fine, but inside they feel insecure and suffer digestive issues, joint pain, and fatigue. You don't have to live your life that way! I did it for too long, but I no longer do. If I can do it, you can do it too!

I don't care if you are under 40, over 40, or over 60. Wherever you are, you can do it, and I will teach you how. I have seen women in their 80s touching bottom and deciding that there will be NO MORE settling; then they turn their lives around. It is doable. You just need help and courage.

If you are reading my book, you are in the right place. We are going to do this together!

Chapter 3

IS IT TIME FOR A DETOX? TAKE THE QUIZ AND FIND OUT MORE

A s a first step in your journey toward getting healthier, losing weight, and feeling happier, I want to invite you to take this free quiz I developed with the help of other health and wellness experts. The quiz will help you learn if it is time for a detox and if it can help your weight and your health.

Go to thelink below to answer a few questions and obtain your FREE report.

http://flacaforever.com/detox-quiz/

Chapter 4

TOP 12 SABOTEURS OF YOUR WEIGHT, HEALTH & LIFE

I t took me thirty years to figure out how to stop struggling with my weight, and unfortunately, by then, my health had been greatly affected. In fact, I had neglected everything in my life for over a decade. I was financially, emotionally, and physically devastated. I don't regret a single second because without my trials, I wouldn't have a message to bring to you and prevent you or save you from similar anguish.

I was never obese, but I was never able to stay at a stable healthy weight for longer than a few days. I was always trying to lose between 5 to 20 pounds. And at one point I was 60 pounds over my healthy weight.

My integrative nutrition education and the access to many health experts was finally the winning combination that supported a healthy weight loss of those extra 60 pounds I was carrying with me. I am happy to say today that I have been able to keep the weight off for four years without the need to count calories, be hungry, feel deprived, or over-exercise. I no longer take medicines or go to the doctor, other than for regular checkups. How I accomplished this stabilization of my weight started with identifying the following key things that were sabotaging my weight, health, and life.

#1 NOT DOING A PERIODIC DETOX

Detoxing is indispensable for losing weight, staying healthy, and feeling great. Your liver is the major site where cleansing and detoxification take place. But there is a limit to how many toxins your liver can clear away. In today's world, there are too many toxins coming into your body daily. Your liver cannot keep up with the load, so toxins accumulate inside your body. Accumulated toxins damage your cells and increase inflammation. This will lead to weight gain and deterioration of your health and wellness. When you reach a high level of accumulated toxins, you are probably going to be feeling frequently tired, overweight, and overburdened. And if you don't do anything about it, you can eventually get sick.

Toxins accumulate in your body as a result of:

- Poor eating choices including sugar, refined carbo-hydrates, saturated fats, junk food, too much red and fatty meat, meat from animals that have received antibiotics and hormones, canned food, and processed foods with lots of additives and preservatives.
- Pesticides in fruits and vegetables are a rapid way to accumulate toxins. You don't need to buy everything organic, but there are certain vegetables and fruits that have the highest level of residual pesticides, so you should buy these organic. For details, refer to Chapter 11 in this book where I show you the list of the Dirty Dozen.
- Unhealthy habits like drinking too much alcohol, smoking, and other addictions.
- Pollutants and chemicals in the environment, air, water, foods and other items of daily use like beauty products and household cleaners.

- High use of medications and supplements can also aggravate the toxicity problem.

It is important to keep toxicity levels as low as possible to avoid weight gain, illness, and unwellness.

If you want to learn more about the way toxins affect you and how to minimize the accumulated toxins in your body, I invite you to:

Go to the link below to Register for my FREE Get Clean and Lean Masterclass:

http://www.flacaforever.com/detox-tutorial

When toxicity in your body starts reaching high levels, your body will start sending you signals to tell you that it is out of balance and requires your attention. Over time, signals will get stronger until you pay attention, which is what happened to me.

As we reviewed earlier in this book, some of the symptoms that you need to pay attention to are the following: difficulty losing weight; fatigue or loss of energy (particularly in the afternoons); digestive issues like bloating, gas, or constipation; water retention and puffiness; increased cellulite; skin that is not clear or lacks a healthy glow; brain fog (lack of mental clarity) or difficulty concentrating; mood swings, anxiety depression, or short-temperedness; persistent cravings for sweets or carbohydrates like pasta, rice, bread, tortillas, or potatoes; lack of restful sleep; achy joints or muscle pain; and frequent colds and congestion.

By doing an effective periodic detox program at least every 3 months, you can reset your metabolism, lose weight, and regain (or maintain) your health and vitality. A periodic detox will also boost your immune system, make your weight loss or weight maintenance efforts more effective, increase energy and mental clarity, reduce cravings and cellulite, make your skin look brighter and younger, improve your quality of sleep, and maximize feelings of wellbeing and happiness. I hope you can now see what a wonderful tool an effective detox program can be.

The Mexican Food Diet™ is your entry gate into a detox lifestyle where the benefits are numerous and GREAT. You will benefit in many ways that you can't even imagine today. I cannot thank God enough for leading me into the detox lifestyle that helped me recover my health, lose the weight, keep it off, and look better than ever without needing to be on a permanent diet or having to depend on extreme exercise. I have recovered my vibe, my drive, my focus, and the confidence I need to take on big challenges.

When you are ready to take your journey of weight loss and health to the next level, take a look at my revolutionary Flaca Detox™ Reset and Renew Program that is the simple, effective, and delicious way to detoxify your body so you can lose the weight and feel great. To learn more, go to www.FlacaDetox.com.

#2 HIDDEN SUGARS

For a long time I thought I was a healthy eater. I knew, like everybody, else that desserts, ice cream, and candy have lots of sugar that cause weight gain. What I did not know until I became a health expert was that sugar is hiding in places you would never imagine and in foods that don't even taste sweet.

Let me share with you my standard "old days" when I thought I was a "healthy eater."

I would start my days with cereal with low fat milk and a banana. The specific cereal was either Go Lean, Raisin Bran, or All Bran.

The criteria I used to select the cereal was the amount of fiber it had and the lack of sugar or something similar in its name. So if it said "Frosted Flakes" or "Sugar Pops," it was out of question.

Throughout the day, I would have a couple venti lattes or cappuccinos with low fat milk or soy milk and sugar substitutes (supposedly to stay healthy and thin). During the day, I would make sure I ate lots of fiber in foods like brown rice or whole wheat pasta. I also loved salads with low-fat dressing, low or nonfat yogurt for snacks, Jamba juice natural fruit smoothies, and ketchup with my hamburger. For drinks, I had many Coke Zeros during the day, and for sweeteners, I used lots of Splenda, and natural agave for some special items (like margaritas). When I was training as a competitive triathlete, I ate protein and energy bars and gels. So a healthy day for me included many grams of sugar, but I was not aware of it.

When I added the total sugar I was consuming, I was in shock. It's not like I was eating cookies or ice cream!

MARU'S SUPPOSEDLY HEALTHY EATING

FOOD ITEM	SUGAR (GRAMS)
1 cup of cereal (Go Lean, All Bran, or Raisin Bran)	6–18 g
8 oz. of 2% milk	11 g
2 venti lattes with low fat milk or soy milk (approx. 12 oz. of milk in each)	34.5 g
4 oz. of low-fat salad dressing	8 g
1 cup of Yoplait light very vanilla yogurt	10 g
1 Jamba Juice Mega Mango smoothie with real whole fruit and 100% juice (16 oz.)	52 g
2 tablespoons of ketchup	7.4 g
1 tablespoon of agave	14.1 g
1 Cliff energy bar	22 g
1 energy gel	5 g
TOTAL	172–184 g; 43–46 teaspoons

There are 4 grams of sugar per teaspoon. So, I was consuming between 43 and 46 teaspoons of added sugar on my average "healthy" day. Forget about counting sugar on my unhealthy days when I would binge. This amount of sugar is almost 8 times (or 800% higher) the maximum daily recommended sugar for a woman, which is a maximum of 6 teaspoons. For days that were not so healthy, add on the particular treat or binge, and you get the picture. The "healthy woman" was not as healthy as she thought.

In addition, sugary foods and drinks have poor satiety when compared to other things like protein, fat, or fiber, so you can eat a lot more sugar than you need because you will not feel full. Or you will fill full for a very short time and then feel very hungry again. Sugar affects the natural hormonal balance that tells you when you are full.

There are three types of simple sugars to know about: glucose, fructose, and sucrose. You must use caution with fructose in particular because it can only be processed by the liver. So, if you are consuming too much fructose, you will be overburdening your liver, storing more fat, increasing toxicity, and making your weight loss and health improvement efforts much harder. In the Reference Chapter you can get some details on each one of these.

I want to make you aware that any sugar, no matter what its color or source, is a sugar that you need to be careful with. Brown sugar is still sugar. Organic sugar is also sugar. Don't let the industry fool you with fancy names. All syrups and honeys also fall into the same category as sugar. Agave, often referred to as a "healthier" sugar option, has 70–90% fructose, which is even higher than the horrible high-fructose corn syrup. And as I said, it all goes into the liver, increasing fat and triggering inflammation, the leading cause of most diseases and weight struggles.

In Chapter 11 you'll find more detailed explanation on why you should minimize your sugar consumption, as well as a list of foods with some of the most common hidden sugars. From that list, you will see that sugar is hiding in too many places. You may be surprised, like I was, when you realize that you have been eating the "high in hidden sugar" foods frequently without being fully aware of their high sugar levels. You really need to become a detective and well-educated to minimize your consumption of hidden sugars and their negative impact on your health, weight and mood.

#3 SUGAR ADDICTION

The more you eat sugar, the more you want. So, if you beat yourself up about constantly succumbing to your sugar cravings, don't feel bad. You are not weak. There are many studies that show that sugar is more addictive than heroine.

Thinking sugar substitutes and diet or sugar-free foods can help you lose weight or not put on weight is another example where you need to correct your thinking (like I had to). "Sugar-free" products use artificial sweeteners instead of sugar, artificial sweeteners like aspartame ("Equal" or "NutraSweet") and sucralose ("Splenda"). If you are still consuming these products, you are not alone. I used to have sugar-free products every day to reduce my calorie intake and to help me be "healthier. " At least that is what I believed.

Although it is true that artificial sweeteners have no calories, there are many studies that show that these sweeteners damage your health (and can even cause cancer), stimulate your appetite, increase your desire for more sweets and carbohydrates, and produce a variety of disorders in your metabolism, leading to accumulation of fat and weight gain. A healthy alternative to replace these sweeteners is stevia, a natural product derived from a South American plant. Stevia can be used to sweeten most dishes and drinks, and does not increase insulin or cravings for sweets and carbohydrates.

In The Mexican Food Diet™, I will guide you through the process of getting rid of your addiction to sugar and your strong cravings for it. This diet is focused on serving your body with the right nutrients and detox support—two essential keys for overcoming cravings and food addictions. For a quicker way to overcome sugar cravings, take a look at my Flaca Detox™ Reset and Renew Program in part 4. In only 14 days, you will be able to see that your cravings are gone, the scale is moving again in the right direction, and you will feel amazing, energized, refreshed, and rejuvenated from the inside out. This program is also based on my principle, "Healthy Eating That Feels Like Cheating™". It is delicious, satisfying, and very easy to do. I have used it and have been able to overcome my food addictions. I have also used it on all my VIP clients, and results have always been amazing. To learn more, go to www.FlacaDetox.com or call me at 858-433-9802.

#4 THE CARBS THAT CAN GET YOU FAT

You need to focus your intake on healthy or what I call S.M.A.R.T. carbs, which are non-starchy veggies, fruits, and some gluten-free whole grains. These S.M.A.R.T. carbs have nutrients and dietary fiber that provide you with gradual and stable energy, preventing blood sugar spikes and reducing the chances of fat storage. The nutrients and fiber will also keep you nourished and feeling satisfied between meals, so you can better resist unhealthy temptations. Unhealthy carbs like a piece of white bread, processed foods and fast foods have almost zero nutrients. Instead of nourishing your body, they add toxins and inflammation. And, they are rapidly converted into sugar, making blood sugar spike, increasing insulin, and leading to fat storage. Over time, frequent or excessive consumption of unhealthy carbs will make you gain weight, get sick and prevent you from feeling great.

I will talk in detail about S.M.A.R.T. carbs in part 2, and you can find more details about unhealthy carbs and where they hide in the Reference Section in the back of the book.

Following The Mexican Food Diet™ will take you by the hand in reducing unhealthy carbs and introducing healthier alternatives that are delicious and nutritious.

#5 BELIEVING FAT IS BAD

You need fat to lose fat and feel happy. For the longest time, I was under the false impression that fat generates fat. I believed that avoiding fat and eating low fat was essential for staying thin. The truth is the opposite. If you eat healthy fat, you will facilitate weight loss and prevent weight gain.

I also avoided fat because it has more than double the calories of carbs. Fat contributes with 9 calories for each gram you eat, whereas carbs give you only 4 calories per gram. Not eating fat seems obvious, right? So the question is: Why is the world, even children, getting fatter?

One of the reasons people have been avoiding fat is that in 1992 the government issued a Food Guide Pyramid with specific nutritional recommendations. The guide suggested to eat fat in very limited amounts and to choose grains instead. As people began avoiding fat, the food industry took advantage, and this led to the existing craze for low-fat supposedly healthy products and the higher consumption of carbohydrates and sugar.

When fat is removed from many products, they lose their flavor and texture. To compensate, manufacturers add sugar and other unhealthy additives. As you can now see, these dietary guidelines incited the multitude of low-fat options currently available like fat-free cookies and cakes, low-fat yogurts, low-fat dressings, low-fat cheese, low-fat milk, etc. Have you noticed how it is harder to find full fat products? I hadn't realized it before, but when I have tried, it has been quite difficult to find them.

Luckily I learned that you need healthy fats or what I call S.M.A.R.T. fats every day in every meal to feel satisfied, burn fat, and feel happy. Your brain needs healthy fats to perform at its best. We will talk about S.M.A.R.T. fats in part 2.

#6 ASSUMING ALL CALORIES ARE THE SAME

I often hear and meet people who complain that they cannot lose weight or maintain their weight loss even when they significantly reduce the calories they consume and/or do a lot more exercise. I personally have also gone through this, and yes, it is frustrating. After so much sacrifice and dedication, you would expect to obtain results and stop struggling with weight problems.

I believed for the longest time that if I wanted to lose weight or avoid gaining weight after I had binged, I just needed to reduce the calories I ate, double the amount of exercise I did, and stay away from fat and junk food. This strategy worked for a while but one day, it just stopped working. I tried eating less and less, and exercising more and more, and I was still not able to not lose the weight or keep it off.

I have also noticed that most of my clients who have the most excess weight are frequently eating very little, yet they are not losing any weight. In both cases, the main explanation is that we were eating the wrong calories and our accumulated toxicity was high.

As I have learned, all calories are not the same, and you cannot undo the damage of bad food choices through exercise alone.

Let's use the example of 300 calories of fresh or cooked veggies versus eating 300 calories from a cake or junk food. Of course, you know veggies are better. But, if you think that the cake is just 300 calories, and you can burn that off, there is a breakdown in the body that affects this mindset.

The veggies provide the elements necessary to support your body's natural detoxification and elimination systems so that waste or toxins get out of your body promptly instead of staying inside, damaging your cells and ending up stored in your fat cells. **Remember that as long as you have toxins stored in your fat cells, you will not be able to lose the fat no matter what you do.** The nutrients also nourish your cells and provide fiber, which will help you stay satisfied and feel energized and sharp.

When you eat the 300 calories from the cake or junk food, the opposite happens. First of all, the cake or junk food adds toxins to your body, and lacks the nutrients that your body needs to stay healthy and strong. Additionally, to process the toxins from these unhealthy foods, your body will need to use most of the nutrients you have consumed earlier in other meals to clean up instead of using them to thrive. Second, the cake and junk food are made of simple carbohydrates that are immediately converted into sugar after you eat them. They are absorbed into your bloodstream, creating a spike in blood sugar. High levels of sugar in your blood can damage your cells and organs. To prevent this, your body will produce insulin, the hormone responsible for bringing sugar levels down and storing fat. If your body needs to produce too much insulin too often, you will be rapidly storing fat and reducing the effectiveness of insulin because the cells start to become resistant to it. As cells become resistant to insulin, more insulin will be produced, and more fat will be stored. Over time, you can also become insulin resistant, and this leads to type 2 diabetes.

Third, the cake or junk food is made of a combination of sugar (or refined carbs), unhealthy fats, and lots of additives and artificial ingredients that when combined, they radically increase inflammation and toxicity, disrupt your hormonal balance and metabolism, and affect your brain, energy, and emotions in negative ways.

#7 UNBALANCED HORMONES

Many hormones contribute to weight gain and weight loss, but the most important ones are insulin, leptin, and cortisol. These three hormones are tightly interrelated, and you must keep the three in balance to stay healthy and keep the weight off.

- **Insulin** is responsible for using sugar and carbs, and converting them into glucose (blood sugar) for energy, then storing any excess glucose as fat. It is also responsible for keeping blood sugar at healthy levels. If you eat too much sugar or carbs, your blood sugar will get high, and this will require ongoing production of insulin, resulting in more fat storage. Over time, it can also result in the diminishing effectiveness of insulin, which can lead to type 2 diabetes. You can find out more details about this in the Reference Section in the back of the book.

- **Leptin** is the hormone responsible for making you feel full after a meal. As you gain weight, production of insulin remains high and affects leptin's effectiveness in communicating to your brain that you are full when you eat a meal. This keeps you hungry no matter what you eat and will make you want to eat a lot more food than your body needs leading to more weight gain and the continuation of the vicious cycle.

- **Cortisol** is the stress hormone. Under high stress, cortisol levels increase making you gain fat around the belly.

The reasons hormones get out of balance are:

- **Poor Food Choices:** Eating foods that promote inflammation, are rich in sugar or simple carbohydrates, or have high levels of unhealthy fats will compromise the effectiveness of insulin and leptin. This will make you gain fat at a quicker rate and at the same time you will get hungrier.
- **Stress:** Continuously exposing your body to high levels of stress increases the levels of cortisol which will make you gain fat.
- **Sleep Deprivation:** When you don't get adequate sleep, your levels of stress and cortisol increase. Lack of sleep also affects leptin. When both cortisol and leptin get affected, you will not feel full after eating, your cravings and hunger will increase, and you will gain fat at a quicker rate.

#8 UNDIAGNOSED FOOD INTOLERANCES OR SENSITIVITIES

A food intolerance or sensitivity means that your body can't digest certain components of food. When this happens, the food passes through your digestive system unprocessed, or it lingers in the gut fermenting and producing excess "gas", and disrupting the healthy bacterial balance. Unprocessed food particles can also sometimes rupture the lining of the intestine allowing foreign particles into the bloodstream. This is known as "leaky gut".

If foreign particles enter your bloodstream, your body will treat them as intruders and will respond with an immune response to destroy them, triggering inflammation, the leading cause of all diseases.

Food intolerances are very different than food allergies. Some people are born with food intolerances while others develop them over time. A poor diet with foods that promote inflammation or eating certain foods too frequently can also result in food intolerances. Other causes can be lifestyle factors, like too much stress, too many medications, or a damaged gut ("leaky gut"). Food intolerances can be permanent, or they can be overcome by staying away from the specific food for a period of time.

When I was competing in triathlons and marathons, I was paying attention to what I was eating because I wanted to be my best at the races, but I was frustrated because I was getting frequently sick with ongoing sinus problems and colds. This was, of course, affecting my performance. There were races where I was taking lots of medicines prior to the race to be able to breathe because I had horrible congestion. There were also races that I had to show up after almost no sleep because of a persistent cough and congestion. I was still doing well in my races, but not as well as I could have if I'd had my full power and health.

At that time, I had no idea that I was highly sensitive or intolerant to some of the "healthy" foods I was consuming like low-fat milk, gluten from my high-fiber cereals and whole-wheat pastas, and the sugar hidden in many things I ate or drank. Eating these foods on a daily basis was keeping my body under a constant state of inflammation, which was affecting my health in many ways, like the respiratory and digestive issues I was struggling with.

At the time, my doctors were just treating my symptoms with continued use of medicines and not looking for the root cause of the repetitive infections. They also suggested that my asthma was sport-induced. Over time, the antibiotics damaged the lining of my intestines leading to leaky gut. This further aggravated my intolerances. The openings in my intestines were allowing unprocessed food, bacteria, and toxins to leak out into my blood, increasing inflammation and damaging my cells. Another bad result from the antibiotics is that they destroyed the balance of the bacteria in my gut. A healthy gut has good and bad bacteria that keep each other balanced. In my case, the antibiotics killed the good bacteria and allowed the bad bacteria to dominate, which contributed to more inflammation and cell damage.

My undiagnosed intolerances were also preventing me from losing my extra weight. Every time I ate one of those foods, I would gain weight from the internal inflammation, increase of toxicity, and the water retention that comes along with inflammation. Fortunately, once I eliminated the foods that were a problem for me, I got rid of all the health issues I described, I no longer needed any medicines, and weight loss became much easier.

Although symptoms are very different for each person, some of the most common symptoms resulting from food intolerances include the following:

- Bloating
- Easy weight gain or inability to lose weight
- Fatigue
- Mental fog
- Irritability
- Moodiness
- Digestive issues
- Respiratory issues

My undiagnosed food intolerances were definitely making my weight struggles harder and were destroying my health.

When I created The Mexican Food Diet™, I made sure to leave out foods that are commonly associated with food intolerances. This will allow your body to heal and make your weight-loss efforts easier.

#9 SKIPPING MEALS

When I ask my clients why they have been skipping meals, here are some of the most frequent reasons they give me: "I didn't have time to eat;" "I ate so much yesterday;" "I am going to eat a big dinner (or going to a party), so I want to save calories;" "I need to fit into some clothing tonight or tomorrow;" "I was not hungry;" or "I want to lose weight."

What they don't know is that when they skip a meal, they are creating a lot of negative effects: 1) Your metabolism becomes slower in order to conserve energy. When you eat again, your metabolism is now slower, so you do not burn calories effectively and end up accumulating fat. 2) You will be very hungry at the next meal; therefore, you will be more susceptible to temptations or excessive eating. 3) You provoke a sharp drop in blood sugar levels, which makes you tired, irritable, and suffer brain fog (lower focus or mental clarity). 4) Your body does not have sufficient fuel, which affects your brain and each of your internal organs as they cannot function properly without adequate fuel. 5) You increase your risk of diabetes by affecting your insulin reactions, and this may eventually create insulin resistance.

#10 "GLUTEN-FREE" PRODUCTS HELP YOU LOSE WEIGHT

Gluten is a protein that is found in all forms of wheat (bulgur wheat, durum wheat, semolina, spelt, farro, and others) and in rye, barley, and triticale. Gluten helps foods keep their shape. It is often found in breads, baked goods, soups, pasta, cereals, sauces, dressings, food colorants, beer, fried foods, and flour containing products, among others.

Many people, like me, have a problem or an inability to digest gluten, so it is important to avoid it. However, the food industry has extrapolated this problem saying that staying off gluten is necessary for every person, and this has promoted the proliferation of "gluten-free" products. "Gluten-free" products are generally perceived as "healthy" and even as dietetic.

Unfortunately, many of these gluten-free products are loaded with calories and sugars to compensate for the lack of flavor and texture. Therefore, it is important to learn how to read the labels to understand a product's nutritional content. With that being said, the best alternative to gluten is to always try to choose unprocessed foods, like fresh vegetables, fruits, lean meats, poultry, and fish.

#11 HIGH STRESS

Stress causes obesity and sabotages your health and your weight-loss efforts. When you hear the word "stress," you probably think about difficult situations, like losing a job or fighting with your loved ones. However, other factors also cause stress: restrictive diets, extreme exercising, lack of sleep, and chronic infections and diseases.

If the stress continues for long periods, you produce high levels of the hormone cortisol. The normal daily production of cortisol has a rhythm during the day: high levels during the morning and low at night. Permanent stress increases cortisol levels throughout the day, disrupting its natural rhythm and causing negative effects. Some of the most common effects are the increase of your blood sugar level, hunger, sugar cravings, and hormonal imbalances; difficulty to burn fat; the acceleration of fat storage; and the increase of fat around the waist and stomach.

Start to identify what changes you can do to reduce your level of stress. For example, dieting continuously is very stressful, especially when it includes significant restrictions of food and/ or calories. It has been confirmed that this type of stress affects the levels of cortisol, and, therefore, it is counterproductive for your weight-loss efforts. A better alternative is to learn what foods work best for your body so you can get healthier, lose weight, and keep it off without restrictive dieting. The good news is that this book will show you how.

#12 LACK OF SLEEP

When you do not sleep enough, it affects your weight in several ways. 1) It affects the areas of the brain that help you make decisions, control impulses, and look for rewards, making it more difficult to resist temptations or make good, healthier decisions. 2) It produces higher levels of the hunger hormone and less of the one that makes you feel satisfied or full, making you hungrier and in need of larger portions. 3) You desire food that is high in carbohydrates, like junk food, pastries, pasta, rice, breads, potatoes, etc. 4) It triggers the hormone that slows down your metabolism. 5) It affects your ability to process insulin.

In conclusion, if you sleep more, you're not going to lose weight, but if you don't sleep enough, you will surely gain weight. The average recommended sleep is between 7 and 8 hours each night. Each person should learn about their number of sleep hours and what amount works best.

Now that you know what can sabotage your weight, health, and happiness, let's get **S.M.A.R.T.** about eating with **Healthy Eating That Feels Like Cheating**™!

PART 2

THE MEXICAN FOOD DIET™ : HEALTHY EATING THAT FEELS LIKE CHEATING™

Chapter 5

MEXICAN FOOD: THE BEST WAY TO GET HEALTHY, LOSE WEIGHT & FEEL GREAT

I am not surprised by Mexican food's popularity in America and in most parts of the world. It is so delicious, satisfying, and affordable. However, most people believe that Mexican food is fattening and unhealthy. Until a few years ago, I did too. When I went back to school to learn about integrative nutrition and health, I discovered that Mexican food is not only delicious and satisfying, but it is also incredibly detoxifying and nutritious, making it amazing for health and weight loss when it is prepared in a certain way.

Through my studies and personal experiences, I learned that the secret for lasting weight loss and maximum health and wellness is to minimize internal inflammation and the toxins that accumulate daily inside your body. As I have shown in part 1, chronic inflammation and accumulated toxins lead to many chronic diseases, depression, and weight struggles. Or said in simple and easy to remember way, inflammation and accumulated toxins can keep you fat, sick, and sad, which is exactly what happened to me for almost two decades.

I also realized that if I wanted to stay on a healthy path for the long run, as opposed to my previous way of permanent yo-yo dieting, I had to find a new way of eating that would be delicious, nutritious, and satisfying. I was done with being on diets that were boring and kept me feeling hungry or deprived.

GET READY TO GET HEALTHY AND LOSE WEIGHT THE SMART AND FUN WAY!

Discovering ways to fight the two enemies (inflammation and toxicity) by cooking the Mexican food I grew up with and love was like a dream come true! What a way to no longer be fat, sick, and sad! Finally, I could have fun while being fit and satisfied! And it was great to know that this type of diet would also be affordable because I am a believer that eating healthy should not cost more. In fact, eating healthy will save you money because it does not cost more and staying healthy does save you money and time.

Once I knew the power of Mexican food, I focused on creating The Mexican Food Diet™. I consulted with other health and weight-loss experts, and then I returned to my birthplace in Mexico to retrieve family recipes from my mother, grandmother, and other friends and family because the women in my family have never been obese. I modified these family recipes to take away any unhealthy elements, maximize the health benefits, all while keeping the exciting and robust flavors that distinguish our foods.

WHO DOESN'T WANT SIMPLE IN THEIR BUSY LIVES?

When I developed **The Mexican Food Diet™**, my goal was to empower you to get on this exciting path to get healthy and lose weight the fun way! To achieve my goal, I focused on creating a delicious, simple, and effective plan to meet your weight and health goals.

The Mexican Food Diet™ is the healthy eating plan you have been waiting for, especially if you have tried programs that don't work or that you just cannot stay on after a few days because you are starving, bored, or just disappointed. In this plan, you will be eating food you love while losing weight and getting healthier. This is what I call **Healthy Eating That Feels Like Cheating**™. It is a simple, easy plan with foods that will give you the satisfaction you crave and the health and weight-loss results you want.

The Top Benefits of Healthy Eating That Feels Like Cheating™ in The Mexican Food Diet™

- **You WILL boost your metabolism to lose weight and fat without starving or feeling bored.**

  You'll be eating delicious meals that are robust and satisfying. They include all the right foods that your body needs to reset, and get clean and fully nourished so that you can lose weight and feel great in a healthy and lasting way.

  The diet is balanced to keep your blood sugar at healthy levels so that your body can stop producing high levels of insulin that are making you store fat. Having high levels of insulin frequently can also lead to diabetes and destroy your hormonal balance, making your weight-loss efforts impossible.

  The meals will provide you with sufficient energy, without providing too much fuel so that your body can tap into your fat reserves, helping you lose inches.

  Through its careful selection of ingredients and combination of recipes, this diet will help you restore the balance in the key hormones that may be currently affecting your weight, your health, and your mood: insulin, leptin, and cortisol. Having hormonal balance will help you boost your metabolism, control your appetite, feel full faster, burn more calories, and get rid of fat instead of storing it.

- **You WILL detoxify and reduce internal inflammation.**
  If you follow this diet, you will begin to detoxify and heal your body. By doing this, you will immediately begin to see weight-loss results as internal inflammation subsides and water retention is reduced.

Reducing chronic inflammation is essential because inflammation is the cause of most of the health issues and diseases in the world today, such as cancer, diabetes, dementia, Alzheimer's, and heart disease, among many others. It is also the source of other issues such as joint pain, arthritis, and asthma.

When toxins are eliminated from your body, you will be able to start getting rid of the fat where toxins had been stored. Remember that if toxins are stored in your fat cells, you will not be able to lose the fat. Getting rid of the toxins will help you lose inches all around, particularly on your waist. Don't forget that accumulated toxins are already making you (or will eventually make you) sick and less smart, so getting rid of them is the best thing you can do for your weight, your brain, and your health.

And, losing fat around the waist and belly is fun for clothes shopping, but also, as we discussed earlier in the book, fat in these areas is the most dangerous fat for your health.

- **You WILL have less cravings.**

  I prepared a meal plan that will keep you full and satiated while fully detoxifying and nourishing your body and brain. Doing this simultaneously will help reduce your cravings for sugar and unhealthy food. I have also eliminated foods that are keeping you addicted and giving you uncontrollable cravings. Some of these foods are so powerfully addictive that they end up ruling your life.

- **You WILL feel energized, focused, calm, and happy.**

  As you implement the changes that we recommend in The Mexican Food Diet™, you will notice that your energy comes back and stays with you throughout the day. When you wake up, you will feel energized and ready to take on whatever challenges come your way.

  Healthy eating will also work miracles in your mental clarity and focus. Unhealthy foods, especially sugar and unhealthy carbs, give you what is known as "brain fog" or an inability to focus and concentrate. As you frequently eat healthier, your focus returns and you think clearly. This is a major aid for dealing with complex situations or difficult times.

  You will also notice how your stress and anxiety are reduced and your mood is more stable. You will feel more calm, happier and have more patience most of the time.

  For some of you, this diet will allow you to discover the connection between some symptoms you are having that you may not currently be associating with the type of diet you are following. For example, you may think that feeling fatigued, stressed, moody, or irritable is a result of your high-stress job, your demanding role as a mother and wife, or the problems in your relationship or with your kids. Soon you will discover how the right food is pivotal to elevating your mood, but the wrong foods can put a damper on everything.

- **You WILL become more beautiful.**

  No matter how you feel today, eating healthier will make you feel and look more beautiful. Listed below are some of the beauty benefits of this diet.

  - **Skin that looks younger and has a clear and healthy glow. The Mexican Food Diet™** will help you get rid of those nasty toxins inside your body that are making you age faster and robbing the healthy glow from your skin.
  - **Reduced cellulite**. Cellulite increases as you accumulate more and more toxins inside your body.
  - **Flatter stomach and leaner body**. By reducing toxicity and inflammation while improving digestion, you will see your stomach get flatter or less bloated, and your body will look leaner.
  - **Better-fitting clothes** will be a great benefit from doing this diet.

- **You WILL be less bloated after eating.**

  This diet will be great for you if you frequently experience digestive issues after eating, such as bloating, gas, or indigestion.

- **You WILL get sick less often.**

  The meals in The Mexican Food Diet™ are nutrient-dense, detoxifying, and anti-inflammatory. This will strengthen the health of your gut and your immune system, making you less susceptible to getting sick or shortening the duration of your colds. And if you suffer from asthma, you may be surprised that it can disappear as you start improving your diet. I used to get horrible colds and sinus infections several times a year, as well as asthma. Today, I rarely get sick, and I no longer have asthma. The last time I got a bad cold was after cutting down on sleep for several days, which weakened my immune system. Since then, if I eat healthy and sleep sufficiently, I have been able to avoid getting sick even when everyone around me is sick.

- **You WILL have less pain.**

  An unhealthy diet will increase toxicity and inflammation, which can result in joint or muscle pain and aches, or arthritis, because toxins are frequently stored in joints. As you lower the toxicity and reduce inflammation, you will begin to see reduction in pain and possibly less injuries.

THE POWER OF MEXICAN FOOD

As you can see by now, Mexican food is a powerful ally in your journey to lose weight and get healthier. Its power comes from the combination of ingredients found in most Mexican dishes.

Mexican food as prepared in **The Mexican Food Diet**™ incorporates some of the best ingredients to boost metabolism, burn fat, control appetite, reduce inflammation, and help your body get rid of toxins that can keep you fat, sick, and sad.

Examples of some of the most common anti-inflammatory and detoxifying ingredients are onions, garlic, cilantro, lime, cinnamon, and many other ingredients and spices that you will discover as you prepare your delicious meals.

Hot peppers can be your best allies to lose weight and feel great.

Hot peppers are included in many of my recipes in **The Mexican Food Diet**™. Hot peppers are rock stars when it comes to weight loss and health benefits. They are full of power. Sure, they can make you cry, but they are POWERFULLY beneficial to your health and weight. Hot peppers have very strong properties for boosting metabolism, reducing appetite, and burning fat.

Hot peppers contain a substance called capsaicin. This substance has proven to be very effective to:

- Boost metabolism, helping you lose weight.
- Help prevent high levels of insulin. Research showed that eating hot peppers reduced the amount of insulin required to lower blood sugar after a meal. And when hot peppers became a regular part of the diet, the level of insulin required became even lower. Avoiding high

levels of insulin will benefit your weight because insulin is in charge of storing fat.

- Reduce inflammation.
- Reduce pain associated with arthritis.
- Reduce cholesterol. ·
- Improve cardiovascular health.
- Clear congestion.
- Help to stop prostate cancer.
- Help prevent stomach ulcers.
- Provide antioxidants that protect you from the damage by free radicals that can make you age faster, look older, and get sick.

Don't worry if you can't eat spicy food because you can minimize how hot or spicy the peppers are by taking away the veins and seeds before cooking them. Most of the time, this will make them not spicy at all. All recipes include this way of preparing peppers.

The key to The Mexican Food Diet™ is the ingredients we use and the foods we absolutely avoid.

Get ready for the next section where I start to teach you about the ingredients you will put in your body and why certain ingredients have been left out of this diet.

Don't worry, you can rest assured that the recipes are flavorful, exciting, and powerful, even without these foods. In fact, once you experience the benefits of not having some of these foods, you may decide to leave them out for good because you don't like how they make you feel or look.

Chapter 6

S.M.A.R.T. & S.T.U.P.I.D. INGREDIENTS

I created the S.M.A.R.T. Ingredients and S.TU.P.I.D. Ingredients to establish the criteria that I would use for selecting what to eat and what to avoid both in The Mexican Food Diet™ or any other plan I would create.

S.M.A.R.T. Ingredients are those that:

S upport health and weight loss, which will help you get healthier and reach and sustain a healthy weight

M inimize toxicity, which could keep you fat, sick, and sad

A ffect your brain, energy, and emotions in positive ways, which will make you feel energized, focused, and happy

R educe inflammation, which is the leading cause of all diseases

T ake care of maintaining hormonal balance, which is essential to lose fat, avoid gaining weight, and to feel happy

S.T.U.P.I.D. Ingredients are those that:

S abotage your health and your weight loss, making you feel and look bad

T rigger inflammation, which makes you gain weight, store more fat, have a greater risk for injuries, be more susceptible to pain, and show more vulnerability to disease

U ndermine your immune system, which makes you get sick frequently and stay sick longer; and leads to multitude diseases

P rovoke hormonal imbalance, which makes you gain weight; sabotages weight loss; increases accumulation of fat; and makes you feel fatigued, have mood swings, feel depressed, and have restless sleep, all of which leads to diseases

I ncrease toxicity in your body, which makes you feel awful, drained, and moody; sabotages your weight and fat loss; gives you brain fog and difficulty in focusing; and leads to diseases, including cancer

D amage your gut's health, which will sabotage your health and your weight-loss efforts; and can lead to multiple diseases

Since I started focusing on eating only meals made with S.M.A.R.T. ingredients and leaving out all the S.T.U.P.I.D. ingredients, I have finally been able to get to a point of healthy weight that I have maintained for four years without relying on ongoing restrictive diets or excessive exercise programs. When I got to this point, I suddenly discovered what feeling amazing and consistent happiness and calm were. It is a feeling of empowerment, lightness, wellbeing, vibrancy, and youthfulness that I love. What a difference from feeling bloated, heavy, burdened, anxious, and stuck. I also realized how great it was to lose the stress of having to be on a constant diet. Today, I eat more than I ever have, but I only eat S.M.A.R.T. ingredients.

And eating this way also helped me recover my health, which I had taken for granted but will never do again. Without health, you cannot be your best self, and it will cost you money and time that I would prefer to spend in other more constructive ways.

You will start your journey by following the meal plan in this diet where I have already done the work for you. All recipes are made with only S.M.A.R.T. ingredients, and the meals have all the elements you need in the right amounts. You just need to pay attention to the recommended portion sizes and meal time. For example, many breakfasts and lunches can be interchanged, but some may not be suitable for dinner because they have more fuel than your body needs after dinner, so you need to keep them for breakfast or lunch.

Use this section as your guide to select what to eat, so you maximize your results. And use the information about S.T.U.P.I.D. foods below in this section and in Chapter 11 to know what to avoid, so you don't sabotage your weight and your health as we discussed in the previous section.

Before I became trained in nutrition, I used to think about losing weight just to look good. Today, I still think that looking good as a goal is perfectly valid, but appearance is no longer only what drives me to eat well. My focus is my commitment to being my best self, empowered, and healthy always. In Chapters 7, 8, and 9, you will learn more about the S.M.A.R.T. ingredients, meals, and snacks, which are the answer to a healthy weight without restrictive diets or excessive exercise. I am confident that I will be able to inspire and lead you to get to this place soon.

EAT MORE S.M.A.R.T. INGREDIENTS

Whenever you are not following **The Mexican Food Diet**™, I want you to use the list of the S.M.A.R.T. ingredients in Chapter 7 to prepare S.M.A.R.T. meals, or to know what to eat when you are out, so that you can keep the results and continue your journey. You will learn the details about how to prepare a S.M.A.R.T. meal in Chapters 8 and 9.

AVOID OR MINIMIZE S.T.U.P.I.D. INGREDIENTS

Make sure you carefully study Chapter 11 for details on S.T.U.P.I.D. ingredients.

Below is the list of the S.T.U.P.I.D. ingredients that will prevent you from achieving your goals. They increase inflammation, toxicity, and get your hormones out of balance, leading to weight problems, disease, and mood problems. It is far more challenging to operate at your best capacity when you are struggling physically and emotionally. I know: I tried, and it didn't work. I want you to reduce the consumption of these foods at a pace that you feel comfortable with until you are no longer eating them or rarely. While on **The Mexican Food Diet**™, you will not be eating S.T.U.P.I.D. ingredients, and believe me, you will not miss them because every recipe is delicious, nutritious, and satisfying.

The S.T.U.P.I.D. Ingredients to Avoid

- Dairy
- Gluten
- Sugar
- Artificial sweeteners
- GMO products
- Soy
- Corn

- Unhealthy oils
- Processed foods
- Unhealthy additives—like MSG and artificial flavors
- The most contaminated vegetables and fruits as found on the list of the Dirty Dozen, which is a list compiled annually by the EWG (Environmental Working Group). The list includes the fruits and vegetables with the most pesticide residues. To get the list for the year, go to https://www.ewg.org/foodnews/dirty_dozen_list.php#.WaDWra2ZNE4. When buying any of the foods in this list, I want you to choose organic in order to keep toxins in your body low.

As I said earlier, the recipes in The Mexican Food Diet™ have been created by using only S.M.A.R.T. ingredients and leaving S.T.U.P.I.D. ingredients out. I guarantee you that you will not miss them because the recipes have sufficient flavor and are going to show you what it feels like to have Healthy Eating That Feels Like Cheating™. You will get the satisfaction you normally get from eating, for example, a desert, but the positive feeling will last. You will be left feeling satisfied, happy, energized, and clear-headed until your next meal, as opposed to feeling hungry, lethargic, unfocused or heavy shortly after.

After you complete this diet, you should continue to avoid or minimize the consumption of these S.T.U.P.I.D. ingredients if you want to stay at a healthy weight and feel happy.

In Chapter 11, I will share with you the reasons why I decided the S.T.U.P.I.D. ingredients should be avoided. Now, let's go to the next chapter where we will go over the good ingredients, the S.M.A.R.T. ingredients that make up each recipe in this book and should become the ingredients for every meal you prepare or eat.

Chapter 7

S.M.A.R.T. INGREDIENTS LIST

B elow is the list you need to get healthier, lose weight, and feel happy. As mentioned earlier, the recipes in this book only use S.M.A.R.T. ingredients. When you eat out or cook other recipes, use this list to make S.M.A.R.T. choices. I am also including some guidance on how to choose certain ingredients because some ingredients, like animal protein, eggs, vegetables, and fruit, are not all healthy. You need to follow my guidelines if you want to stay on track.

To get a printable version of the S.M.A.R.T. and S.T.U.P.I.D. Ingredients list go to www.flacaforever.com/SmartnStupid

S.M.A.R.T. PLANT-BASED PROTEINS

PROTEIN POWDERS

- Flaca Stay Lean™ All-In-One Shake—Vanilla or Chocolate
- Flaca Get Lean™ —Vanilla or Chocolate
- Flaca Detox™
- Other plant-based protein powders (must be dairy-free, gluten-free, soy-free, sugar-free, non-GMO)

NUTS AND NUT BUTTERS

From raw nuts and unsweetened butters: almonds, Brazilian nuts, cashews, hazelnuts, pecans, pine nuts, pistacchios, walnuts.

SEEDS

Chia seeds, flax seeds, hemp seeds, pumpkin seeds, sesame seeds, sunflower seeds.

S.M.A.R.T. ANIMAL PROTEINS

- Chicken and turkey—organic and free-range
- Eggs—organic and free-range
- Pork—organic and pastured
- Red meats—organic, grass-fed, lean beef, game, or lamb; see section below on how to buy meat

FISH

Check the section below on how to buy fish.

- Anchovies
- Butterfish
- Clams
- Cold-water fish and shellfish, preferably wild-caught
- Halibut
- Herring
- King crab
- Lobster
- Sardines
- Scallops

- Shellfish
- Sole
- Tilapia
- Trout
- Whitefish
- Wild salmon

S.M.A.R.T. FATS
- Almond meal
- Almond milk—unsweetened
- Avocado
- Cashew milk—unsweetened
- Coconut butter
- Coconut milk—unsweetened
- Flaxseed meal
- Olives

HEALTHY OILS
- Flaxseed oil
- Avocado oil
- Coconut oil—extra virgin
- Olive oil—extra virgin
- Palm fruit oil

NUTS (From raw nuts and unsweetened butters)
- Almonds
- Brazilian Nuts
- Cashews

- Hazelnuts
- Macadamia nuts
- Pecans
- Pine nuts
- Pistachios
- Walnuts

SEEDS (Raw)

- Chia
- Flax
- Pumpkin
- Sesame
- Sunflower

S.M.A.R.T. VEGETABLES: NON-STARCHY (UNLIMITED)

- Arugula
- Asparagus
- Bamboo shoots
- Bean sprouts
- Beet greens
- Bell peppers: red, green, and yellow (Dirty Dozen, so they need to be organic)
- Broccoli
- Brussels sprouts
- Cabbage: red, yellow, and green
- Cauliflower
- Celery (Dirty Dozen, so it needs to be organic)
- Chayote
- Cherry tomatoes (Dirty Dozen, so they need to be organic)

- Chives
- Collard greens
- Cucumber - (Dirty Dozen so it needs to be organic)
- Dandelion greens
- Eggplant
- Endive
- Fennel
- Garlic
- Ginger
- Green beans
- Green onions
- Hot peppers
- Jalapeño peppers
- Jicama
- Kale
- Leeks
- Lemon
- Lettuce
- Limes
- Mushrooms
- Mustard greens
- Onions: yellow, red, and white
- Parsley
- Poblano peppers
- Radishes
- Scallions
- Serrano peppers
- Shallots
- Snow peas

- Spaghetti squash
- Spinach (Dirty Dozen, so it must be organic)
- Sugar snap peas (imported are Dirty Dozen, so they need to be organic)
- Summer squash
- Swiss chard
- Tomatoes
- Turnip greens
- Water chestnuts
- Watercress
- Zucchini
- Zucchini flowers

S.M.A.R.T. CARBS

FRUITS:

- Apples
- Berries: acai, blackberries, blueberries, boysenberries, elderberries, goji berries, goose berries, loganberries, raspberries, strawberries (strawberries should be organic as they are part of Dirty Dozen)
- Cranberries
- Grapefruit
- Nectarines
- Oranges
- Passion fruit
- Peaches
- Persimmon

VEGETABLES

- Acorn squash
- Artichokes
- Butternut squash
- Carrots
- Leeks
- Okra
- Parsnip
- Pumpkin
- Sweet potato/yam
- Winter squash

GRAINS

- Amaranth
- Brown rice and brown rice pasta (no corn)
- Quinoa and quinoa pasta (no corn)
- Millet
- Oatmeal
- Teff
- Wild rice

BEANS AND LEGUMES

- Chickpeas or garbanzo beans
- French beans
- Hummus
- Kidney beans
- Lentils

- Lima beans
- Pinto beans
- Split beans
- White beans

S.M.A.R.T. CONDIMENTS AND SPICES (UNLIMITED)

- Apple cider vinegar
- Black pepper
- Cayenne
- Cinnamon
- Coriander
- Cumin
- Dijon or spicy mustard—no sugar added
- Dried bay leaf
- Garlic
- Oregano
- Rosemary
- Sea salt
- Shallots
- Thyme
- Turmeric

S.M.A.R.T. SUPERFOODS

- Acai
- Cacao nibs
- Cacao powder—organic, raw,
- Coconut chips—unsweetened
- Maca powder
- Seaweed

S.M.A.R.T. DRINKS

- Coffee—organic and dark roasted
- Flaca Forever Stay Lean, Get Lean, or Detox Shakes
- Green tea
- Teas—no caffeine
- Teas—with caffeine
- Water—plain water only

CHOOSING S.M.A.R.T. ANIMAL PROTEIN

All protein is not the same. You need to know how to select a S.M.A.R.T. animal protein to achieve your goals of losing weight and transforming your health. Animal proteins, when not chosen correctly, can be unhealthy for you and sabotage health and weight-loss efforts.

You are what you eat and how you live your life, but you are also what the animals you consume eat or live their lives. Let me give you some quick examples, so you get the picture.

If the animals you are eating were given hormones, so they would grow faster, or antibiotics so they wouldn't get sick, you will be getting those hormones and antibiotics in your body. If the animals were kept under very unsanitary or stressful conditions, or they were killed in a stressful way, they will be stressed, and stress creates toxicity, so you will be adding those toxins to your body.

Characteristics of S.M.A.R.T. Animal Protein

Here is your summary of what to look for. Also, read the details below to understand the reasons why and how to choose each specific animal protein.

- Grass-fed, instead of corn-fed
- Organic
- Free-range
- No antibiotics used
- No hormones added
- Nitrate-free
- For fish: smaller-sized fish that were wild-caught

Why Is Grass-Fed Better than Corn-Fed?

There are many benefits from choosing grass-fed versus corn-fed meat. The way the animals are fed has a major impact on the nutrient component of the meat and the impact on your health. Grass-fed is superior on both counts. It will be more nutritious and will support your health and weight-loss efforts. Here is a clear comparison on why you should select grass-fed.

1. **Grass-fed cows are healthier**. They have better living environments and are not confined, which allows them to get exercise. Corn-fed cows live confined in large feedlots that are unsanitary and unhealthy.

2. **Grass-fed cows mainly eat grass** while corn-fed cows eat genetically modified corn that can rapidly fatten them. They often receive drugs and hormones to grow even faster, some of which you will also get by eating their meat.

3. **The meat of grass-fed cows is leaner, and its fatty acid composition is better**. Fatty acids are essential for your body and brain to function at their peak.

4. **Grass-fed beef has 5 times more omega-3**, which has very important health and weight-loss benefits. Some of the benefits are:

- Reduced inflammation and insulin resistance, key causes for obesity and diseases like diabetes and cancer.
- Lowered risk of heart disease.

5. **Grass-fed meat has 2 times more conjugated linoleic acid (CLA)**, which is associated with reduced body fat and other health benefits.

6. As far as fats, they both have saturated fat, monounsaturated fat, and omega-6 polyunsaturated fats.

Why Is Organic Better?

When meat is certified as organic, you will have the assurance that it will be S.M.A.R.T. Getting these certifications requires that farms and ranches follow a strict set of guidelines that the USDA (US Department of Agriculture) has established. Following these guidelines results in healthier, non-toxic animals that will provide S.M.A.R.T. protein for your diet.

To receive the USDA organic certification, the livestock (chickens, cows, and pigs) must be:

1. Raised organically on certified organic land, which decreases the amount of pesticides or toxins that they will be exposed to, which could end up in your body.

2. Fed certified organic feed. This feed cannot contain animal byproducts or genetically engineered grains. This feed cannot be grown using persistent pesticides or chemical fertilizers.

3. Raised without antibiotics or added growth hormones.

4. Living in non-confined environments with frequent outdoor access.

Why Is Free-Range Better?

Free-range, as defined by the USDA, is a term that is applied to chickens that can have some access to an outside area instead of spending their entire lives in small areas and frequently confined in cages.

Poultry that can feed from pastures has demonstrated to be healthier. Having access to the outside encourages movement, which encourages muscle growth and reduces fat accumulation. This combination results in a leaner, meatier chicken. Animals allowed to feed from pastures also contain more omega-3, which is healthy fat that you need for your body and brain to perform at their best. It also helps reduce inflammation.

It is important to note that having a "free-range" label could mean that the chickens get outside for a very short period of time and the rest of the time they are confined. It could also mean that they get access outside but only to a tiny area. A free-range label does not guarantee that they have not been fed GMO grains or been given antibiotics or hormones.

To get S.M.A.R.T. poultry, you need to make sure it is labeled both "organic" and "free-range." Having these 2 labels will guarantee that the animals have frequent access to pasture areas that are large enough and that they were not fed animal byproducts, GMO grains, or given antibiotics or hormones.

Why Is Cage-Free Not Recommended?

Being labeled "cage-free" does not ensure the poultry will be a S.M.A.R.T. protein. "Cage-free" does not mean the animal had free access to an adequate-sized outside area where there is pasture. It frequently means that the animals were out of a cage but crammed together in an indoor place, preventing them from eating in pastures. On top of that, a "cage-free" label does not guarantee that the animals are not eating GMO grains, animal byproducts, or receiving antibiotics and hormones. As a conclusion, "cage-free" does not guarantee much. If you want to have S.M.A.R.T. protein, you need to choose "free-range" and "organic" poultry.

Why Is It Important to Have Animals Raised without the Use of Antibiotics or Hormones?

It is also a common practice in the meat industry to mix antibiotics with animal food and water every day to compensate for the unhealthy living conditions when animals are raised in crowded and confined areas. Antibiotics help the farmers to prevent the spread of infections that could kill most of the animals, affecting the farm's economics. Growth hormones are also given to animals to promote rapid growth so that animals are ready for market sooner, which will help profits.

One of the problems with using antibiotics for animals that are not sick is that it kills weak bacteria and creates the perfect environment for antibiotic-resistant bacteria to multiply and thrive. If you eat these meats, you may be getting some of these bacteria that are now resistant to antibiotics, and they would be hard to treat if you acquire them. Furthermore, many of the antibiotics given to animals remain in their meat, ending up in your body and increasing toxicity.

Regarding hormones, they can remain in the meat increasing the risk of certain cancers, such as breast cancer and prostate cancer.

It is important to specify that the USDA does not allow the use of hormones at all in raising chickens, turkeys, or other fowl. So, you will not see any labels of "no hormones added" on the meat of these animals. Choosing organic poultry is still the safer way to go.

Why Is Nitrate-Free Recommended?

Nitrates and nitrites are chemicals that are added to certain foods, such as cured meats. These chemicals give the meats color and extend their shelf life but can also increase your risk of developing certain cancers and can affect pregnancy. When buying sliced turkey, look for nitrate-free or "no nitrates added."

Why Is Wild-Caught Fish Better?

There is a lot of confusing information out there. It used to be that wild-caught fish was considered significantly healthier. Some of the reasons were that most fish farms were feeding fish unnatural diets and raising them in cramped, unhealthy enclosures that were breeding disease and leading to the heavy use of antibiotics.

However, today, there are also important concerns about wild-caught fish because of the effects that concentrations of heavy metal contaminants, pollutants, pesticides, fertilizers, and trash have on the waters and the fish that live in them.

Fortunately, fish farming practices have been improving, and there are now options of healthy farmed fish.

The best option for you today is to get wild-caught fish and only strategically select farm-raised fish. What I mean by "strategically select" is that you know the source and their practices.

In terms of what fish to buy, smaller types of fish are better. Research has found that the larger top predator fish have more mercury in their blood and have no better nutrients than the smaller fish. For what specific fish to buy, refer to the S.M.A.R.T. ingredients list in Chapter 7.

Chapter 8
S.M.A.R.T. MEAL

O ne of the most frequent questions I get from my clients is what they should be eating for each meal when they are not following **The Mexican Food Diet**™ meal plan, how to select it, and when can they get this accomplished in their busy life! I created the S.M.A.R.T. plate as the guiding principle when selecting each of your 3 meals.

In this section, you will find the answers and a simple guide to ensure that each meal has on the plate the right players or food elements to support your journey towards looking and feeling great.

In the next chapter, you can see what a S.M.A.R.T. plate would look like for a snack.

SMART PLATE

The S.M.A.R.T. plate includes the different categories of food that your body needs to operate at its peak. The first thing you will notice is that every meal should be dominated by S.M.A.R.T. Veggies. You need at least 5 servings per day of non-starchy veggies. The more, the better. You can find the list on Chapter 7. These type of veggies are unlimited. Have as much as you feel like. They will nourish your body and your brain, and they are fuel for your detox system. They also help you feel satisfied longer and also help with keeping your blood sugar more stable. All of these will help you stay healthy and energized throughout the day while burning more fat.

While you are following **The Mexican Food Diet**™ you do not need to worry about what to have in your plate. I got you covered. The meals have all you need for reaching your weight and health goals. To know what to eat when you are not eating the meals on The Mexican Food Diet™ use the S.M.A.R.T. ingredients list in Chapter 7 and avoid the ingredients in Chapter 11.

Here are the elements you need to include in every meal. In the section below, you will find the reasons why you need each.

THE ELEMENTS OF A SMART PLATE

S.M.A.R.T. Clean Proteins

- At least 0.36 g multiplied by your bodyweight in pounds. The total amount should be distributed between your daily meals and snacks.
- For example, if you were to weigh 100 lbs.: 0.36 X 100 = 36 g of protein per day.

S.M.A.R.T. Healthy Fats

- 3 servings per day. Include them in every meal every day.
- A serving is 1 tablespoon of a healthy oil or nut/seed butter, ½ avocado, or ¼ cup of raw nuts or seeds.

S.M.A.R.T. Veggies

- You need 5–10 servings per day of non-starchy veggies. A serving is 2 cups of raw leafy greens or 1 cup of cooked or raw non-starchy veggies. Consult Chapter 7 to find the long list of alternatives to meet this very important need.

S.M.A.R.T. Healthy Carbs

- These are certain veggies with high-carb content, fruits, gluten-free grains, and legumes.
- You need 1–2 servings per day of fruits and a maximum of 1 serving of a high-carb veggie, gluten-free grain or legume. A serving of fruit is 1 cup. A serving of high-carb veggies, gluten-free grain or legumes is ⅓ cup. Consult Chapter 7 to find the long list of alternatives to meet this need.
- You don't need healthy carbs for your dinner because they provide too much fuel that you will not need at night and will only increase your fat. The dinner recipes in this diet do not use healthy carbs, only at breakfast and lunch. This does not apply to your kids.

S.M.A.R.T. Spices and Condiments (optional).

- These add flavor, and many also have health benefits. Use them as you like and need. Experiment with them. There is no minimum or maximum for this category.

S.M.A.R.T. Superfoods (optional)

- These types of foods are nutrient-dense and add flavor. They are called superfoods because in a small amount you get a lot of the benefits. There are a lot to choose from, and you should also experiment. The serving size varies for each food. No minimum is required. Consult Chapter 7 to find the long list of alternatives to choose from.

CLEAN PROTEIN OR S.M.A.R.T. PROTEIN

You must have clean protein at each meal if you want to lose weight and keep it off because:

- Protein helps you feel full faster and stay satisfied for longer periods.
- Protein helps you control your cravings for sugar and unhealthy carbs. In fact, it has been proven that people's cravings frequently mean they are low on protein. When levels of protein are low, your body feels a need for energy and will lead you towards quick energy source foods, such as sugar and carbs. These will satisfy the immediate craving and need for energy, but shortly after, will make blood sugar spike, trigger an insulin response, and promote fat accumulation.
- Protein slows the absorption and release of sugar into your blood from the carbs you eat, thus keeping blood sugar levels more stable and helping you reduce cravings, energy crashes, and mood swings. This will help you be less hungry. It will also help you stay energized, focused, and in better mood than when you eat sugar or unhealthy carbs.

- Sufficient amounts of protein are required for effective detoxification. Without sufficient protein, toxins cannot be fully processed, and they get sent back to the bloodstream damaging cells along the way and ending up stored mainly in your fat cells.

- Protein requires more energy to be digested, so you will burn more calories by eating protein than by eating carbs or fat.

- Protein is the fuel that your body needs to burn fat. Your body cannot use fat for energy (which means burning your fat) unless it has the help of carbohydrates or protein.

- Protein is needed to preserve lean muscle while you are losing weight. Lean muscle will help you look better and burns more calories.

S.M.A.R.T proteins come from animals or plants. Examples of animal protein are meat, fish, poultry, or eggs. Most animal proteins tend to deliver all the amino acids your body needs to make new protein and cells. It is important for you to know that not all animal proteins are S.M.A.R.T. You need to know how to buy them. In the previous Chapter 7, you can find details of how to make sure your animal proteins are S.M.A.R.T.

Examples of non-animal proteins are nuts and seeds, grains, and legumes. Most non-animal proteins lack one or more essential amino acids. The challenge for people that depend on this non-animal protein is that they need to make sure they include a very wide variety of foods to get all the essential amino acids that are needed to make new protein and cells.

S.M.A.R.T. HEALTHY FATS

Fat is INDISPENSABLE for reaching absolute wellness and is EXTREMELY important for weight loss and weight maintenance. The S.M.A.R.T. meal uses S.M.A.R.T. fats as a critical player, making your weight-loss efforts easier. S.M.A.R.T. fats are the healthy and helpful fats. For now, just remember that good fats should be part of your daily diet and part of every meal. Also know that not all fats are the same.

When you make sure you include S.M.A.R.T. fats in your diet, you will be able to notice that you do not get hungry as fast. You also will be surprised as to how much less cravings you will have. S.M.A.R.T. fats give you a stable source of energy, slowing down the digestion of carbs, allowing for a consistent release of energy throughout the day. They also speed up metabolism and stimulate fat burning.

Healthy fat does not lead to heart disease, nor does it increase cholesterol as we used to believe. On the contrary, healthy fat benefits you in many ways:

- It helps you burn fat.
- It fuels your brain so you stay focused, calm and happy.
- It keeps you satisfied and reduces your cravings.
- It strengthens your immune system.
- It reduces inflammation most of the time.

S.M.A.R.T. HEALTHY CARBS

Most healthy carbs are leafy greens or non-starchy vegetables.

In **The Mexican Food Diet**™, we use carbs, but mostly in the form of non-starchy vegetables. We also use moderate amounts of select fruits, gluten-free grains and legumes. In the S.M.A.R.T. plate, veggies are a category on their own, so we have a smaller percentage of other carbs, which is what we call S.M.A.R.T. carbs. These include fruits, some veggies that are considered more as fruit because of their sugar content (like sweet potatoes, beets, carrots), legumes like beans or lentils, and select gluten-free grains like quinoa, amaranth, and brown rice.

Carbs are the preferred source of energy for your body. And some of them, like vegetables, and select grains and legumes, also provide you with a wide variety of necessary nutrients and fiber.

In the S.M.A.R.T. carbs group, I have included fruits, starchy veggies, and gluten-free grains that are the best for your health and weight goals. These select S.M.A.R.T. carbs are good for the following reasons:

- They are the easiest source of energy and can also be stored as energy for later use.
- They lower blood pressure.
- They lower cholesterol.
- They protect you from heart disease.
- They are needed for the central nervous system.
- They are needed for the proper functioning of the brain, kidneys, and muscles.
- They are vital for the health of your digestive system and the proper elimination of waste and toxins that could damage your health and wellness.

S.M.A.R.T. VEGGIES

Veggies are the best carbs for you. They provide you with lots of fiber, nutrients, and are very low in sugar. They are also one of the

2 key fuels required for effective detoxification and elimination of toxins and waste that can keep you fat, sick and sad. You must have them with each meal. No maximum on this category, just minimum. You must have no less than five servings a day. The more you have, the better for you. Each serving consists of 1 cup of cooked or raw veggies or 2 cups of green leafy greens. But like I said, you can have unlimited amounts.

The ones you can eat in unlimited amounts are the non-starchy vegetables like all the green plants, broccoli, cauliflower, peppers (bell peppers and hot peppers), cucumber, mushrooms, onions, garlic, tomatoes, lemons, limes, and a lot more that you can find in Chapter 7. The more colorful your selection, the better for your health. It is important to rotate the veggies in your meals. You will be getting more variety of nutrients and preventing the possibility of developing an intolerance to a specific vegetable.

This type of carb also provides you with energy but in more stable and healthier ways. I used to think that non-veggie carbs like grains were the only ones that could keep me energized. But to my surprise, lately, I have been able to get all my energy from non-starchy veggies and limited fruits. And believe me, I am extremely energized throughout the day.

Some specific benefits of veggies are:

- They are a major source of vitamins, minerals, fiber, and phytochemicals.
- They are required for your body's detoxification process.
- They strengthen your digestive health and improve elimination of waste and toxins.
- They have strong anti-inflammatory properties.
- They boost your immune system.
- They help maintain blood sugar at healthy levels.

- They protect you from most major diseases like heart diseases, diabetes, and cancer.
- They provide antioxidants that protect your body from free radicals.
- They protect your vision.

Weight Loss and Maintenance

Non-starchy veggies will be your secret weapon in your weight-loss and weight-maintenance efforts. They should fill up most of your S.M.A.R.T. plate. Veggies will fill you up with little calories and a lot of nutrients. They strengthen your metabolism, so you can burn more fat. They help your body get rid of toxins that can keep you fat. They provide with stable and healthy energy, and reduced calories, so your body can start tapping into your fat reserves. If you don't crave veggies today, don't worry, as you get more into clean eating, you will start craving them. I found that preparing veggies with some added flavor and healthy fats is much better than eating them steamed and bland. The recipes in this book include your veggies in a fun and delicious way.

S.M.A.R.T. SPICES, CONDIMENTS & SUPER FOODS

S.M.A.R.T. Condiments and Spices: These add flavor to your meals. You can have unlimited amounts. Many of these are also beneficial to your health.

Condiments and spices are your tools in making your meals exciting and adding flavor. They do not affect your weight or your blood sugar. In **The Mexican Food Diet**™, we use a variety of condiments. Many of these are great aids in your body's detoxification process and in the control of blood sugar, both of which are very important for your health and your weight.

Some examples of condiments and spices are cinnamon, cumin, paprika, vanilla, vinegar, sea salt, rosemary, thyme, cayenne pepper, and black pepper, among many others.

Some of the most relevant benefits of spices and condiments are:

- Boost metabolism
- Reduce fat accumulation
- Reduce cravings and appetite
- Improve digestive health
- Reduce inflammation
- Provide detoxification support
- Boost immune system
- Maintain blood sugar at healthy levels and improve insulin sensitivity
- Provide antioxidant protection
- Lower cholesterol and triglycerides (fat) in the blood
- Prevent or reduce allergy and nasal congestion

S.M.A.R.T. Superfoods: These are optional but very powerful for your health and weight-loss goals. Superfoods are nutrient-rich foods that in small amounts can supply you with a large dose of antioxidants, protein, essential fats, vitamins, minerals, and other key nutrients. They are great sources of energy and major tools to strengthen your physical and emotional health.

You can experiment adding them to your diet. **The Mexican Food Diet**™ uses many of these in the recipes. Some of my favorites: chia seeds, raw cacao powder, cacao nibs, maca powder, green powder, acai, goji berries, and many others.

Some of the benefits:

- They are a condensed source of powerful nutrients, protein, fatty acids, and fiber.

- They have powerful antioxidant properties, which protect from the damaging effects of free radicals that can make you age faster and get sick.
- They can help overcome fatigue and increase stamina.
- They can enhance mood and boost libido.
- They can help reduce stress.
- They can help maintain blood sugar at healthy levels and improve insulin sensitivity.
- They can have important anti-aging properties.
- They can strengthen the endocrine system.
- They can strengthen your digestive health.
- They can strengthen your heart's health.
- They can have anti-inflammatory properties.
- They can boost your immune system.
- They can help improve brain function.

Weight Loss and Maintenance: Superfoods, condiments and spices are great help for weight loss too.

- They can help reduce cravings and appetite.
- They can slow down the breakdown of carbs, reducing the amount of sugar in the blood and minimizing the amount that gets converted into fat.
- They can improve insulin sensitivity.
- They can interfere with the formation of fat cells.
- They can increase the body's ability to use food as energy and minimize the amount of fat accumulation.
- They can increase metabolism.

S.M.A.R.T. Drinks: The only one you must have is water. And you need to have a lot of this. Not unlimited but at least half of your body weight (measured in pounds) in ounces of water each day. So, if you were to weigh 100 pounds, you need to drink 100/2 = 50 ounces of water every day. One glass is 8 ounces, so you would need 50/8 = 6.25 glasses of water. It is easy to forget to drink water. I recommend that you keep a big thermos or glass water bottle with you at all times. The only time you don't need water is during meals. Water interferes with digestion. I recommend drinking water throughout the day except thirty minutes before and thirty minutes after your meals.

Chapter 9
S.M.A.R.T. SNACK

When you begin your health journey, you may feel hungry between meals and will need a S.M.A.R.T. snack to satisfy your hunger. As your body gets fully nourished, you will start to get hungry right around 4–6 hours after each meal. In this case, you do not need a snack between meals.

You should eat a S.M.A.R.T. snack if you will not be able to eat for a period longer than 6 hours or when you are going to a place where there are no healthy options available.

If you get hungry after dinner, you should focus on veggies, protein, or fat. Healthy carbs, like fruit or gluten-free grains, should be left for snacks during the day if you are truly hungry, instead of just emotionally hungry. And, if you do get hungry at night, you will need to increase your protein and/or veggies portions at dinner.

When you are planning or preparing your snacks, you want to always include a protein or a fat, and try to avoid eating a non-veggie carb, such as a fruit alone, because that will spike your blood sugar, affect your energy, and lead you to store fat. When you combine a fruit with a protein or fat, this will slow down digestion and will allow for the gradual release of sugar into the blood resulting in a more stable source of energy that your body can use throughout the day instead of storing it as fat.

The following are good alternatives for a S.M.A.R.T. snack. You can test different combinations to find out the one that works best for you.

Based on the above, the ideal snack would be any of the following combinations:

- A clean protein + a veggie or fruit
- A healthy fat + veggie or fruit
- A healthy fat
- A clean protein

Here are some recommended serving sizes for the elements in a snack:

- **Protein**: 2–3 oz, 1–2 eggs, or ½–1 scoop of protein powder
- **Healthy Fat**: 1 tablespoon of healthy oil or nut butter, ¼ cup of nuts or seeds, ½ avocado
- **Fruit**: ½ cup or ½ fresh fruit
- **Veggies**: Unlimited servings of leafy greens or non-starchy veggies; ½ cup of high-sugar veggies like sweet potatoes or beets.

Chapter 10
THE RULES

N ow that we have covered the players in your S.M.A.R.T. meals and snacks, let's review some of the rules you should follow if you want to succeed.

- **There is NO skipping meals ever**, especially breakfast. Skipping meals is one of the worst things you can do for your weight and your health. It slows down your metabolism. It compromises your supply of energy. And, it makes you very susceptible to overeating in your next meal, snacking in between meals, and choosing unhealthy foods.
- **You should aim to eat every 4 to 6 hours** to keep your metabolism functioning at its peak, maintain healthy levels of blood sugar and ensure a steady supply of energy.
- **Afternoon snack**. You can have the afternoon snack only when you are truly hungry (not just emotionally hungry), if you are very active, if your dinner will be delayed, or if you are going to a place where there may be no healthy options.
- **S.M.A.R.T. carbs need to always be accompanied by S.M.A.R.T. fat and/or S.M.A.R.T. protein**. When you do this, you will be slowing down the conversion of carbs into sugar.
- **Unlimited amounts of S.M.A.R.T. veggies are allowed**. The more you eat, the better. Strive for variety and lots

of color in your veggies. Ensure rotation of veggies. One way to make it easier for you is to pick two veggies at a time. That way you don't run out of veggies in your next meals. You can repeat them for a couple of days but change on the third day.

- **Limited amounts of S.M.A.R.T. carbs while trying to lose weight**. You will need to control the amount and frequency. These include healthy fruits, vegetables like sweet potatoes, beets, and butternut squash, and legumes like beans and grains.

- **No S.M.A.R.T. carbs after 4 pm**. You will not have any of the S.M.A.R.T carbs listed in Chapter 7 after 4 pm. You don't need them, and when you do consume them, you will be sabotaging your weight-loss efforts and increasing the chances that they end up as fat.

- **Limited wine**. You can have wine a few times a week (1 glass) with rest days in between.

What Comes After the 7-Days of The Mexican Food Diet™

While following the meal plan in this diet, you can rest assured that your plate includes all you need to be fully nourished, so you will not be hungry, tired, or crave unhealthy foods between meals. Eating this way will help you feel much better and will also save you money as you will not be eating out as often. The recipes I selected are quick to prepare because I believe that you should not have to spend all day in the kitchen to eat delicious and nutritious meals.

After you finish the 7-day plan of **The Mexican Food Diet**™, if you want to maintain the results, you can continue eating in a similar way by using the guides in this book. If you want to accelerate your journey to get healthier, leaner, and happier, I have created a program that is very easy to follow and in only 14 days will take you to the next level in your weight loss and health. It is the **Flaca Detox™ Reset and Renew Program**, the simple, delicious, and nutritious way to get your body clean and set the strong foundations needed to turn your body into a fat-burning machine. If you want to learn about it, go to:

www.FlacaDetox.com.

Chapter 11

WHY YOU MUST AVOID S.T.U.P.I.D. INGREDIENTS

A s I mentioned in the previous chapter, S.T.U.P.I.D. ingredients are those that sabotage your health and your weight in too many ways keeping you fat, sick, and sad. They increase inflammation, toxicity, and get your hormones out of balance, leading to weight problems, disease, and mood problems. It is far more challenging to operate at your best capacity when you are struggling physically and emotionally. I know: I tried and it didn't work.

Let me share with you the reasons why I have decided each S.T.U.P.I.D. ingredient should be avoided.

THE PROBLEM WITH DAIRY

Dairy is a S.T.U.P.I.D. ingredient because **dairy is one of the most inflammatory foods in our world, second only to gluten**.

Dairy causes inflammation in a large percentage of the population and inflammation is the cause of major chronic diseases like cancer, diabetes, and dementia. Inflammation also causes skin, health, and digestive issues, such as acne, bloating, gas, constipation, and diarrhea—and even brain or mood disorders.

About 75% of the world's population have some problem with dairy, and most don't know it.

Having a problem with dairy is usually inherited and varies among different ethnic groups. According to Harvard Medical School, as many as 90% of people from some areas of Eastern Asia, 80% of American Indians, 65% of Africans and African-Americans, and 50% of Hispanics have some degree of a problem with dairy. In contrast, most Caucasians (80%) have a gene that preserves the ability to tolerate dairy into adulthood.

Milk does not reliably prevent osteoporosis.

A 1992 review revealed that fracture rates differ widely between various countries and that calcium intake demonstrated no protective role at all. (*Abelow B.J., Holford T.R., Insogna K.L. Cross-cultural association between dietary animal protein and hip fracture: a hypothesis. Calif Tissue Int. 1992; 50:14-18.*)

In fact, those populations with the highest calcium intakes had higher, not lower, fracture rates than those with more modest calcium intakes.

There are several ways dairy can cause problems:

- Contains lactose which some people cannot digest.
- Contains the proteins casein and whey that cause health and weight problems in a large percentage of people.
- Non-organic dairy comes from animals that were given antibiotics and hormones.

The Problems with Lactose

Lactose intolerance is the most common problem. Lactose intolerant people do not produce the enzyme required to break down lactose and this creates digestive issues when they consume dairy products such as bloating, gas, constipation, diarrhea, and stomach pain.

Problems with Casein and Whey Are Less Known

Milk contains two types of proteins: casein and whey. Casein is 80% of the protein in milk and whey is 20%. Cheeses are mainly casein.

Intolerance to casein is the second most common problem for people, after lactose intolerance. Most people and conventional doctors are still unaware of this widespread problem today. Whereas lactose intolerance is an inability to digest lactose, the problem with casein or whey is characterized by immune reactions when the body is exposed to cow's milk protein. This happens because the body does not recognize one or more of the cow's milk proteins, so it treats it like an invader, triggering a reaction and internal inflammation. For people with a problem with casein or whey continued exposure to dairy triggers chronic inflammation that could lead to diseases.

Most conventional doctors are still using antibiotics and steroids for treating problems that are a result of sensitivities or intolerance to casein and whey. Both my daughter and I were given antibiotics and steroids for several years to treat our asthma and sinus and ear infections when all we needed was to stay away from dairy. Since we eliminated dairy from our diets, we no longer have any of those health problems.

Problems with Casein

1. **Casein triggers inflammation** when the body has difficulty breaking down this protein. When you can't digest casein properly, the partly digested proteins and sugars damage your small intestine, creating tiny holes in the tissue lining. These tiny holes allow unfamiliar protein pieces to get into the bloodstream. The immune system considers these undigested protein dangerous and sets up inflammation

to fight them off. This type of inflammation starts slowly at first but quietly builds up over time. At some point, it starts to create health symptoms until it reaches a point where a diagnosis of a chronic disease is given.

2. **Casein is a frequent cause of respiratory problems**. It is a strong mucus-forming substance that when consumed in high amounts, irritates and clogs your respiratory system leading to a runny or stuffy nose, thick throat, asthma, bronchitis, sinusitis, colds, ear infections, hay fever, and the common allergy to dairy.

3. **Casein can create food addiction equivalent to heroine**. When casein is digested, it produces morphine-like substances (casomorphins) that when they enter the bloodstream act like an opiate. An opiate is a substance that acts on the nervous system to relieve pain. Opiates are components of legal drugs, as well as illegal drugs like heroin or opium. Continued use of opiates can lead to physical dependence. So, when you consume dairy, the casein releases the drug-like casomorphins that attach to opiate receptors in your brain, and this leads to strong addictions to dairy. Casein can cause such a strong food addiction that it has been compared to heroin addiction. Cheese is the most concentrated source of casein among all dairy products. This is the reason why it is much harder to let go of it than other dairy products.

Problem with Whey

1. **Whey can make you fat and sick**. Whey is digested quickly and absorbed rapidly into the bloodstream, provoking a spike in insulin. Insulin spikes reduce blood sugar, increase fat storage, and disrupt your hormonal balance, negatively affecting your metabolism and mood, making you feel

sluggish or depressed. People with low blood sugar or diabetes need to be careful with food that can trigger spikes in insulin because this can lead to very low blood sugar. Low blood sugar affects your energy and makes you want to eat more than you need. Continued spikes in insulin make cells less sensitive to insulin, resulting in insulin resistance. When this happens, the body must produce higher levels of insulin, thus further increasing fat storage and decreasing insulin sensitivity. Over time, cells can become resistant to insulin, the cause of diabetes.

2. **Whey can make you hungry fast**. Whey is digested quickly and absorbed rapidly into the bloodstream. This is one of the reasons many people seek whey, especially after workouts so that they can replenish muscle cells. However, if you are using a meal replacement shake made of whey, you will probably feel hungry very quickly, leading you to cravings for more food and leaving you easily tempted by the unhealthy foods that will surround you throughout the day.

3. **Whey can also trigger inflammation**. People that have difficulty breaking down this protein can also damage their intestinal tissue if they consume dairy. The damage allows undigested food parts to get into the bloodstream, triggering an immune reaction that leads to chronic inflammation the same way as it happens with casein. And, as you know by now, inflammation is the leading cause of most major diseases and the most common health issues.

4. **Whey is associated with a wide variety of health issues**. When people with an allergy or sensitivity to milk consume whey, they can have reactions like diarrhea, failure to thrive, infant colic, rashes, or vomiting. Whey can also cause abnormal heart rhythms, changes in cholesterol levels, headache, increased diabetes risk, increased fracture or osteoporosis

risk, kidney dysfunction, liver damage, stomach or intestine symptoms (acid reflux, bloating, constipation, cramps, gas, increased bowel movements, movement problems, nausea, reduced appetite, swelling of limbs, and upset stomach), and thirst.

5. **Whey promotes aging and increases risk of several cancers**. Whey stimulates what is called insulin growth factor (IGF-1), one of the body's important growth promoters during pregnancy and childhood growth. Later in life, IGF-1 promotes the aging process. Studies have shown that reduced IGF-1 signaling in adulthood is associated with decreased inflammation and cell damage, and increased sensitivity to insulin. When cells are sensitive to insulin, less insulin needs to be produced, leading to less fat storage and a longer life. Conversely, high levels of IGF-1 are linked to increased risk of several cancers because it has been shown to promote the growth, proliferation, and spread of cancer cells.

6. **Whey can also cause respiratory problems.** People that are sensitive to whey will get a strong inflammatory immune response that provokes high production of mucus. This irritates and clogs your respiratory system, leading to a runny or stuffy nose, thick throat, asthma, bronchitis, sinusitis, colds, ear infections, or hay fever. As mentioned above, this happened to my daughter and me.

Products with Dairy

Some of the most common products that contain dairy include the ones listed below. However, dairy can also be easily hidden in many other foods and products, so you need to read labels carefully and directly ask restaurants whether their dishes are prepared using dairy.

- Cheese
- Chips
- Crackers
- Creams
- Dressings
- Ice cream
- Milk
- Processed foods
- Sauces
- Soups
- Yogurt

Over time, people that have a problem with dairy can have some or all the following issues:

- **Skin problems like acne or rosacea.** Dairy contains hormones that increase the production of certain oil glands creating skin congestion even in adults.
- **Excessive production of mucus** is a common sign that people can get when they are sensitive to dairy. I remember having excessive mucus whenever I ran. So much that I had to carry a big package of tissue. Since I removed dairy from my diet, I do not have the mucus and may need one tissue if any during a long run.
- **Frequent sinus infections, colds, congestions, and asthma.** Many people may notice or experience these symptoms when they are adults as it happened to me. I only started getting asthma and recurrent sinus infections in my 40s. As mentioned earlier, since I removed dairy from my diet 3 years ago, I have not had a sinus infection or a cough. However, a year ago I decided to have a cheese plate after dinner and the next day I had

a cough attack while giving a public presentation. It was embarrassing, but it did not last more than that day. So, no more dairy for me since then.

- **Bloating, gas, or constipation** is another common issue associated with dairy sensitivities.

So even if you believe you are not sensitive to dairy, I always recommend experiencing how you feel after not having dairy for 3 weeks. You may be surprised by how much better you feel and look. After 3 weeks, you can go back to it and notice if you like what you feel or not. If you are interested in knowing for sure, you can get tested. Contact me at info@flacaforever.com so I can help you identify the right test for you.

THE PROBLEM WITH GLUTEN

Gluten is a general name for the proteins found in certain grains. **Gluten** helps foods like bread products maintain their shape and plays a key role in allowing bread to rise. Wheat is referenced predominantly in this section because it is the primary way we consume gluten.

Gluten is a S.T.U.P.I.D. ingredient for many reasons:

- **It makes you gain weight, store fat, and feel hungrier**. Gluten-containing products create a very high spike in blood sugar, leading to a high spike in insulin to bring blood sugar levels down. This then results in increasing fat storage, affecting your energy and breaking the hormonal balance. When your hormones are out of balance, you will store more fat, be hungrier, and have a hard time feeling full or satisfied.

  I bet you did not know that gluten-containing products like whole-wheat bread increase blood sugar more intensely than table sugar. There is a measure called the glycemic index (GI) that measures how much blood sugar levels increase in the 90 to 120 minutes after a food is consumed. The "healthy" whole wheat bread has a GI of 72 while the unhealthy table sugar has a GI of 59. In fact, the wheat carbohydrate has demonstrated to create a higher spike in blood sugar than most other carbs, including candy and ice cream. A severe drop in blood sugar soon after eating the wheat-containing product will give you an irresistible hunger that will send you off in search for any food you can find. I am not suggesting you dump whole-wheat bread and go back to sugar. This only shows that wheat is as bad for your weight and health as sugar.

- **It has a negative influence on your brain and your mood**. It can irritate your nervous system, which can lead to headaches, anxiety, depression, and dementia. When people get off gluten, they normally feel major mood improvements, fewer mood swings, and a better ability to focus. I have experienced this. Whenever I eat anything that contains gluten, not only do I get some digestive issue like bloating or indigestion, I also feel down and lethargic for almost 24 hours. This is one of the main reasons I no longer eat gluten. The other one being that I have a high intolerance to it, so eating it will eventually get me sick.

- **It is highly addictive**. People struggle with getting rid of cravings for bread, muffins, donuts, and cookies due to its highly addictive properties (stronger than drugs like heroine) and the extreme withdrawal symptoms that people experience when they stop eating gluten-containing products.

Gluten-Containing Grains

Wheat is the predominant grain today and the main source of gluten in our diets. The other grains are:

- Barley
- Bulgur
- Durum
- Einkorn
- Emmer
- Farina
- Farro
- Fraham
- Kamut
- KAMUT® khorasan wheat
- Rye
- Semolina
- Spelt
- Triticale
- Wheat berries

Common Gluten-Containing Foods

- Additives—most contain gluten
- Bran products
- Breads, cakes, and cookies
- Breakfast cereals
- Cheese spreads
- Gravies
- Margarines
- Meatballs
- Pasta
- Processed foods
- Salad dressings
- Sauces
- Some alcohols
- Soups
- Soy sauce

Gluten Intolerance or Sensitivity

When most people think about gluten intolerance, they are thinking about extreme reactions such as those seen in people with celiac disease. People with celiac have an extreme reaction to gluten, which damages their small intestine. However, there are many people like me with a moderate to high sensitivity to gluten. When we eat gluten-containing foods, it triggers an aggressive immune reaction inside our bodies. This can occur because our body lacks the right enzymes to digest some of the protein composites in gluten. As these undigested particles enter our digestive system, they are immediately labeled as enemies or invaders. The resulting immune response sends out inflammatory chemicals to try to destroy these invaders. As this process continues over time, it can end up damaging the walls of our intestine, making it permeable or compromised. In a healthy intestine, the walls act as a protective barrier. In a damaged intestinal wall, known as "leaky gut," food particles can escape and enter our blood, leading to additional food sensitivities.

For many people today, wheat is still thought as the "whole" healthier carb and is part of every meal and snack they have. This was my belief when I was trying to eat healthier to lose weight. As you remember, it backfired on me because my high consumption of gluten-containing carbs was keeping me fact, sick, and sad.

THE PROBLEM WITH SUGAR

It should not surprise you that sugar is a S.T.U.P.I.D. ingredient that makes you fat. But it may be news to some of you that sugar can also make you tired, sick, and sad. Sugar is highly addictive, which makes it difficult to break the vicious cycle. Sugar or sugar-containing products are also the emptiest calories, providing little to no nutrition but lots of excess energy that may end up stored as fat.

Sugar Makes You Fat.

- High sugar consumption makes blood sugar and insulin spike, increasing fat storage. And over time, this can lead to insulin resistance, the leading cause of diabetes.
- Excess consumption of sugar disrupts your hormonal balance affecting your metabolism and making you gain weight and feel lousy or moody.
- Sugar does not fill you up, so you can eat more than you need or should.

Sugar Makes You Sick.

- **It increases inflammation** in your body and your brain. Chronic inflammation is the leading cause of most diseases like diabetes, cancer, and dementia, among many others.
- **It increases toxicity** in your body. Fructose is a component of sugar that can only be processed by the liver. So, if you are consuming a lot of sugar, you are distracting your liver from its more important function of getting rid of the toxins that enter your body daily.
- **It weakens your immune system.** Sugar compromises the ability of white blood cells to fight infections and viruses, leaving you more subject to infections and diseases.
- **It disrupts the delicate balance of gut bacteria,** which leads to digestive issues and inflammation of the gut. You cannot lose weight or be healthy without a healthy gut.

Sugar Makes You Tired.

- Sugar provides a quick source of energy that is followed by an energy crash soon after, leading to increased hunger and more cravings

Sugar Keeps You Addicted.

It is more addictive than heroin or cocaine. The more you eat, the more you will want and crave sugar or carbs, creating a vicious cycle.

These are only some of the sugar-containing products. You need to make sure you read labels carefully because sugar can sneak into many places.

- Agave syrup
- All processed foods
- BBQ sauce
- Beer
- Beet juice
- Breads
- Breakfast bars
- Breakfast cereals
- Cakes
- Candies
- Carrot juice
- Champagne
- Cocktail sauce
- Coffee creamers (refrigerated or dry)
- Coffee drinks
- Dried fruit or dried fruit snacks
- Energy and protein bars
- Frozen yogurt
- Fruit juices (all, even the natural ones)
- Granola and granola bars
- Half-and-half
- Honey
- Hot cocoa
- Ice cream
- Ketchup

- Low-fat and fat-free yogurts, both dairy and non-dairy, such as coconut, almond, and soy
- Maple syrup
- Milk alternatives that are sweetened and the ice creams made with them (almond, soy, coconut, and rice)
- Muesli
- Pastas
- Protein bars and powders (not all)
- Salad dressings
- Sauces
- Smoothies
- Table sugar
- Tomato sauce
- Wine

THE PROBLEM WITH ARTIFICIAL SWEETENERS

Artificial sweeteners are S.T.U.P.I.D. ingredients because they offer the taste of sweetness without any calories, fooling you into thinking you are taking care of your weight and health when you are doing the opposite. They also damage your hormonal system making you gain weight and feel lousy or moody. They are also highly addictive.

Artificial Sweetener-Containing Products

- Splenda or sucralose
- Equal or NutraSweet
- Sweet'N Low or saccharin

What Artificial Sweeteners Do to Your Health and Weight

- Promote metabolic dysfunction
- Disrupt gut bacteria, the same as regular sugar. An out-of-balance gut will prevent you from staying healthy or losing weight

THE PROBLEM WITH GMOs (Genetically Modified Products)

A GMO is created through artificially injecting the DNA of a species into a plant's DNA to achieve characteristics that are more desirable, such as a faster growth cycle, bigger size, higher nutrition, stronger resistance to disease or bugs, or greater tolerance to harsh temperatures. Many of these characteristics help to improve the economics of growing crops.

Genetically modifying an organism is different from the traditional plants crossbreeding where farmers produce hybrid products.

There is a lot of controversy on whether GMO foods are safe to consume. One of my biggest concerns about them is that they are often designed to resist pesticides, which has led to higher levels of pesticides remaining in food you eat and more toxins accumulating inside your body. Remember that accumulated toxins can keep you fat, sick, and sad. And some of the most common pesticides used have been linked to cancer and many other disease and health issues.

One of the most well-known pesticides is Roundup, whose active ingredient is glyphosate. Glyphosate is extremely toxic to almost every form of life, even when consumed at low levels. Glyphosate has been linked with chronic fatigue, birth defects and cancer. Most GM foods have shown to have doses of glyphosate.

In recent years, many research papers have shown that GMOs are extremely detrimental to human health. A French scientist, Seralini, showed that rats fed Monsanto's GM corn developed severe liver and kidney damage, and malignant tumors in just 4 months. Other reports have shown that GMOs are associated with a broad range of health issues, such as organ failure, autism, allergies, asthma, infertility, infant mortality, digestive disorders, bowel disease, Crohn's disease, constipation, kidney disease, heart disease, and more.

The most frequently genetically modified foods are cottonseed (94%), soy (93%), canola (90%), corn (88%), Hawaiian papaya (75%), and most processed foods (70%).

THE PROBLEM WITH CORN

Corn is the number 1 crop grown in the US and 88% is genetically modified. Corn has always been an essential part of the Mexican cuisine and an important part of the American diet, but you need to be aware of the health and weight problems that result from the corn produced these days.

Genetically modified corn increases toxicity. The company Monsanto has genetically engineered a type of corn called BT corn. This corn has been modified to produce, as it grows, an insecticide that kills pests. The problem is that when you eat this type of corn and digest it, BT corn does not stop producing pesticides inside of you.

Corn, and the ingredients derived from it, are a major source of sugar in your diet, keeping you fat and increasing your risk of diabetes, cancer, heart disease, and dementia. Corn has a very high carbohydrate content. All carbs, when digested, are rapidly converted into sugar and absorbed into your blood. If the amount of carbs is high, blood sugar will rise. Your body cannot have high levels of sugar in the blood because they damage your cells and organs, so it will have to produce high levels of insulin, the hormone responsible for bringing blood sugar down to healthy levels; part of the way it accomplishes this is by storing fat. Additionally, if you need to produce insulin too frequently, your body becomes resistant or less sensitive to it, needing higher and higher levels of insulin to bring blood sugar down. This will mean faster accumulation of fat and eventually resistance to insulin, which leads to diabetes.

One cup of corn provides 123 g of carbs and 606 calories. Remember that all carbs are converted into blood sugar to be used as fuel for energy. Unused fuel is converted into fat. Although corn does have high fiber content, it is still very high in carbs for somebody who wants to lose weight.

Corn is frequently contaminated with fungi and mold that increase toxicity. Research has shown that corn is an easy food for certain fungi and molds to infest in. These organisms produce very toxic chemicals that can be very harmful to your health. Toxicity is the leading reason for weight struggles, health issues, and mood problems.

Limiting corn consumption can be tricky because it is not only the corn on the cob that you need to limit. Corn is hidden in too many products, mainly processed foods you may be consuming today. Once again, you need to learn how to read labels carefully.

Corn-Containing Products

- Breakfast cereals

- Corn chips
- Corn cobs
- Corn oil
- Corn starch
- Gluten-free products
- High-fructose corn syrup
- Hominy
- Maize
- Margarine
- Popcorn
- Tortillas

What Corn Does to Your Health and Weight

- It increases body inflammation.
- Its high level of carbohydrates provokes a spike in blood sugar and insulin, leading to more fat storage and an out-of-balance hormonal system.
- It is linked to gut issues. Corn stimulates the bacteria in your gut. Once the bacteria growth gets out of hand, they start to ferment starches, turning them into gas, which in turn makes you bloat up.
- It increases the amount of toxicity in the liver, making fat loss difficult and increasing the risk of liver issues.
- It decreases the ability of the kidneys to detoxify the body, increasing the risk of kidney issues.
- It increases the risk of heart diseases.
- It increases the risk of blood-related disorders.
- Corn is also one of the most common genetically modified (GM) foods. I spoke about GM foods earlier in

this section, but I recently came across research on the side effects of GM corn species on a person's health. Even I was alarmed to see so many side effects that the researchers reported with the use of such corn species. I don't recommend eating such corn.

THE PROBLEM WITH SOY

While soy is commonly perceived as a health food and a good source of protein, it is on the S.T.U.P.I.D. ingredients list because 94% of the soy consumed in the US is genetically modified to increase farming efficiency and lower the cost of producing it. What this means for your health is that it is loaded with toxic pesticides. It is not ideal to eat this food too frequently.

Some people may also be sensitive to soy or may have certain health issues for which soy is not ideal, such as estrogen or thyroid issues.

What Soy Does to Your Health and Weight

- **Soy disrupts your hormones**. Its plant-based estrogen can affect the hormonal balances of both men and women. It has also been linked to impaired fertility.
- **Soy has been linked to breast cancer**.
- **Soy affects your thyroid**, which will sabotage your weight loss efforts. When eaten too frequently, soy can decrease thyroid function. It has also been linked to thyroid diseases like thyroid cancer and autoimmune thyroid disease.
- **In adults, soy has shown to affect memory and increase the risk of dementia.**

- **Soy has certain elements called phytates that block the absorption of minerals,** particularly calcium, magnesium, copper, iron, and zinc.
- **Soy has certain enzymes that can interfere with protein digestion and lead to problems with the pancreas.**
- **Soy contains a substance called hemagglutinin that promotes blood clotting,** causing red cells to clump together. This affects the absorption and distribution of oxygen to your tissues.

Common Soy Products

- Edamame
- Soy infant formula
- Soy meat
- Soy milk—this can have a high amount of sugar. They serve it in many coffee shops as the "healthy" alternative to milk, but beware, it is loaded with sugar.
- Soy protein powders or snacks
- Soybean oil
- Soy sauce
- Tofu

THE PROBLEM WITH UNHEALTHY FATS

Fat is required in your diet. However, just like many other foods, not all fats are the same. Some of the dominant players in the market of fats today are refined oils, which are S.T.U.P.I.D. ingredients. Processed from seeds, grains, and beans, refined oils are very high in omega-6, which triggers inflammation.

Hydrogenated fats or trans fats are the worst of all oils. These types of fats are man-made and mainly used in processed foods, shortenings, margarines, fried foods, and commercially baked goods. Trans fats have been ruled by the FDA as "not safe to eat."

Unhealthy Oils

- Canola oil
- Corn oil
- Crisco
- Peanut oil
- Rapeseed oil
- Safflower oil
- Soybean oil
- Sunflower oil
- Most oils used in restaurants

Products Containing Unhealthy Oils

- Baked goods
- Coffee creamers
- Fast food
- Fried food
- Frozen meals
- Margarine
- Pam spray
- Pre-made frostings
- Processed foods (most of them)
- Restaurant food (in many of them)

What Unhealthy Fats Do to Your Health and Weight

- Unhealthy fats increase inflammation, the leading cause of most major diseases and mood problems.
- Unhealthy fats compromise your immune system, making you get sick more often or stay sick for longer.
- Unhealthy fats cause weight gain.
- Unhealthy fats increase risk of heart disease, cancer, and autoimmune diseases.

THE PROBLEM WITH PROCESSED FOODS

Processed foods are S.T.U.P.I.D. ingredients that require a factory or a lab to produce them, instead of whole foods that nature produces. They are generally unhealthy, fattening, and have lower nutrients than whole foods. They are all man-made.

What Processed Foods Do to Your Health and Weight

- Processed foods cause spikes in blood sugar and insulin, promoting weight gain and disease.
- Processed foods increase cravings for more unhealthy food.
- Processed foods prevent you from feeling full, leading you to eat more than you need.
- Processed foods promote inflammation.
- Processed foods increase risks of many diseases.
- Processed foods promote skin reactions.

THE PROBLEM WITH UNHEALTHY ADDITIVES AND ARTIFICIAL INGREDIENTS

There are too many additives and artificial ingredients that are S.T.U.P.I.D. ingredients because they have no nutritional or health benefit, and they increase toxicity and overburden your liver.

One of the worst additives, very common in Mexican and Chinese foods is MSG or monosodium glutamate. It is a flavor enhancer used in canned soups, sauces like "Maggi," meats, dressings, and processed foods. In the US one of its most common presentations is in "Accent" powder.

What Unhealthy Additives Do to Your Health and Weight

- **They increase toxicity** sabotaging your efforts to lose fat and at the same time keeping your liver working overtime, which will eventually make it slower and less able to process all the toxins that come into your life daily.
- **Some additives like MSG overstimulate your brain cells**, increasing the risk of brain damage and worsening learning disabilities and other mental diseases like Alzheimer's and Parkinson's.
- **They can make you gain weight and store fat.**
- **MSG is linked to eye damage.**
- **MSG is linked to headaches, fatigue, and depression**.

Unhealthy Additive-Containing Products

- Accent powder
- Chinese food

- Junk food and snacks
- All packaged and processed foods
- Restaurant foods
- Salsa Maggi

THE DIRTY DOZEN

It is widely known that pesticides are not good for your health and weight. Conventional-grown fruits and vegetables are exposed to high levels of pesticides. And these pesticides remain in the products even if you wash and rinse them well. Unfortunately, not everyone can afford or locate organic produce, which does not use pesticides but is more expensive.

Understanding this challenge and to help people reduce their exposure to pesticides, the USDA Environmental Working Group (EWG) produces an annual report that singles out produce with the highest pesticide loads. It is currently known as the Dirty Dozen, and they are part of S.T.U.P.I.D ingredients when conventionally grown (i.e., non-organic). I recommend that you try to search for the organic versions of these Dirty Dozen. This list can change year to year although many products are constantly on the list. To check on any updates, you can go to: www.ewg.org/foodnews/dirty_dozen_list.php

At the time of writing this edition (2017), the Dirty Dozen includes the products listed below. The products are listed starting with the most contaminated fruit/vegetable as number 1.

1. Strawberries

2. Spinach

3. Nectarines

4. Apples

5. Peaches

6. Pears

7. Cherries

8. Grapes

9. Celery

10. Tomatoes

11. Sweet bell peppers

12. Potatoes

What Pesticides Do to Your Health and Weight

- They increase the levels of accumulated toxicity, leading to diseases and problems with losing weight.
- They increase the risk of cancers.
- They disrupt the endocrine system, breaking the hormonal balance, thus leading to disease and weight gain.
- They increase the risk of infertility and birth defects.
- They strongly affect the development of the central nervous system in children under the age of 12. The reason is that scientific evidence has shown that the brain is not fully formed until the age of 12.

CONCLUSION: Avoid S.T.U.P.I.D. Ingredients If You Want to Be Healthy and Lose Weight

The S.T.U.P.I.D. ingredients are going to sabotage your health and weight, trigger inflammation, undermine your immune system, provoke hormonal imbalance, increase toxicity in your body, and damage your gut's health.

You may disagree with me, but I urge you to try to see how you feel without S.T.U.P.I.D. ingredients for a few weeks. You need at least 3 weeks for your body to heal and inflammation to decrease. Although you will start to feel the positive benefits in less than a week, to get the full results, you need to leave them out of your diet for 14–21 days at least. In **The Mexican Food Diet**™ you will start with 7 days. If you love how you feel, then I urge you to continue.

There are several ways to continue your health journey. The fastest way is to try a safe and effective detox that will provide everything you need to maximize results—get rid of cravings, minimize toxicity and inflammation, and prepare your body to become a fat-burning machine instead of a fat-storing machine.

I invite to check out our **Flaca Detox**™**, Reset, and Renew Program** in part 4 of this book. It is the simple, effective, and delicious way to lose weight and quickly get on a healthy path. **The Flaca Detox**™ is a medically formulated plan that is super easy. I use it regularly to stay in the best shape possible—physically, mentally, and emotionally. I have also had great success with my private clients who all have lost weight in a sustainable way. But even more fascinating than the great weight loss is that my clients start to feel so great and focused that most of them have taken big steps to transform their lives in many positive ways after having managed little to no changes for years. I have seen clients change careers, go back to school, or take bold moves towards their dreams. One of the changes that I love hearing about is that their families also benefit from better health and experience less visits to the doctor.

If you want to learn more about this great program, turn to part 4 or check out my revolutionary Flaca Detox™, Reset, and Renew Program at www.FlacaDetox.com.

Chapter 12
THE S.M.A.R.T. SCHEDULE

I t is very important that you stick to a S.M.A.R.T. schedule when eating and not skip meals so that you can maintain your blood sugar at healthy levels. Steady blood sugar will help you keep cravings away, stay energized and feel great throughout the day.

It may be challenging for you to stick to a schedule at first, especially if your current diet is filled with a lot of carbs and sugars. As you have learned, carbs and sugars create a spike in your blood sugar that is closely followed by a blood sugar crash. The frequent crashes are preventing you from going without food for more than three to four hours. You may get frequently hungry between meals and are used to snacking throughout the day. If you stick it out and fill your plate with the right foods, it will become much easier after the first few days of your diet.

When it comes to creating a schedule for eating, there are several important decisions you need to make.

First, have a regular schedule. You want to wake up and eat breakfast at the same times each day. The time when you have breakfast will determine when you will eat the rest of your meals. It is very important to remember that you should never skip breakfast, or any meals for that matter. Doing this will sabotage your weight and health.

Second, plan your meals ahead of time to guarantee that all your meals are made in accordance with your diet, empowering you and not sabotaging you. If you know that you are out all day and will not have access to healthy food, prep your food and bring it with you. This allows you to stick to your diet and eat your meals on time. Skipping meals and eating S.T.U.P.I.D. or unhealthy foods will set you back and sabotage your progress, your health, and your weight.

Third, eat meals 4 to 5 hours apart. Your three main meals, breakfast, lunch, and dinner, should be made according to the S.M.A.R.T. meal as described in Chapter 8. These meals need to include all the players, so don't skip even just one of them, or you will be missing out on valuable nutrients and potentially end up hungrier sooner than you need to.

Whenever I don't have time to eat healthy, I will take with me one of my **Flaca Stay Lean™** or **Flaca Detox™ Shakes**. They are made with very clean plant-based protein, nutrients, and fiber. I use it to make healthy shakes or protein balls that are quick, easy, and portable. They provide me with all the nutrients and satiety to keep me powering through my day no matter where I am. They also taste great too! I love to add S.M.A.R.T. fats and S.M.A.R.T. superfoods to them. (For my favorite recipes, refer to the Recipes Section.)

If you find yourself hungry in between meals, you may have the optional S.M.A.R.T. snack between lunch and dinner. Many times, a snack is necessary because your time between lunch and dinner is too long (if longer than six hours). It is important to have a snack rather than being so hungry at dinner that you pick unhealthy foods or overeat. You can also bring a small bag of nuts or seeds that are easy to carry and can keep you satisfied if there are no healthy choices.

For me, lunch is normally at 12 noon, and dinner is not until 6:30 or 7 pm. At the beginning of my journey, that was too long of a time between meals, and I would normally get hungry around 3:30 or 4 pm. This is when I would have a S.M.A.R.T. snack. Today, I am not hungry anymore except if I have an intense workout during the day or if I don't eat enough protein or fat at breakfast or lunch.

The type of snack you eat for your afternoon snack will depend on how active you are. When I am more active, I will eat a snack that has some carbs, like a healthy fruit, and a healthy fat, like almonds. When I am less active, I will eat some veggies like celery, seaweed, or avocado. If you are not very active, you will only need a very small portion of a S.M.A.R.T. snack, or pick from the S.M.A.R.T. veggies list, which have no limit. The Mexican Food Diet™ has a 7-day plan that will guide you on how your plates should look, including snacks.

At dinner, the only carbs allowed are S.M.A.R.T. veggies. As discussed in previous sections, carbs quickly convert into blood sugar for use as an energy source. After dinner, you do not have major energy needs, which means that the energy your carbs will produce will not be used and will most likely end up as fat. Therefore, you want to avoid eating non-veggie carbs at dinner time. They provide too much energy for what you need at that time. You will get sufficient energy from the protein, fat, and veggies in your dinner plate to take you through the evening and night, and it will not affect your weight.

Your goal should be to stop eating 3 hours before bedtime. That means there is NO after-dinner snacking. If you ate the elements in your S.M.A.R.T. plate, in the recommended amounts, you should be feeling full and satisfied. The elements are more than enough to keep you going until breakfast. If you feel hungry, it may be other things causing it, such as anxiety, stress, or thirst.

Many times, when you feel hungry, your body is just thirsty. When this happens, try drinking water or a non-caffeinated tea.

On most days, try to have your breakfast 60–90 minutes after you wake up. Here is an example of a smart schedule if you wake up at 6am. If you wake up later or earlier, adjust accordingly. When I grew up in Mexico, the schedule was different. We had lunch at 3 pm and dinner around 8 pm. I am aware that many people of Hispanic heritage are following similar schedules. Read my recommendations below on how to do it.

The Lunch at Noon Schedule

- 6 am—Drink a cup of hot or warm water with half a lemon. You can also have up to 2 cups of coffee. For your coffee, you may add an envelope or drops of stevia and some unsweetened non-dairy alternative if you'd like. My favorite is unsweetened almond milk. To add more flavor, you can use cinnamon and raw cacao.
- 7 am—Full breakfast with all players in the S.M.A.R.T. plate.
- 12 pm—Full lunch with all players in the S.M.A.R.T. plate.
- 3:30 pm—Snack if you are hungry or if your dinner is more than 6 hours after lunch. Small snack if you are not very active. Green tea is great at this time of day because it has many powerful health benefits and is a healthy source of energy. No more caffeine after this time. You want to avoid affecting your sleep.
- 6:30 or 7 pm—Full dinner with all players in the S.M.A.R.T. plate—NO carbs except veggies. S.M.A.R.T. veggies are unlimited and highly encouraged. Get creative!

- If you get hungry after a meal, look at what you ate, and make sure your plate had a large amount of S.M.A.R.T. veggies and sufficient protein and fat. Non-starchy veggies, protein, and fat should help you feel full for longer periods of time. If you are very active, you may need to increase your protein amounts. The same would apply for men and growing teenagers. They need additional healthy protein to fulfill their needs.

The Lunch at 3 pm Schedule

If you are following this type of schedule then I would recommend:

- 6 am—Drink a cup of hot or warm water with half a lemon. You can also have up to 2 cups of coffee as described above.
- 7 am—Full breakfast with all players in the S.M.A.R.T. plate.
- 12 pm—Small snack if you are not very active. Larger if you are very active.
- 3 pm—Full lunch with all players in the S.M.A.R.T. plate. Green tea is great at this time of day because it has many powerful health benefits and is a healthy source of energy. No more caffeine after this time. You want to avoid affecting your sleep.
- 7:30pm or 8pm—Full dinner with all players in the S.M.A.R.T. plate—NO carbs except veggies. S.M.A.R.T. veggies are unlimited and highly encouraged. See recommendations above.

When you feel hungry, you can also drink water or prepare a decaf tea and get busy. A lot of times, when you reach for a snack in the mid-morning or afternoon, it is not out of hunger but rather out of boredom or cravings. Therefore, reaching for water or decaf tea is a good compromise. Remember, you must drink at least half of your body weight in ounces of water each day. So, for example, if you weigh 140 pounds, you should be drinking 70 ounces of water each day, which is almost 9 glasses. Try to keep a big glass of water with you always as it is easy to forget, and you don't want to feel obligated to drink a large amount of water right before bed just to meet your daily requirements.

When you feel hungry between meals, you can also try doing something you enjoy or getting something done on your to-do list. Keeping your mind off food will help. It is very unlikely that you are hungry. As you improve your eating habits, these fake hunger situations will be a thing of the past.

THE CALENDAR SCHEDULE

There is another type of schedule that is very important too. This is the scheduling of your day, your week, your month, your year. I have learned over and over that whatever I don't schedule never gets done. There is always too much going on, and believe me, you will never do it. And remember, nothing feels better than being able to cross something off your to-do list!

To get your full health and weight transformation so that you experience absolute wellness, here are the things you need to make sure you schedule in your calendar. You should separate these into two groups: those that are non-negotiable and that you need to do every week; and those that are optional and can be postponed or rescheduled if you have a busy week or a project deadline.

NON-NEGOTIABLE WEEKLY ACTIVITIES THAT NEED TO BE SCHEDULED

- **Eating times for the day**. This doesn't have to be written down. You just need to have it in your head, but you should look at your calendar the day before to see if you need to do any special planning or prepping because you will be on the go or traveling.

- **Prepping and cooking meals for the week**. It is recommended that you prep and plan things 3 days in a row and that you cook in bulk when possible.

- **Food shopping**. You can schedule a bigger shopping trip once a week and another shorter trip a second time to replenish fresh produce in the middle of the week.

- **S.M.A.R.T. exercising**. Gone are the days when I exercised for 2–6 hours. Today I have short but very focused, intense, and effective exercising sessions of 30 to 60 minutes, depending on the day. I also try adding walking as much as possible or fitting in a few minutes of core workout every several hours.

- **Family (includes your other half and kids)**. Find those quality times in the week that you will spend doing special activities with each person in your family. Feeding them while you are rushing to get them to school does not count. That is important, but it is not a quality activity. You don't have to have extended times or every-day activities. Just plan a few times each week, and then work everything else around those.

- **Self-care**. Plan one activity that you enjoy, just for yourself, at least once a week. Remember how important it is to find time to put yourself first. It could be having a massage, taking a nice bath, getting your nails done, going for a walk, or taking a fun class. Whatever helps you take care of your most valuable asset: yourself. Keeping yourself healthy and happy allows you to be the best possible you for everyone else in your life.

OPTIONAL ACTIVITIES THAT CAN BE DONE LESS FREQUENTLY

- **Social life**. This is important, but you need to be realistic. You cannot be with your friends having coffee all the time and getting your things done. So, plan a day once a week, or two times per month, depending on the free time you have. But don't neglect your health, your family, or your self-care in exchange for spending more time with your friends.

- **You may want to start searching for groups of friends with similar or bigger goals than you**. They will inspire you, motivate you, and support you. They will not be obstacles in your health and weight transformation because they understand how important it is for your future and your happiness. Perhaps now is the time to start to move away from those friends who are negative and don't uplift you or bring out the best in you.

- **Joy**. These are additional things that will bring more joy to your life. For example, a trip, going out and experimenting at new restaurants, or visiting a new museum. Sometimes it can be something as simple as buying yourself some nice flowers to brighten up the house, listening to music, watching a movie, going for a walk, sitting out in a beautiful place outdoors and enjoying nature, or getting rid of clutter. Whatever brings you joy and makes you feel happy. You should try to do at least a couple of these a month.

In general, the non-negotiable group is exactly that. It includes things that should be non-negotiable. You cannot just skip them. Of course, if an unexpected thing comes up that is critical for you to deal with, then fine. Ideally, you should reschedule if possible, or do the best you can. If it is a timed activity like exercise, maybe do a shorter session or break it down into parts. Don't allow yourself to continually put off the "you time" you have added into your schedule because more things keep coming up. Sometimes it is even important to learn how to say no and to stop taking on so many tasks. Often, tasks that seem so important can be done later, and you do not need to sacrifice your own happiness and health to get them done.

Chapter 13

S.M.A.R.T. KITCHEN

COOKING AT HOME: It Is Essential and Does Not Have to Be Hard

I care about my family's nutrition, so meal planning and meal cooking are a big part of my day. I know how much food can determine the type of future each family member will have; therefore, I refuse to sacrifice their nutrition by serving them fast food, processed food, frozen food, or take out. I plan all their meals, coordinate the food shopping required, and personally cook 2–3 meals and 1–2 snacks every day. I love doing it. It makes me feel great to know that I am empowering them and making them as strong as possible so that they can have bright and healthy futures.

You may be saying, "But Maru, that is what you do for a living. I don't have time for all that. I can barely get my laundry done."

I too have a business as a health and wellness coach, which requires me to be working with clients, speaking at events, traveling all over the country to appear on TV, touring with my book, and teaching. I am a member of multiple groups and educational courses, which also takes a lot of my time. I can accomplish both parts of my life—nurturing my family and running a business—because I eat well and take care of myself daily.

Even with limited time, I make sure I have time to do the most important things to take care of myself. Of course, the first thing is feeding myself appropriately. I cook for myself and prepare my food on the go when I need to, so that I don't have to eat junk or skip a meal, which is not healthy. Most of the times that I travel I take food with me because I don't want to compromise the way I feel when I don't have sufficient veggies, healthy fats, or clean protein.

The S.M.A.R.T. kitchen does not have to be huge or have fancy equipment. You just need to be smart about what you will have so that you can prepare the healthy meals that your body requires for you to experience absolute wellness.

In fact, you probably have many, if not all, the basic tools already in your kitchen.

BASIC TOOLS

To be able to prepare the recipes in The Mexican Food Diet™, you will need the following basic tools, which will also be needed for the healthier meals you will want to prepare after completing The Mexican Food Diet™.

- Blender or NutriBullet
- Baking pans—2 full-size
- Cooking knives—1 set
- Cooking pans—1 medium and 1 large
- Cooking sheets—1
- Cutting boards—1 small and 1 large
- Food processor
- Food scale
- Garlic presser

- Julienne peeler
- Lemon squeezer
- Measuring cups—1 set
- Measuring spoons—1 set
- Meat thermometer—1
- Mixing bowls—1 set
- Potato masher—1
- Pots—1 medium and 1 large
- Prepping bowls—1–2 sets
- Sauce pans—1 small, 1 medium, 1 large
- Skillet—1 medium-size
- Silicone head spatulas—1 small, 1 medium, 1 large
- Spice grinder or cheap coffee grinder to be used for grinding spices
- Strainer—1 medium
- 1 set of collapsible silicone strainers
- Zester

Chapter 14
S.M.A.R.T. COOKING

O ne of the most important aspects to making a S.M.A.R.T. meal is to ensure that every ingredient that goes into it is of the highest quality possible, particularly the oils that are used for cooking these meals. For these reasons, I have provided you in **Chapters 7** and **11** with a list of the oils that are best and those that you should stay away from.

Here, you can find my three favorite oils, along with my recommended safe temperatures for cooking with them, as well as the temperatures recommended for cooking meat and poultry. You need to ensure you don't surpass the maximum recommended temperatures for each oil because they become toxic, and that you cook your meats to at least the recommended temperature.

Olive Oil

This is no doubt my favorite oil. I recommend using extra virgin olive oil. Extra virgin olive oil is better for your health than traditional vegetable oil. While vegetable oil may sound healthy, most of them are not really from vegetables. They are also highly unstable (which means they can become toxic more easily), and they trigger inflammation. Olive oil is a monounsaturated fat which is a heart-healthy fat and helps to reduce inflammation. High quality olive oil (extra virgin) also has a higher smoke point, around 350 degrees Fahrenheit. Lower quality olive oil has a lower smoke point, 320 degrees Fahrenheit. Olive oil adds a nice flavor to cooked foods and is also affordable enough to use in larger amounts. However, it can have a stronger taste when used for baking.

Avocado Oil

Avocado oil is like extra virgin olive oil in that it is also a heart-healthy monounsaturated fat. Avocado oil has a light and delicious flavor and has a higher smoke point, over 500 degrees Fahrenheit. This makes avocado oil a great oil for cooking with. However, it can be quite expensive. Because of avocado oil's great flavor and heart-healthy benefits, I find it to be perfect for making home-made salad dressings, cooking delicious eggs, and roasting veggies.

Coconut Oil

My third favorite oil for cooking is coconut oil. Coconut oil has a smoke point around 350 degrees Fahrenheit. Coconut oil imparts a delicious coconut flavor when used in its raw form and comes completely flavorless in its refined form. Coconut oil was avoided for a long time because the media was pushing that saturated fats were unhealthy. However, many studies have shown that naturally occurring saturated fats, such as coconut oil, are not known to be unhealthy and that coconut oil has amazing health benefits. It can boost your immune system and help with your gut's health. I like to use coconut oil for snacks and for baking because it is healthier than using vegetable or canola oil, and can add a delicious light coconut flavor. To use coconut oil in baking, simply use a 1:1 substitution for whatever fat is called for in the recipe. Before using it, melt the coconut oil by placing it in a bowl surrounded by warm water.

I like all three of the oils above for their flavors, heart-healthy benefits, and high smoke points. These oils are very versatile and can be used for cooking, baking, and dressing. You can play around with these oils and see which ones you and your family prefer, and then use these to replace the traditional, unhealthy oils, such as vegetable and corn oil.

COOKING TEMPERATURES

It is suggested that you cook meat, poultry, and fish to their recommended safe temperatures to ensure their safety. Below are the suggested internal temperatures (in Fahrenheit) for traditional proteins:

- Steak—145 degrees
- Chicken and poultry—165 degrees
- Pork—145 degrees
- Fish—145 degrees
- Lamb—165 degrees

TIPS ON HEALTHY STORAGE OF FOOD

Storing food wisely is easy and convenient. All you need to do is plan innovatively. Some general tips on storing different food are as follows:

- Store your food in containers or plastic bags. They keep them fresh and don't allow foods to dry out while in the refrigerator.
- Don't reuse plastic bags or bottles if they are damaged.
- Keep raw meat away from cooked ones. Raw meat should be separately stored away from all other food products.

- Store raw meat in lowest shelf of the fridge, so that it doesn't drip on other food items.
- If you store fish, poultry, or meat in the refrigerator instead of freezing them, use them within two to three days.
- Avoid putting food in the refrigerator while it is still warm.
- Keep your vegetables and fruits in separate drawers.
- Always keep items covered in the fridge.
- If you want to store something for a long time, you will need to freeze it or use advance storing methods like canning or drying.

Chapter 15

S.M.A.R.T. SHOPPING

The following list is for you to check which items you already have in your pantry. You will then go shopping for the missing items to complete the 7-Day Mexican Food Diet™. Even if you are not planning to do the whole plan, this list will stock up your refrigerator and pantry with powerful nutrition.

The amounts you will need will depend on what you have and the portions you will be preparing. For fresh produce, buy ingredients for the first 3 to 4 days. Then do a second shopping trip to buy for the second half of the diet.

You can download the shopping list in pdf format for printing or in jpg format for storing as an image in your mobile device. Go to www.FlacaForever.com/TMFDShoppingList to download the list.

Where to Buy

You may have most of these ingredients already. I buy my food at the following places:

- Grocery store - most of the products and produce
- Shakes and snacks - at the shop at www.FlacaForever.com. Remember that if you registered this book you get at $20 dollar coupon to try our products.
- Protein - local farmers market or www.vitalchoice.com
- Non-perishable products at Thrive Market or go to http://go.thrv.me/SH2HX.

Protein Shakes

Flaca Stay Lean™ All-In-One Protein Shakes (plant-based)—Chocolate or Vanilla. You can buy them at the shop at www.FlacaForever.com

Proteins

- Beef (organic, grass-fed)
- Chicken breasts (organic, free-range)
- Chicken leg with thigh (organic, free-range)
- Eggs (organic, free-range)
- Flank steak (organic, grass-fed)
- Pork (organic, pasture-raised)
- Salmon (wild)
- Shrimp (wild)
- Tilapia (wild)
- Turkey ground (organic, pasture-raised)

I like to buy most of my proteins at the local farmer's market or at www.vitalchoice.com

Non-Dairy Milks

- Almond Milk (unsweetened)
- Coconut Milk (unsweetened)

Oils and Vinegars

- Olive oil (extra virgin)
- Rice wine vinegar
- Sesame oil

- White vinegar
- Wine vinegar (red, white, or champagne)

Nuts/Seeds

- Almonds (raw, organic)
- Chia seeds (organic)
- Pecans (raw, organic)
- Pumpkin seeds (raw) (pepitas)
- Walnuts (raw)

Produce (Fruits and Veggies)

- Apples (organic)
- Anaheim chile
- Arugula
- Asparagus
- Avocado
- Blueberries
- Broccoli
- Butternut squash
- Cabbage
- Carrots
- Cauliflower
- Celery (organic)
- Chayote
- Cherry tomatoes (organic)
- Cucumber (organic)
- Cilantro (fresh)
- Garlic
- Green onions

- Habanero chiles
- Jalapeño chiles
- Jicama
- Lemon
- Lime
- Mint (fresh)
- Oranges
- Poblano chiles
- Red bell peppers (organic)
- Red cabbage
- Red onion
- Roma tomatoes (organic)
- Serrano chiles
- Shallots
- Strawberries (organic)
- Tomatillos
- Yellow bell pepper (organic)
- Yellow onion
- Zucchini

Frozen Produce (Fruits and Veggies)

- Frozen peas

Grains and Legumes

- Amaranth
- Black beans (dried)
- Brown rice
- Quinoa

Spices and Condiments

- Allspice (ground)
- Ancho chile (dried)—you can buy online at Thespicehouse.com
- Ancho chile (ground)—you can buy online at Thespicehouse.com
- Annatto seeds—you can buy online at Thespicehouse.com
- Bay leaves
- Black pepper (freshly ground)
- Cayenne pepper
- Chili pepper flakes
- Chili powder ("Tajin" is my favorite. You can find it at Walmart or Amazon)
- Cinnamon (ground)
- Cinnamon stick
- Cloves (ground)
- Clove (whole)
- Cumin (ground)
- Guajillo pepper—you can buy online at Thespicehouse.com
- Mulato chile—you can buy online at Thespicehouse.com
- Nutmeg (ground)
- Onion powder
- Oregano (dried)
- Paprika
- Pasilla chile—you can buy online at Thespicehouse.com
- Sea salt

- Sriracha sauce
- Tabasco sauce
- Tequila

Jarred/Canned

- Almond butter (unsweetened, organic)
- Chicken stock (organic and low sodium)
- Chipotle peppers
- Diced tomatoes (organic)
- Garbanzo beans or chickpeas
- Prunes (unseeded)
- Tomato paste (organic)
- Vegetable broth (organic)

Miscellaneous

- Epson salts (great for relaxing baths before bed)
- Stevia (pure)
- Vanilla extract
- Flaca Choco-Coconut™ Healthy Snack Bars - great healthy choice to have for when you are on the go and need a quick healthy snack. You can find it at the shop at www.FlacaForever.com

Drinks

- Coffee (organic and dark roasted)
- Green tea
- Herbal teas
- Sparkling water

Chapter 16
S.M.A.R.T. PREPPING

I f you are like me, your days are full of a variety of responsibilities and activities so every minute counts. I am very sensitive and aware of using time effectively and efficiently. I have said that cooking at home is the best thing you can do for you and your family, so finding ways to prep ahead of time is critical for success. Here is the list of things you need to consider for S.M.A.R.T. prepping so that you can always be prepared.

Advance Preparation

Each recipe in The Mexican Diet™ plan has specific indications as to what can be prepared in advance and how long you can store things in the refrigerator. This will help you manage your time better. I have noticed that the days when I do not have a plan, I spend a lot more time at the kitchen, and it is not because I am cooking more complex recipes. Most of the time is inefficient time trying to figure out what to do for the meal.

Repurpose and Reuse

Another good tip for saving time is to cook more than you will need and then repurpose it over the next two days. You could use the leftover food in a different way, or you can also use the food in the same way if it does not bother you or your family to repeat meals. Each recipe includes a comment on how to reuse leftovers or extra amounts you may have prepared. When I cook,

I like to do double the amount needed, so I have another day ready to go.

You should create a list that has meals that are very quick to assemble or to prepare. When you don't have a plan, you can always look at your emergency meals list and pick something. Ideally, you should always have in stock the ingredients needed for this type of meals.

An Example of my Emergency Meals List

Breakfast

- Protein shake (recipe in book). These are my best friends for when I am on the run or traveling.
- Vanilla chia pudding (recipe in book). Another great alternative for when I am traveling.
- Cinnamon quinoa with apple and almond butter (recipe in book)
- Mexican-style scrambled eggs (recipe in book)
- Fried eggs with sautéed veggies

Lunch

- A S.M.A.R.T. plate with leftovers. Always look at the leftovers in the fridge first and see if you can assemble a S.M.A.R.T. plate.
- Protein shake (recipe in book)
- Green salad with a S.M.A.R.T. protein and a serving of almonds, chia seeds, or avocado
- Fish ceviche (recipe in book)
- Salmon ceviche (recipe in book)

- Cooked beans (recipe in book) and veggies. I always have cooked beans in the fridge, ready to go.
- Pan-seared or baked protein (chicken, fish, or meat) and 2–3 veggies. Oven baking is great because you don't have to oversee it.
- Fried eggs with sautéed veggies (recipe in book). This assumes you did not eat eggs for breakfast.

Snack

- Almond butter and apple (organic)
- Almond butter and chia seeds
- Almond butter and protein powder
- Almond butter, raw cacao, cacao nibs and a little stevia
- Apple (organic)
- Avocado slices
- Blueberries and nuts
- Cucumbers (organic)
- Jicama strips
- Hummus and veggies

Dinner

- A S.M.A.R.T. meal with leftovers. Always look at the leftovers in the fridge first and see if you can assemble a S.M.A.R.T. meal.
- Protein shake (recipe in book)
- Pan-seared or baked protein (chicken, fish, or meat) and 2–3 veggies. Baking is great because you don't have to oversee it.
- Some type of egg-white omelet with 2 veggies and avocado.

Chapter 17
MARU'S TIPS & TRICKS

Here is a list of my favorite tips and tricks for staying in shape and in the best health possible:

1. I NEVER skip a meal.

2. I always eat at the same times: 7:30, 12:30, and 7:00. I sometimes have a snack at 3:30, but I normally don't need one.

3. I start my day with 20 minutes of meditation.

4. After meditation, I get a cup of warm water and half a lemon, and then 2 cups of coffee with unsweetened almond milk foam and some drops of stevia.

5. While my coffee is brewing in the French press, I do sit-ups and squats to get part of my daily exercise out of the way, get my blood pumping, and feel like I am using my time productively. Although this is only 5-7 minutes, everything counts when you are busy.

6. I restock my favorite foods list for my family weekly so that I have the necessary elements to prepare simple, yet powerful S.M.A.R.T. plates at any given time. Of importance to me is having a variety of frozen proteins, such as fish, meat, and poultry. Protein does not last for long in the fridge, so I cannot buy all the week's supply at once. I am always prepared by having frozen protein

available. I defrost it in the morning by putting it in cold water for 20 minutes, then I transfer it into the refrigerator until I am ready to use it later in the day. If I remember, I can also thaw it by moving it to the refrigerator the day before. Some days I have even put it on the grill frozen and it is fine.

7. My favorite emergency meals:

   • Breakfast: Flaca Stay Lean™ shake chocolate with almond milk, chia seeds, raw cacao powder, cacao nibs, Maca powder, and almond butter. You can find the recipe in the Recipes Section. I also have 1 cup of blueberries or a mix of blueberries and organic strawberries. And to finish it up I have 1 cup of cooked veggies leftover from the previous days.

   • Lunch: A green salad with some protein and other non-starchy veggies. I season it with lemon and sea salt.

   • Snack: Almond butter. I sometimes have it alone. Other times with things like Flaca Stay Lean™ protein powder, chia seeds, raw cacao powder, cacao nibs, and stevia. I include these added things when I can, when I need more power, or when I need to stay full longer. I sometimes accompany almond butter with celery or apple slices.

   • Dinner: I defrost a healthy protein, such as turkey, chicken or fish, then bake it in the oven or grill it in a pan. I then find 2 or 3 veggies in my refrigerator, and bake or sauté them. I use olive oil, sea salt, and garlic powder for both the protein and the veggies.

8. I try to always cook double amounts of foods so that I can have leftovers that I reuse or repurpose by serving them in different ways.

9. I have a time scheduled daily in my calendar to plan for all the meals of the day and the following days. I then decide when I am going to do the prepping and cooking, set it in my calendar with an alarm, and then forget about it until then. I am never stressed because it is all written down. I don't use paper because when I need it, I usually can never find it. I use the notes app in my iPhone, iPad, or computer.

10. I don't drink water during meals except for a few sips if I need to. I try to drink my water before and after. The reason for this is that water, when it is drunk together with food, interferes with digestion.

11. When I go to conferences, I take emergency food options that I can eat as snacks when the food alternatives are not healthy (which is most of the time). The Flaca Stay Lean™ shakes are great help in these occasions.

12. When I am anxious and feel like I need something to eat or drink, but I am not hungry, I prepare a tea or a hot chocolate made with unsweetened almond milk, raw cacao, and stevia. If it is still before 4 pm, I do green tea. If it is after 4pm, I do an herbal tea. I love to have a variety of teas in my pantry. Another favorite one is making foam from unsweetened almond milk, then adding raw cacao and stevia. I love this.

13. When I get off track or start feeling not at my best, I do a few days of my Flaca Detox™. It always works to reset and renew my metabolism, my wellness, and keep my health and weight in top shape. It also helps me tremendously with my focus and mental sharpness.

14. If I have a big project and need to work for long hours, I put my daughter to bed and work a few more hours. I then try

to get a decent night's sleep. I prefer to wake up super early (4 am) than stay up too late. I find that after 10 pm I cannot think clearly, but at 4 am I am clear and focused. I no longer do caffeine to force myself to stay awake longer. I know this messes up my systems and hormones. I also try to sleep as close to 7 hours as possible.

I can't express enough how **The Mexican Food Diet™** will not only change your body and mental state, but it will become a new way of living for you and your family. No more questioning what to eat and then regretting unhealthy choices. I have laid out in the simplest way all the S.M.A.R.T and S.T.U.P.I.D ingredients, S.M.A.R.T. plates, and for those of you who desire to know so much more about what goes into your body, extensive information on the S.T.U.P.I.D. foods.

I look forward to you diving into the recipes with me!

PART 3

GETTING STARTED!

Chapter 18
GETTING STARTED CHECKLIST

Now that you have learned all the health-related reasons as to why you should lose weight and how the **Mexican Food Diet**™ is structured, it is time to put your new knowledge into action!

You will start by completing the *Getting Started Checklist*. After that, I offer the meal plans and recipes. I am excited to think about the positive impact **Healthy Eating That Feels Like Cheating**™ will have in your weight, health, and whole life.

1. **Take the Detox Quiz**. The quiz is a great tool to help you identify some of the things that can be behind your difficulty losing weight or struggling with your health. If you don't have health struggles, taking the quiz can identify things that could affect you in the future if you don't address them now. So, go ahead and take the detox quiz now.

It will be a good base of where you are starting.

To take your test now, copy the following link into your browser: https://goo.gl/dMyYPS

If you have any problems, please contact us at support@flacaforever.com or call 1-858-433-9802.

2. **Take Your Initial Photo, Weight and Measurements**. Having a baseline for how you look, your weight and key measurements is critical to monitor your progress. Once you get on your way, it is easy to forget how far you have come. Regularly weighing yourself and checking your key measurements is also important to keep you accountable to yourself but also to help you identify potential threats for your health. It is better to weigh yourself around the same time, and it is best right after you wake up. Weigh yourself daily; then calculate your BMI and measure your waist once per month. For details, read below.

Assessment of your health risks involves using Body Mass Index (BMI) as well as your waist circumference.

BMI is calculated from your height and weight to estimate your body fat. It is a good indicator of your risk for diseases that can occur with more body fat. The higher your BMI, the higher your risk for certain diseases, such as heart disease, high blood pressure, type 2 diabetes, gallstones, breathing problems, and certain cancers. Keep in mind that it has some limits. It may overestimate body fat in athletes and others who have a muscular buildup; and it may underestimate body fat in older people and others who have lost muscle. But even with these limitations, it is a good thing to know. To use the BMI calculator copy this link into your browser: https://goo.gl/cUwuBe. Your goal is to get your BMI in the normal weight range of 18.5–24.9 because doing this will not only make you look great, feel great, feel less pain, but it will also help you reduce your risks for the health risks associated with being overweight or obese.

If your BMI is on the obese range of 30 or greater, it is very important to start making changes immediately. The Mexican Food Diet™ is a great way to start, but be aware that it will take more than this diet. I am here for you, and if you let me, I will help you get to your goal.

Waist Measure. Measuring the circumference of your waist can help you identify possible health risks that come with being overweight or obese. In earlier sections of this book, we saw that the fat around your waist or belly is the most dangerous type of fat because it produces a higher amount of toxins. According to the National Institute of Health (NIH), "If most of your fat is around your waist rather than at your hips, you're at a higher risk for heart disease and type 2 diabetes. This risk goes up with a waist size that is greater than 35 inches for women or greater than 40 inches for men. To correctly measure your waist, stand and place a tape measure around your middle, just above your hipbones. Measure your waist just after you breathe out." The NIH has produced the table below to give you an idea of whether your BMI combined with your waist circumference increases your risk for developing obesity-associated diseases or conditions.

Classification of Overweight and Obesity by BMI, Waist Circumference, and Associated Disease Risks

	BMI (kg/m²)	Obesity Class	Disease Risk* Relative to Normal Weight and Waist Circumference	
			Men 102 cm (40 in) or less Women 88 cm (35 in) or less	Men > 102 cm (40 in) Women > 88 cm (35 in)
Underweight	< 18.5		-	-
Normal	18.5-24.9		-	-
Overweight	25.0-29.9		Increased	High
Obesity	30.0-34.9	I	High	Very High
	35.0-39.9	II	Very High	Very High
Extreme Obesity	40.0 +	III	Extremely High	Extremely High

* Disease risk for type 2 diabetes, hypertension, and CVD.
+ Increased waist circumference also can be a marker for increased risk, even in persons of normal weight.

3. **Initial Measurements**. Record your initial weight and measurements below, and then do it again after being 2 weeks on the program where you are eating either the meal plans in this book or using the guides in this book to prepare other types of S.M.A.R.T. meals that will help you get healthy, lose weight, and feel happier.

- Date and time of measurements:
- My initial weight is:
- My waist measure is:
- My initial BMI is:
- I currently wear a size:
- My most frequently used jeans or pants are a size:
- My hips measure:
- My right upper arm measure is:
- My right thigh measure is:
- My right calf measure is:
- My wellness level is:

Rate your general wellness level from 1 to 5, with 1 meaning you have no problems and 5 meaning you are really struggling with any or all the following: weight, health, energy, or mood.

4. **Define a Start Date for Your Diet**. Remember that there will never be the perfect time.

5. **Go Shopping for Missing Ingredients**. Use the shopping list in Chapter 15 to check your pantry and refrigerator and see what is missing. If you are buying fresh food, plan to buy ingredients for the recipes for 3–4 days at a time to ensure food freshness and safety. Also, check if you will need to make any substitutions so that you can buy the items when you go to the store. Each recipe talks about recommended substitutions. Try to go shopping no more than 2 times a week for efficiency purposes.

6. **Prep Ahead**. Look at the recipes for the first 3–4 days, and see what things you can prepare ahead of time and refrigerate or freeze. Each recipe talks about what you can prepare ahead and how long you can store things in the refrigerator.

7. **Schedule 2 Bulk Cooking Days**. Now that you know what can be prepped ahead of time, find a time in your calendar when you can do a day of bulk cooking. You will need two of these days, one for the first 3–4 days of the diet, and the other one for the last days of the diet. On your bulk cooking days, you will be doing a few hours of cooking everything that can be prepared ahead of time so that you can minimize the time required during the rest of the days.

8. **Schedule Daily Eating and Cooking Times**. You will need to know ahead of time what times you will be eating and where, so that you can be appropriately prepared. Remember that you need to keep a regular eating schedule and eat every 4 hours. Look closely at your time availability and the cooking time required for the day's meals, and schedule the block of time in your calendar. Remember that you only need to do some steps because you already did some of the prepping on the bulk day.

9. **Anticipate Challenges**. One of the secrets to staying on a healthy diet is anticipating challenges. Make sure you look at your day ahead of time and find some of the challenges. Some of the most common challenges I have found are:

   - **Days On the Go**. If you cannot take the meal with you, a perfect substitution is a healthy all-in-one protein shake with an unsweetened non-dairy milk and a good source of healthy fat. For ideas, look at my best tips and tricks in **Chapter 17** and the yummy shake recipes at the end of the **RECIPES section**.
   - **Eating at the Office**. Pack your meals the night before and reheat them at your office, or eat them cold if you don't care. When I travel, I take precooked meals and eat them cold.

- **Eating Out**. If you are eating out, order using the S.M.A.R.T. ingredients and meal guidelines in Chapters 7 and 8.
- **Late Eating**. If your next meal will be out of schedule, and the period between that meal and the previous one is more than 6 hours, make sure you have a good healthy snack that has a healthy fat or protein in it. This will keep you full and supply you with a steady source of energy. One of the quickest snacks to prepare is a serving of the nuts or nut butters with a half of an apple or a veggie. Seeds are also great portable choices. Or look at the snack recipes in the **RECIPES section**.

10. **If you have certain food intolerances or certain medical conditions, it can be challenging to find a diet that suits your needs. For medical conditions, always consult your doctor first**. If you have been told by your doctor that you need to reduce your sugars, fats (the doctor probably referred to unhealthy fats), and processed carbs, you are in a good place. All the recipes in the Mexican Food Diet™ are low in carbs and sugars, and use mainly whole, fresh foods and unrefined carbs.

This diet can be the perfect lifestyle choice for people with dietary restrictions and food intolerances or sensitivities. If you have a specific allergy to some of the foods used in the recipes, I have included some substitution ideas in each recipe. You can also feel free to modify the recipe, removing the foods you can't tolerate and replacing them with a similar ingredient that fits your needs. To find substitute ideas, refer to the S.M.A.R.T. ingredients in Chapter 7. The recipes are very versatile and allergy-friendly, so you should not have many problems.

Here are some comments for each of the most common dietary restrictions:

- **Gluten-Free**. YES. All recipes are gluten-free.
- **Dairy-Free**. YES. All recipes are dairy-free.
- **Sugar-Free**. YES. If you are following a sugar-free diet because you need to monitor your blood sugar, you won't need to make any modifications. All the recipes have no added sugar, use ingredients that have a low impact on your blood sugar, and there are no processed carbs.
- **Diabetics**. Always consult your doctor. The recipes are all low in carbs and have no added sugar. If you are a diabetic, the recipes should fit into your suggested diet very well. If you know there are certain foods that raise your blood sugars easily, then simply avoid them and swap them out with something else from the S.M.A.R.T. ingredients list in Chapter 7.
- **Paleo**. MOST recipes ARE paleo. Some recipes use gluten-free grains. But most of the recipes are Paleo-friendly. I also advocate a low-carb, high-protein diet making it the perfect paleo-friendly fit!
- **Cholesterol**. Always consult with your doctor. This diet is also friendly and can be beneficial for people with high cholesterol levels. If you are overweight, it is likely that your doctor has already warned you of high levels in the bad cholesterol and low levels in the good cholesterol. This diet kicks out all the unhealthy, processed carbs and fats that you are used to and replaces them with whole foods and cholesterol-friendly carbs. Following this diet, along with exercise, will help to lower your bad cholesterol and raise your good cholesterol.

11. **Track your progress**. Each week, measure your progress. Take your weight, your key measures as described in point 3 above, and a photo. Compare them with your starting numbers and photos. Review the results from your detox quiz and check out the improvements you begin to have in those areas that came up as challenges for you. Pay attention to how you look, how you feel and how you think. Are you looking less bloated? Is your skin looking healthier? Remember that the skin is a clear reflection of your internal health. Are you feeling less tired or lethargic after eating? Are you needing less caffeine to get through your day? How is your mood? Do you feel your brain fog is going away and your mental clarity or focus is improving? If you follow the plan, results will start to be noticeable very soon. And don't worry, if you fall off the plan, just get back on track as soon as you can. Be patient. The greatest results are achieved gradually. Keep moving forward.

12. **Share your progress and stay accountable**. Post your results and progress in our Facebook page:

https://www.facebook.com/TheMexicanFoodDiet

Post your progress also in your social media and use our hashtag #themexicanfooddiet or #flacaforever so we can follow you, celebrate and recognize your achievements. A great way to keep you moving forward is to define goals and share them with your world. This will ensure you have supporters, cheerleaders and loving people who can keep you accountable. If possible, choose an accountability partner. A friend or family member that can support you to make sure you reach your goal of losing weight and getting healthier.

Chapter 19

THE MEAL PLAN

The Mexican Food Diet™ is your first step to an amazing journey that will help you jump-start your weight loss and health transformation. I have selected a diverse and balanced sample of your favorite Mexican food recipes and made them healthy.

MY MAIN GOALS FOR YOU ARE THE FOLLOWING:

1. During the **7 days of the Mexican Food Diet™**, I want you to always feel like you are cheating because everything tastes too good. You will feel very satisfied after every meal, and you will have less cravings for unhealthy foods.

2. I want to jump-start your weight loss by helping you lose up to 7 pounds in 1 week. How much you lose will depend on the state of your health, how much excess weight you are starting with and how close you follow the diet. But no matter what, you will benefit in too many ways so give it a try.

3. I want to help you take the first step of your detox journey.

4. I want you to experience how amazing you feel when you eat meals that satisfy you, empower your body and brain, and make you feel happy and satisfied for an extended period.

This book includes 7 days of 3 meals per day and 1 optional afternoon snack. As mentioned before, you will only want to eat the snack if you are hungry or are very active. You will also want to take the snack if your next meal is going to be more than 6 hours after your last meal or if you are going to a place where there will be very little or no healthy alternatives.

If you follow this plan as presented, you will be more likely to lose the weight you want. You can also test the recipes before you decide to follow the plan. Any steps you take will be improving your nutrition and health anyway.

You can extend the diet for a longer period by cooking double amounts and repeating each meal plan the following day. In other words, you would be eating the meals for **Day 1** two days in a row, then moving on to the meals in **Day 2**.

Or you can repurpose leftovers. Each recipe has ideas for repurposing or reusing leftovers in a different way for the following days. To ensure you have a complete meal, refer to the S.M.A.R.T. meal in **Chapter 8** or the Getting Started checklist in **Chapter 18**.

Flaca Stay Lean™ Shakes are the perfect meal replacements

When you are on a rush or on-the-go, you can substitute one of your meals with a Flaca Stay Lean™ shake as prepared in the recipes section. This plant-based all-in-one shake is the great way to eat a nutrient-dense meal when you have no time to prep, cook or eat. They have all the clean nutrients, vitamins, minerals and fiber that your body needs to stay energized, satisfied and healthy. You can take them with you and drink them at your first opportunity or while driving. If you are interested in getting them, go to the shop at www.FlacaForever.com. These shakes are my go-to breakfast every morning. I also take them with me always when I travel.

In the next Chapter, you can find the recipes for the 7-day diet, as well as for the shakes. If you want all the recipes in full color and in a pdf file that you can print, register your book at www.flacaforever.com/TheMexicanFoodDiet.

	BREAKFAST	LUNCH	SNACK	DINNER
DAY 1	Ranchero Eggs with Quinoa	Chicken with Blueberry Mole	Guacamole de Spa	Mexican-Style Chicken Soup
DAY 2	Cinnamon Quinoa with Apple and Almond Butter	Mango Soup Carne Asada Salad	Cabbage, Jicama, and Carrot Slaw	Roasted Cauliflower with Pepitas Chicken with Tarasco Sauce
DAY 3	Spicy Chipotle Chicken	Quinoa with Cilantro and Almonds Salmon Ceviche with Avocado Cucumber Salad with Strawberries and Avocado	Spicy Jicama Strings	Chayote Pasta with Turkey Meatballs
DAY 4	Vanilla Chia Pudding	Butternut Squash with Chile Ancho Beef Adobo	Jalapeño Hummus	Zucchini Pasta with Mexican Pesto Tomato Shrimps
DAY 5	Fried Eggs Over Brown Rice	Vegetarian Butternut Squash Chili	Black Bean Hummus	Guajillo and Tomato Soup with Vegetables Cochinita Pibil
DAY 6	Amaranth Pudding with Blueberries and Pecans	Fish Ceviche Mexican-Style Brown Rice	Almond Butter and Apple	Zucchini, Cilantro, and Poblano Soup Tequila Salmon
DAY 7	Mexican-Style Scrambled Eggs with Beans and Green Sauce	Chicken with Chile Mulato and Prune Sauce	Blueberries with Nuts	Mexican-Style Fish Chayotes with Spicy Tomato Sauce

THE MEXICAN FOOD DIET™ MEAL PLAN

RECIPES

BREAKFAST DAY 1:

Ranchero Eggs with Quinoa

This is one of my family's favorite breakfasts, created especially for Isabel (19-year-old). They have named it "The Power Breakfast". It is a perfect mix to keep anybody going through the first part of their day. Good combination of protein, fat and carbs with a great touch of spice given by the 2 sauces.

TOTAL TIME: 25 min.
Prep: 19 min.

Unattended: 6 min.

Storage Notes: Quinoa and salsa keep well for 4 days when refrigerated

Equipment Required: None

Gluten-Free, Dairy-Free, Sugar-Free, Soy-Free
[2 Servings] [6 Servings]

INGREDIENTS:

- Quinoa – uncooked [½ Cup] [1 ½ Cups]
- Water [1 Cup] [3 Cups]
- Jalapeño pepper [1] [3]
- Tomato – organic [1 med.] [3 med.]
- Onion [1 med.] [3 med.]
- Garlic cloves – peeled [2] [6]
- Cilantro – fresh [½ Cup] [1 ½ Cups]
- Lime [2] [6]
- Sea Salt [¼ tsp.] [¾ tsp.]
- Cumin [¼ tsp.] [¾ tsp.]
- Chili Powder [¼ tsp.] [¾ tsp.]
- Paprika [⅛ tsp.] [¼ + ⅛ tsp.]
- Salt and Pepper [As desired]
- Eggs - organic [4] [12]
- Olive oil - Extra Virgin [2 Tbsp.] [6 Tbsp.]
- Green Sauce [As desired- recipe in this book]
- Avocado [1] [3]

PROCEDURE:

1. Place quinoa in a strainer and rinse it thoroughly with water. Then place in a medium-sized pot.

2. Add water to the pot and cook on high heat until it boils. Turn heat down to simmer, cover pot and cook for 20 minutes until water is absorbed. While it is cooking, start preparing the salsa.

3. **SALSA** | Remove Jalapeño seeds.

4. Chop jalapeño, tomato, onion, garlic and cilantro. Place on a medium-sized bowl.

5. Squeeze the limes into the bowl.

6. Add the salt and mix all ingredients. Taste for seasoning.

7. When quinoa is done, add ½ cup of the salsa to the cooked quinoa and turn heat to low. Set aside the rest of the salsa.

8. Add the seasonings to the quinoa plus the salsa mix. Stir well until quinoa is warm.

9. Heat a pan on medium heat. When pan is warm, add the olive oil and immediately add the eggs. Cook them until desired doneness.

10. Slice the avocado.

11. Divide the quinoa mix equally among the plates. Serve the eggs on top of quinoa. Add the avocado slices and the salsa on the side. You can also add green sauce as prepared in the recipe from this book (see breakfast day 7).

S.M.A.R.T. TIPS

Prep in Advance: You can do the quinoa and salsa the day before and store them in the refrigerator (steps 1-6).

For Kids: Set apart the Jalapeño pepper from step 3. After completing step 6, separate a portion for kids and add the jalapeño pepper to the rest of the salsa.

Repurposing: You can cook additional quinoa to use for other meals during the next days. Extra salsa can be used to accompany other meals during the week.

Substituting: If you do not eat grains, you can skip the quinoa and replace it with grilled vegetables such as peppers, cauliflower, broccoli or whatever you like.

Adapted from Gringalicious.com

BREAKFAST DAY 2:

Cinnamon Quinoa with Apples and Almond Butter

Finding a variety of powerful breakfasts is quite challenging, particularly if you are focused on having all the S.M.A.R.T. players required: S.M.A.R.T. protein, fat, and carbs. Quinoa is a great breakfast alternative. It has the feeling and flavor of a warm cereal, but it carries the power of real protein, has good amounts of fiber, and a multitude of important nutrients. Adding the apples and the almond butter makes it even better both in taste and nutrition.

TOTAL TIME: 19 min.
Prep: 6 min.

Unattended: 13 min.

Storage Notes: Quinoa keeps well for 4 days when refrigerated.

Equipment Required: None

Gluten-Free, Dairy-Free, Sugar-Free, Soy-Free
[2 Servings] [6 Servings]

INGREDIENTS
- Quinoa - uncooked [½ Cup] [1 ½ Cup]
- Coconut milk - unsweetened [¾ Cup] [2 ¼ Cups]
- Cinnamon - ground [½ tsp.] [1 ½ tsp.]
- Nutmeg - ground [¼ tsp.] [¾ tsp.]
- Stevia [2 tsp.] [2 Tbsp.]
- Vanilla [1 tsp.] [2 Tbsp.]
- Apple - organic [1] [3]
- Almond Butter [2 Tbsp.] [6 Tbsp.]
- Pecans [1 Tbsp.] [3 Tbsp.]

PROCEDURE
1. Place quinoa on a strainer and rinse it thoroughly with water. Then place in a medium-sized pot.
2. Add all the ingredients to the pot except the apple, almond butter and pecans. Cook on high heat until it boils. Once it boils, turn heat down to simmer, cover pot, and cook for 15 to 20 minutes until liquid is absorbed. While it is cooking, prep the rest of the ingredients.
3. Slice the apples to serve on top of the quinoa.
4. Serve the cooked quinoa with the apple slices, 1 Tablespoon of the almond butter, and some pecans on each plate.

S.M.A.R.T TIPS

Prep in Advance: You can cook the quinoa the day before and store it in the refrigerator (steps 1-2). You can eat it cold or warm it up briefly in a saucepan.

For Kids: This recipe is perfect for kids. No adjustments needed.

Repurposing: You can cook additional quinoa to use for other meals or snacks during the next days.

Substituting: You can substitute coconut milk for almond milk and use another type of unsweetened nut butter or nuts. Not peanuts.

Adapted from How Sweet Eats

BREAKFAST DAY 3:

Spicy Chipotle Chicken

What I love about this breakfast is that you can prepare most of it ahead of time and just do the last-minute things the day of. It has great spicy flavor, great protein and fat. It will keep you energized and satisfied for a long time.

TOTAL TIME: 22 min.
Prep: 13 min.

Unattended: 9 min.

Storage Notes: Sauce can be stored in the fridge for 4 days.

Equipment Required: None

Gluten-Free, Dairy-Free, Sugar-Free, Soy-Free, Paleo
[2 Servings] [6 Servings]

INGREDIENTS

- Chipotle chiles – canned [2] [6]
- Canned diced tomatoes – organic – with liquid [14 oz.] [42 oz.]
- Onion [½ med.] [1 ½ med.]
- Garlic cloves – peeled [2] [6]
- Serrano peppers [1] [3]
- Cilantro [¼ Cup] [¾ Cup]
- Paprika [Dash] [¼ tsp.]
- Water [½ Cup] [1 ½ Cups]
- Olive oil Extra Virgin [1 Tbsp.] [3 Tbsp.]
- Sea Salt [Season] [Season]
- Pepper [Season] [Season]
- Chicken breasts - organic - free range [1.5] [4.5]
- Eggs - organic - free range [3] [9]
- Avocado [1] [3]
- Tomato – organic [½] [1 ½]
- Cilantro – fresh [to garnish] [to garnish]

PROCEDURE

1. Take out the stems and seeds from the Chipotle chiles.
2. Place in a blender the following ingredients: chipotle, tomatoes, onion, garlic, Serrano peppers, cilantro, paprika and water. Blend until ingredients combine into a smooth puree.
3. Place the blended mixture in a large saucepan and bring it to a boil. Reduce heat to medium, cover, and simmer for 15- 20 minutes until the sauce thickens. While this sauce is done, cook the chicken and eggs as specified on steps 5-6. When this sauce is ready, proceed to step 4.
4. Heat a large sauce pan on medium heat. When it is warm, add the olive oil and immediately add the sauce. Stir frequently for 10 minutes. Then add salt and season to taste.
5. Bake or cook the chicken depending on your preferences.

6. Beat the eggs and cook them to your desired level of doneness.

7. Slice avocado just before serving the plates.

8. Chop tomatoes for garnishing and set aside.

9. Serve each plate with½ cup of the cooked sauce. Divide the chicken, eggs, and avocado among the plates. Garnish with the chopped tomatoes and cilantro. Add more sauce if desired.

S.M.A.R.T. TIPS

Prep in Advance: You can do the sauce a few days in advance (steps 1-4). Chicken and eggs can be cooked the night before (steps 5-6). Just before serving, heat chicken and eggs in a pan and sauce in another one. Then proceed with steps 7-9.

For Kids: You can put all ingredients in the blender except the chipotle and serrano. Once blended, take out a part of the salsa to be used for the kids and add the chiles to the rest. Proceed with steps 3-4 using 2 different pans. For steps 5-9 you can do all at once.

Repurposing: You can use the extra sauce for eggs or to accompany another main dish (fish or meat). You can also cook more chicken to have it ready for a salad or a dinner/ lunch.

Substituting: You can use real chopped organic tomatoes instead of the canned tomatoes. Just add ¼ more water to the blend.

Inspired by boulderlocavore.com

BREAKFAST DAY 4:

Vanilla Chia Pudding

I love this breakfast. It is so easy and quick to make. You can have this on your fridge as an emergency breakfast for those days when you are very short on time or for healthy afternoon snacks. Easy to take on the go too. Chia is a superfood, very nutritious, filling, and a great source of fiber. Fabulous for weight and health. My kids love this one. You can also turn it into a chocolate one by adding organic raw cacao.

TOTAL TIME: 65 min.
Prep: 5 min.

Unattended: 60 min.

Storage Notes: Keeps for 3 days when refrigerated

Equipment Required: None

Gluten-Free, Dairy-Free, Sugar-Free, Soy-Free, Paleo
[2 Servings] [6 Servings]

INGREDIENTS
- Almond milk – unsweetened [2 Cups] [6 Cups]
- Chia seeds – organic [½ Cup] [1 ½ Cups]
- Vanilla extract [½ tsp.] [1 ½ tsp.]
- Stevia [1 tsp.] [1 Tbsp.]
- Mixed organic berries: blueberries, strawberries [1 Cup] [3 Cups]
- Almonds – sliced or slivered [⅓ Cup] [1 Cup]

PROCEDURE
1. Combine all ingredients except berries and almonds. Mix well for 1 minute until the mix begins to thicken.
2. Store mix in the refrigerator for at least 1 hour but preferably overnight.
3. Stir mix well. Divide mix, berries and almonds into individual cups.

S.M.A.R.T. TIPS

Prep in Advance: You can do the pudding the night before or several days ahead. You can have this pudding available for snacks, on-the-go meals, or fast breakfasts.

For Kids: No adjustment needed. If they like it sweeter, you can add more Stevia.

Repurposing: You can add this to your protein shakes, mix it up with other nuts, or use it as a meal or side dish.

Substituting: You can use coconut milk (unsweetened) instead of the almond milk. You can also use other nut butters or raw nuts instead of the almond butter (no peanuts).

BREAKFAST DAY 5:

Fried Eggs Over Brown Rice with Chia

This is a very tasty breakfast. It takes some time, but most of it is unattended time for the rice. You can cook the rice ahead of time. Great balance of S.M.A.R.T. protein, fat and carbs. This combination will keep you full and provide you with a slow release of energy without the unwanted sugar crashes that can lead you into temptation.

TOTAL TIME: 70 min.
Prep: 21 min.

Unattended: 49 min.

Storage Notes: Rice and chia gel can be stored for 4 days.

Equipment Required: None

Gluten-Free, Dairy-Free, Sugar-Free, Soy-Free
[2 Servings] [6 Servings]

INGREDIENTS
- Brown rice – organic [½ Cup] [1 ½ Cups]
- Chicken stock – organic [1 Cup] [3 Cups]
- Green onion - white parts [2] [6]
- Vegetable broth – organic [½ Cup] [1 ½ Cups]
- Chia seeds – organic [2 Tbsp.] [6 Tbsp.]
- Sesame oil [1 ½ tsp.] [4½ tsp.]
- Eggs - organic and free range [4] [12]
- Chia seeds – organic [1 Tbsp.] [3 Tbsp.]
- Green onion- green parts [1] [3]

PROCEDURE
1. Rinse rice thoroughly with water using a strainer. Place rice on a medium pot.
2. Add chicken stock. Bring to a boil over medium-high heat. Reduce the heat to medium-low, cover the pot, and simmer for 40 minutes until stock is completely absorbed and rice is just tender. Turn off the heat and leave covered for 10 minutes. Then uncover and fluff rice with a fork. Place rice in fridge to cool.
3. Cut the onions in diagonal slices, separating the white parts from the green parts. Put the green parts aside and use the white parts in the following steps.
4. Put the white parts of the green onion, vegetable broth and chia seeds in a small sauce pan and stir without heat. Let sit for 20 minutes without heat.
5. Bring the mixed ingredients to a boil over high heat.
6. Add the rice and stir for 30 seconds. Cover the pan and lower the heat to low. Let it cook for about 4 minutes until the rice is steaming hot and has a sticky consistency.
7. Heat a nonstick or cast iron pan over medium low heat. Once the pan is hot, add the oil and immediately add the eggs. Cook until desired doneness.

8. Serve the eggs over the rice mixture and sprinkle with chia seeds and the green onion parts.

S.M.A.R.T. TIPS

Prep in Advance: You can cook the rice a day or two ahead of time and reheat it before serving (steps 1-2) or eat it cold. You can also cook the chia gel ahead of time (steps 3-4) and refrigerate until you are ready. This will save you a lot of time.

For Kids: No adjustment needed.

Repurposing: You can cook more rice than you need so that you have it for other meals. I like always having some ready to go. I just add veggies and it's a great side dish for the family.

Substituting: You can substitute the rice with quinoa if you like it better. Or if you don't eat grains, you can do a base of sautéed veggies.

Adapted from Dailyburn.com

BREAKFAST DAY 6:

Amaranth Pudding

Amaranth is a healthy grain that is well-known in Mexico and South America. This grain contains high levels of calcium and of several minerals. It is considered a protein powerhouse, so a great option for vegetarians. In fact, it is one of the grains that has the highest protein content. It is also great for your heart, and it is gluten-free. Another good option to bring variety to your breakfasts without sacrificing the protein content. You can make it chocolate too for those chocolate lovers.

TOTAL TIME: 32 min.
Prep: 7 min.

Unattended: 25 min.

Storage Notes: Amaranth can be stored for 4 days.

Equipment Required: None

Gluten-Free, Dairy-Free, Sugar-Free, Soy-Free
[2 Servings] [6 Servings]

INGREDIENTS
- Amaranth [½ Cup] [1½ Cups]
- Coconut milk – unsweetened [1 Cup] [3 Cups]
- Coconut milk – unsweetened [6 Tbsp.] [1 Cup + 2 Tbsp.]
- Cinnamon – ground [½ tsp.] [1½ tsp.]
- Stevia [2 tsp.] [6 tsp.]
- Walnuts [⅔ Cup] [2 Cups]

PROCEDURE
1. Place the amaranth on a strainer and rinse it thoroughly with water. If amaranth is not rinsed well, it can taste bitter.
2. Place the first coconut milk on the saucepan over high heat until it boils. Once it reaches boiling point, pour the amaranth and turn the heat down to low and cook for 20-25 minutes or until most of the coconut milk is absorbed. Be careful not to burn or overcook.
3. Serve the cooked amaranth on individual bowls.
4. Divide the second coconut milk in equal parts over each bowl, and sprinkle with cinnamon.
5. If you prefer it sweet, add 1 envelope or 1 teaspoon of stevia per bowl.
6. Divide the nuts equally between the bowls.

S.M.A.R.T. TIPS

Prep in Advance: You can cook the amaranth a day or two ahead of time and reheat it before serving (steps 1-2) or eat it cold. This will save you a lot of time.

For Kids: Adjust sweetness. Add banana or berries for kids.

Repurposing: You can cook more amaranth than you need so that you have it for other meals.

Substituting: You can substitute the amaranth with quinoa if you like it better. You can substitute walnuts with raw pecans or almonds, or an unsweetened nut butter, except peanuts. The portion for a nut butter would be 1-2 Tablespoons. You can substitute coconut milk with unsweetened almond milk too. Make sure the almond milk does not have carrageenan.

Adapted from Dailyburn.com

BREAKFAST DAY 7:

Mexican-Style Scrambled Eggs

Eggs are a great way to start your day. This recipe in Spanish is called "Huevos a la Mexicana" or Mexican-style eggs. They are delicious and add power to your day. In this diet, we accompany them with typical side dishes in Mexico: beans and hot sauce. Our beans (next recipe) are cooked and not fried. The hot sauce is homemade green sauce (recipe following beans).

TOTAL TIME: 13 min.
Prep: 13 min.

Unattended: 0 min.

Storage Notes: Cooked eggs can be stored for 2 days.

Equipment Required: None

Gluten-Free, Dairy-Free, Sugar-Free, Soy-Free
[2 Servings] [6 Servings]

INGREDIENTS
- Eggs – free-range, organic [4] [12]
- Onion [¼ med.] [¾ med.]
- Garlic clove - peeled [2] [6]
- Serrano chile [1-2] [3-6]
- Tomatoes - Roma – Organic [3] [9]
- Cilantro – fresh [¼ Cup] [¾ Cup]
- Olive oil - Extra Virgin [1 Tbsp.] [3 Tbsp.]
- Sea salt [½ tsp.] [1 ½ tsp.]

PROCEDURE
1. Beat the eggs and set aside.
2. Chop the onion, garlic, Serrano peppers, tomatoes and cilantro and set aside separately on a cutting board. Do not mix them all together.
3. Heat the pan on medium temperature. Once it is hot, add the olive oil and immediately add the chopped onion. Cook for 1 minute.
4. Add the chopped garlic and serrano chile and cook for 1 more minute.
5. Add the tomato and cook for 2 more minutes.
6. Add the chopped cilantro and the salt.
7. Add the beaten eggs and cook for 2 minutes, stirring constantly until they are done to your desired consistency/cooked level.

S.M.A.R.T. TIPS

Prep in Advance: You can chop all the ingredients the night before (step 2) and then cook them and the eggs the day you need them.

For Kids: Before adding the Serrano peppers on step 4, separate ingredients in 2 different pans, keeping one without the Serrano peppers and the other one with the peppers.

Repurposing: You can chop extra ingredients and save them to do a fresh sauce (just add lime and salt) or cook more eggs in the following days. You can also cook the eggs all the way and save part of them to be reheated in the next few days for breakfast or even for lunch.

Substituting: If you want to do egg whites you can. Just eat them with additional fat from avocado so you can stay full for a longer period.

Adapted from Dailyburn.com

Cooked Beans

Beans are a special plate for Mexicans. The good thing is that they are a powerhouse. They provide a high content of protein, fiber, and minerals. You can eat them boiled or fried. If you fry them, they need to be with olive oil or avocado oil, and at the right temperature. Beans are great side dish for eggs or a good meal on their own, accompanied with veggies. They can also be blended with veggies to provide a delicious soup with a creamy texture.

TOTAL TIME: 9.75 hrs.
Prep: 14 min.

Unattended: 9.5 hrs.

Storage Notes: Beans can be stored in the fridge for up to 4 days

Equipment Required: None

Gluten-Free, Dairy-Free, Sugar-Free, Soy-Free
[2 Servings] [6 Servings]

INGREDIENTS

- Beans - dried black or pinto [0.25 lbs.] [0.75 lbs.]
- Yellow onion [1 med.] [3 med.]
- Bay leaves [1] [3]
- Sea Salt [season] [season]
- Black pepper – ground [season] [season]
- Olive oil - Extra Virgin [1 Tbsp.] [3 Tbsp.]

PROCEDURE

1. Spread beans in a single layer on a large sheet tray. Pick through to remove and discard any small stones or debris and then rinse well with a strainer.

2. In a large bowl, cover beans with 3 inches of cold water, cover, and set aside at room temperature for 8 hours or overnight.

3. Cut the onion in quarters and set aside.

4. Drain soaked beans and transfer to a large pot. Cover pot in 2 inches of cold water.

5. Add onion and bay leaves and bring to a boil. Use a large spoon to skim off and discard any foam on the surface.

6. Once it reaches boiling point, reduce heat, cover, and simmer, gently stirring occasionally until beans are tender, 1 to 1½ hours.

7. You can drain beans, if desired, and discard onions and bay leaves. Season with salt and pepper.

8. If you like refried beans or dried beans, you can heat up in a medium-sized pan by adding the olive oil and squashing the beans until they reach the desired consistency.

S.M.A.R.T. TIPS

Prep in Advance: Beans can be cooked several days in advance and refrigerated until needed.

Kids: All ingredients are kid friendly.

Repurposing: You can use beans as a high-protein soup by mixing them with vegetables (with or without blending them), or as a side dish to another vegetarian plate or mixed with your scrambled eggs.

Substituting: If you don't like beans or can't eat beans you can substitute them for lentils, quinoa, sweet potato, or brown rice. You can also experiment with other types of beans.

Green Sauce

Green sauce is one of my favorite staples. I love to always have some in the fridge. I use it with eggs, with veggies, with any protein. Whenever I want to give flavor, spice, and detox power, I add it.

TOTAL TIME: 33 min.
Prep: 22 min.

Unattended: 11 min.

Storage Notes: You can store the sauce for 1 week. You can also freeze it and then reheat in a saucepan later.

Equipment Required: None

Gluten-Free, Dairy-Free, Sugar-Free, Soy-Free, Paleo
[2 Servings] [6 Servings]

INGREDIENTS
- Green tomatillos [1 lb.] [3 lb.]
- Water [4 Cups] [12 Cups]
- Serrano chiles [4] [12]
- Onion [3 oz.] [9 oz.]
- Garlic cloves - peeled [2] [6]
- Olive oil - Extra Virgin [2 Tbsp.] [6 Tbsp.]

- Sea salt [1 tsp.] [1 Tbsp.]
- Cilantro - fresh [0.5 oz.] [1.5 oz.]

PROCEDURE

1. Peel and rinse the tomatillos. Put them on the large pot with the water.
2. Cook the tomatillos on high heat for 15 minutes. While they are cooking, continue with step #3.
3. Take out the seeds and stem of the chile.
4. Chop the onion and the garlic.
5. Heat a deep pan on medium heat. When hot, add the olive oil and immediately add the onion. Cook for 2 minutes, stirring so it cooks evenly.
6. Add the garlic and cook for 1 more minute, stirring. Remove from heat.
7. Place the cooked tomatillos, onion, garlic, chiles, and salt in the blender. Blend on high speed for 10 seconds.
8. Pour the blend into the frying pan and cook for 5 minutes on high heat. When boiling, reduce the heat to medium.
9. Pour the sauce into the blender. Add the cilantro. Blend on medium speed for 2 seconds.

S.M.A.R.T. TIPS

Prep in Advance: You can cook the sauce once a week and have it ready for any day you desire. You can also cook double and freeze half or more of it to use whenever you need it or crave it. You can also have the tomatillos peeled and cleaned, and the vegetables chopped ahead of time.

For Kids: You can separate a part of the mix in step 7 to be without chiles and the other part with chiles.

Repurposing: You can use this sauce again to accompany fried eggs, grilled veggies, meats and fishes, healthy burritos, or whatever your imagination suggests.

Substituting: If you want to do egg whites you can. Just eat them with additional fat from an avocado so you can stay full for a longer period.

LUNCH DAY 1:

Chicken with Blueberry Mole

This recipe has been a great success. People don't expect to eat mole that is healthy. It is a nutrition powerhouse with the combination of ingredients. It is very satisfying and delicious.

TOTAL TIME: 90 min.
Prep: 30 min.

Unattended: 60 min.

Storage Notes: Sauce can be stored in the fridge for 4 days.

Equipment Required: None

Gluten-Free, Dairy-Free, Sugar-Free, Soy-Free, Paleo
[2 Servings] [6 Servings]

INGREDIENTS

- Ancho chile [2] [6]
- Guajillo chile [1] [3]
- Onion [3 oz.] [9 oz.]
- Garlic cloves - peeled [1] [3]
- Tomatoes – organic [1] [3]
- Cinnamon stick [¼] [¾]
- Pecan [1 oz.] [3 oz.]
- Almonds [1 oz.] [3 oz.]
- Clove [1] [3]
- Sea salt [½ tsp.] [1 ½ tsp.]
- Water [5 oz.] [15 oz.]
- Blueberries [3 oz.] [9 oz.]
- Chicken stock - organic - reduced sodium [⅓ Cup] [1 Cup]
- Stevia [1 tsp.] [1 Tbsp.]
- Olive oil [1 oz.] [3 oz.]
- Chicken stock - organic - reduced sodium [6 oz.] [18 oz.]
- Chicken thighs or chicken legs with thighs - organic - free range [8 oz.] [1 ½ lbs.]

PROCEDURE

1. Preheat the oven at 350 F.
2. Wash the chiles and remove the seeds and the veins. Soak the chiles on water while you measure the rest of the ingredients.
3. Heat a large pan over medium high to high heat. Roast the chiles, onion, garlic, tomatoes and cinnamon sticks. Turn around making sure they are well roasted on all sides.
4. Place the roasted ingredients in a blender.
5. Add the pecans, almonds, clove, sea salt and water to the blender.
6. Heat a small sauce pan over medium heat. When hot, add blueberries, the first chicken stock and stevia.
7. Bring it to a boil and then reduce heat to simmer. Cook for 5 minutes stirring frequently.

9. Add ½ cup of the sauce to the blender if you are doing 2 servings, or 1½ cups if you are doing 6 servings.
10. Blend all ingredients in the blender on high speed for 30 seconds.
11. Heat a large sauce pan over medium heat. When hot, add the olive oil and the blended ingredients. Bring to a boil and then reduce heat to simmer. Cook for 30 minutes, stirring occasionally.
12. Add the second chicken stock and the remaining blueberry sauce. Bring to a simmer and cook for 20 minutes.
13. Pour all the ingredients into the blender and blend for 15 seconds on high speed.
14. Place the chicken thighs on an oven tray and cover with the mole. Cook until the internal temperature reaches 165 F.
15. Serve the chicken with additional mole on top and garnish with some pecans and blueberries.

S.M.A.R.T. TIPS

Prep in Advance: You can prepare the mole a day or two in advance (steps 2-12). Then continue with the remaining steps when you are ready.

For Kids: The mole is not spicy at all. If you want to do it for them without chile, in step 4 you can separate a kids' portion and continue with the next steps doing two different sauces.

Repurposing: You can use the extra mole for other meals with a different S.M.A.R.T. protein.

Substituting: You can substitute chicken for red meat, pork, fish. Follow the S.M.A.R.T. Protein guidelines to ensure quality protein.

Inspired by Thermomix

Cauliflower Tortillas

These are healthy versions of tortillas. When you prepare them, you will be surprised to see how much water cauliflower has. The liquid that comes out also tastes good, too. I have kept it and drank the liquid afterwards. You can make these tortillas as small as you want. Cauliflower is a great source of vitamin C which will boost your immune system.

TOTAL TIME: 39 min.

Prep: 15 min.

Unattended: 24 min.

Storage Notes: You can keep the tortillas in the refrigerator for 3 days. Reheat in a pan when you are ready to use.

Equipment Required: Food processor

Gluten-Free, Dairy-Free, Sugar-Free, Soy-Free, Paleo
[2 Servings] [6 Servings]

INGREDIENTS
- Cauliflower [½] [1 ½]
- Eggs - organic and free range [1] [3]
- Serrano chile [1] [3]
- Cilantro – fresh [¼ cup] [¾ cup]
- Lime [½] [1 ½]
- Sea Salt [½ tsp.] [1 ½ tsp.]

PROCEDURES
1. Preheat the oven to 375 F. Set up a baking sheet with parchment paper.
2. Cut the cauliflower into small pieces and put it in a food processor until it looks like rice.
3. Place the cauliflower in a microwave-safe bowl and microwave for 2 minutes, then stir and microwave again for another 2 minutes.
4. Place the cauliflower in a fine cheesecloth or similar and squeeze out as much liquid as possible. It is very hot, so you will need to be careful. If you have gloves, you should use them.
5. In a medium bowl, whisk the eggs.
6. Take the seeds out of the Serrano chile and then chop it. Now chop the cilantro. Keep them separate.
7. Add the Serrano chile, cilantro, lime and sea salt to the bowl with the eggs.
8. Add the cauliflower.
9. Mix all ingredients until they are well combined.
10. Shape the tortillas in the size that you desire and place them on the cooking sheet.
11. Bake the tortillas in the oven for 10 minutes, then flip them and cook for another 5-7 minutes. You need to make sure they are completely set.

12. Let the tortillas cool in a wire rack for 3 minutes.
13. Heat a medium-size pan on medium heat. Place the tortillas and let them brown for 1 to 2 minutes on each side.

S.M.A.R.T. TIPS

Prep in Advance: You can prepare the ingredients up to step 9 ahead of time. When you are ready to serve, continue with steps 10-13.

For Kids: In step 7, separate a portion for the kids and then add the chile to the rest.

Repurposing: You can serve this as a snack or a side dish to anything. They can also be used as a base for other vegetables or as a sandwich.

Substituting: You can substitute the Serrano chile for a Jalapeño.

Adapted from Recipegirl.com

LUNCH DAY 2:

Carne Asada Salad

This is a very easy salad that provides you with all your needs for protein, veggies and fat. You can get creative and add more veggies from the S.M.A.R.T. veggies list. It takes a long time to marinate but you can do it the night before.

TOTAL TIME: 8 hrs. 30 min.
Prep: 30 min.

Unattended: 8 hrs.

Storage Notes: Cooked steak can be stored in the fridge for 3 days. Dressing refrigerated for 1 week.

Equipment Required: None.

Gluten-Free, Dairy-Free, Sugar-Free, Soy-Free, Paleo
[2 Servings] [6 Servings]

INGREDIENTS

- Oranges [¼ Cup] [¾ Cup]
- Garlic clove - peeled [2] [6]
- White vinegar [¼ Cup] [¾ Cup]
- Olive oil - Extra Virgin [2 tsp.] [2 Tbsp.]
- Cumin [½ tsp.] [1 ½ tsp.]
- Chili powder [2 tsp.] [2 Tbsp.]
- Sea Salt [½ tsp.] [1 ½ tsp.]
- Flank steak - grass- fed [8 oz.] [1.5 lb.]
- Red bell peppers - organic [1] [3]
- Lime [2] [6]
- Olive oil - Extra Virgin [1 Tbsp.] [3 Tbsp.]
- Sea Salt [1 tsp.] [1 Tbsp.]
- Arugula - organic [3 Cups] [9 Cups]
- Avocado [1] [3]
- Cilantro - fresh [½ Cup] [1 ½ Cups]

PROCEDURE

1. Squeeze orange juice and put it into a medium-sized bowl.
2. Chop garlic and add to bowl.
3. Add the following ingredients to the bowl: white vinegar, olive oil, cumin, chili powder, and salt.
4. Place flank steak in a one-gallon Ziploc plastic bag and pour the mix from step 3 over it. Refrigerate bag for at least 8 hours or overnight.
5. Once the steak has been marinating for at least 8 hours, preheat a grill pan over medium high heat. Cook the steak for approximately 4 to 5 minutes on each side, pouring the marinade on as it cooks. This will give you a medium rare cook. You may need to adjust cooking if the steak is thick.
6. Once the steak is cooked, set it aside.
7. Roast red peppers on all sides. When done, slice them and set aside.

8. In a small bowl, mix the lime, olive oil and sea salt.
9. Divide the arugula among the plates.
10. Pour the dressing from step 8 over each plate.
11. Slice the avocados.
12. Add the peppers and avocado on top of the salad, leaving space in the center for the meat.
13. Cut the steak on a cutting board in thin slices and divide it among the plates.
14. Chop cilantro and use it to garnish the plates.

S.M.A.R.T. TIPS

Prep in Advance: The steak needs to be marinated for at least 8 hours so you need to prepare it the night before or 2 days before you want it. The rest of the salad is best to do it just as you need it because it does not keep well in the refrigerator.

For Kids: All ingredients are kid friendly.

Repurposing: You can cook double amount so you can have it in a few days without cooking again. You can also put the steak over a different type of salad and veggies mix. Or you can eat it alone with another healthy side dish.

Substituting: You can substitute red meat for pork, chicken, or fish. Follow the S.M.A.R.T. Protein guidelines to ensure quality protein. And adjust the cooking to the type of meat or fish you are having.

Adapted from Foodfantastic.com

Mango Soup

Mango soup is a very refreshing soup. You may struggle to find mango in certain times of the year. It is produced throughout the year, but most of it reaches the U.S. in spring and summer. It is a great combination of fruit and veggies. The jicama and cucumber garnishes add a very interesting texture. The contrast of the chili powder is great too. My favorite chili powder is Tajin. You can buy it online or in certain grocery stores. It has a lime flavor to it that I love.

TOTAL TIME: 45 min.
Prep: 15 min.

Unattended: 30 min.

Storage Notes: This soup can be stored for up to 4 days.

Equipment Required: Food processor or blender. If you don't have either, then use a sharp knife.

Gluten-Free, Dairy-Free, Sugar-Free, Soy-Free, Paleo
[2 Servings] [6 Servings]

INGREDIENTS
- Oranges [5] [15]
- Limes [2] [6]
- Garlic cloves - peeled [1] [3]
- Jicama [½] [1 ½]
- Cucumber - organic [1] [3]
- Mangos [2] [6]
- Onion [¼ small] [¾ small]
- Yellow bell pepper [1] [3]
- White vinegar [1 ½ tsp.] [4 ½ tsp.]
- Sea Salt [to season] [to season]
- Chile powder [to garnish] [to garnish]
- Cilantro - fresh [to garnish] [to garnish]

PROCEDURE
1. Squeeze the juice of the oranges and limes into a small bowl and set aside.
2. Chop garlic and set aside.
3. Peel the jicama and cucumber and cut them into medium-sized chunks.
4. Place the jicama and cucumber into a food processor or blender at medium speed for 4 seconds. Set aside.
5. Cut the mangos, onion and yellow bell pepper, into medium-sized chunks, then place these ingredients into the food processor or blender.
6. Add the garlic, orange and lime juices from steps 1-2.
7. Add the vinegar. Blend these ingredients at high speed for 10 seconds.
8. Add salt to season and blend again. Add more salt if needed.
9. Pour into a container and refrigerate for 30 minutes.
10. Serve soup chilled in a small bowl. 1 Cup is a serving if you are trying to lose weight.

11. Add some of the jicama and cucumber mix from step 4 on top and sprinkle with chili powder.
12. Garnish with cilantro.

S.M.A.R.T. TIPS

Prep in Advance: You can make this soup up to step 9 in advance, up to 3 days. The day of, continue with steps 10-12.

For Kids: Just skip the chili powder from step 11.

Repurposing: You can use the mango soup and add berries instead of jicama and cucumber.

Substituting: You can try making this soup with any type of mango that you find at the store.

Adapted from Thermomix

LUNCH DAY 3:

Cucumber Salad with Strawberries and Avocado

A very fresh and light salad. It works very well with the Veggie Bullet or Spiralizer, which are smart gadgets that turn vegetables into pasta-like noodles. You don't need to rush out and buy one. It tastes just as yummy if you use a vegetable peeler and do nice shaves from the cucumber. Or you can cut it into very fine strips. Whatever you decide, be creative and enjoy the combination of sweet and sour that this recipe brings.

TOTAL TIME: 12 min.
Prep: 12 min.

Unattended: 0 min.

Storage Notes: This salad can keep for 1 or 2 days in the fridge. The cucumber and strawberries start to turn soggy after this period.

Equipment Required: Veggie bullet, spiralizer. If you don't have one, then use a vegetable peeler.

Gluten-Free, Dairy-Free, Sugar-Free, Soy-Free, Paleo
[2 Servings] [6 Servings]

INGREDIENTS
- Cucumber, organic [½] [1 ½]
- Strawberries, organic [¾ Cup] [2 ¼ Cups]
- Avocado [½] [1 ½]
- Cilantro - fresh [1 Tbsp.] [3 Tbsp.]
- Red onion [¼ Cup] [¾ Cup]
- Jalapeño chile [½] [1 ½]
- Lime [1] [3]
- Stevia [1 tsp.] [1 Tbsp.]
- Salt and pepper [to season] [to season]

PROCEDURE
1. Attach cucumber to the veggie bullet or spiralizer. Use the veggie bullet or spiralizer with the appropriate blade to produce noodles that are like linguine or spaghetti. Set the noodles aside in a mixing bowl of appropriate size for all the ingredients in the recipe.
2. Cut the strawberries and avocado into smaller pieces for the salad and add to the cucumber bowl.
3. Take out the seeds of the Jalapeño. Chop the cilantro, red onion and jalapeño. Add these ingredients to the cucumber bowl.
4. Combine all the ingredients from steps 1-3 in the bowl.
5. In a small bowl, mix together the lime, stevia, salt and pepper. Pour the dressing over the rest of the ingredients and mix together.
6. Serve on individual bowls or as a side dish with the other parts of the day's meal.

S.M.A.R.T. TIPS

Prep in Advance: You can prepare this recipe a day before, but it is always better to do the same day. The ingredients in step 3 (except cilantro) can be perfectly prepped the night before. The dressing in step 5 can also be prepped ahead.

For Kids: When you get to step 3 separate a portion for the kids before adding the jalapeños and then keep going with the recipe in 2 versions.

Repurposing: You can cook double amount so you can have it in a few days without prepping again.

Substituting: You can try this recipe with blueberries or a mix of berries. You can add more or less chile according to your preference. You can also use another vegetable like jicama.

Adapted from Inspiralized

Salmon Ceviche with Avocado

Ceviche is one of the easiest ways to eat a powerful meal. It takes very little time to prep and can be stored for up to 3 days. This

ceviche can be eaten in the fancy way, on top of avocado, like in the photo or just mixed in a plate. You can reuse it for grilled salmon and eat the next day or eat it again as ceviche. You can also add other ceviche-style ingredients like cilantro, chiles, and onion.

TOTAL TIME: 65 min.
Prep: 5 min.

Unattended: 60 min.

Storage Notes: Ceviche can be stored for 3 days in the refrigerator.

Equipment Required: None

Gluten-Free, Dairy-Free, Sugar-Free, Soy-Free, Paleo
[2 Servings] [6 Servings]

INGREDIENTS
- Wild salmon [8 oz.] [1.5 lbs.]
- Limes [5] [15]
- Sea salt [1 tsp.] [1 Tbsp.]
- Avocado [1] [3]

PROCEDURE
1. Cut the salmon into small cubes and place in a medium bowl.
2. Squeeze the lime juice into the bowl to cover the salmon with it.
3. Add the salt and mix well.
4. Cover and refrigerate for at least 1 hour so that it cooks in the lime juice.
5. After 1 hour, taste it and add more lime juice or salt as needed.
6. Smash the avocado and place it on a mold to get a shape and then mount the salmon on top.

S.M.A.R.T. TIPS

Prep in Advance: You can do ceviche steps 1-5 the day before.

For Kids: All ingredients are kid friendly.

Repurposing: You can prepare double amount so you can have it in a few days without prepping again. The second time, you can put it in a pan and cook it so it is warm. You can also add other ingredients like cilantro, onion, garlic, tomato and chiles. It will make a great S.M.A.R.T. Meal for another day.

Substituting: If you can't find wild salmon you can buy farm-raised salmon but only from a source that you trust.

Quinoa with Cilantro and Almonds

Quinoa is a nutrient-rich, easy to digest and gluten-free grain that provides a high level of protein. It is very versatile and easy to combine with a variety of things. You can have it with fruit, with veggies, with protein or just alone. It is a S.M.A.R.T. source of carbs and fiber which means a healthy and stable source of energy and a support to your digestive system. This recipe incorporates also the power of cilantro and the healthy fats from almonds.

TOTAL TIME: 36 min.
Prep: 20 min.

Unattended: 16 min.

Storage Notes: This complete dish can be kept in refrigerator up to 4 days.

Equipment Required: None

Gluten-Free, Dairy-Free, Sugar-Free, Soy-Free
[2 Servings] [6 Servings]

INGREDIENTS

- Quinoa [½ Cup] [1 ½ Cups]
- Onion [½ med.] [1 ½ med.]
- Garlic cloves - peeled [2] [6]
- Serrano chiles [2 oz.] [6 oz.]
- Jalapeño chiles [½] [1 ½]
- Olive oil - Extra Virgin [1 Tbsp.] [3 Tbsp.]
- Vegetable broth- organic [1 Cup] [3 Cups]
- Green onions [½ Cup] [1 ½ Cups]
- Lime juice [1 Tbsp.] [3 Tbsp.]
- Lime zest [¼ tsp.] [¾ tsp.]
- Cilantro - fresh [½ Cup] [1 ½ Cups]
- Salt and pepper [to taste] [to taste]
- Almonds [½ Cup] [1 ½ Cups]

PROCEDURE

1. Rinse the quinoa in a strainer over water until very well rinsed. If you do no rinse it, it will taste bitter. Set aside.
2. Chop onion, garlic, serrano and jalapeño peppers.
3. Heat a medium saucepan over medium high heat. As soon as it is hot, add the olive oil and immediately add in onions. Sauté for 2 minutes.
4. Add garlic and sauté for 1 to 2 minutes.

5. Don't let it brown.
6. Stir in serrano and jalapeño chiles and cook for another 2 minutes.
7. Add in quinoa and vegetable broth and bring to boil. Reduce heat to a gentle simmer, cover and cook for 20-25 minutes until the quinoa is tender and most of the liquid has been absorbed.
8. Chop the green onions and add to the quinoa.
9. Add in remaining ingredients and fluff with a fork. Serve immediately.

S.M.A.R.T. TIPS

Prep in Advance: You can cook the full dish up to 3 days in advance and store in the fridge for a total of 4 days.

For Kids: Before you go to step 6, separate a portion without the chiles.

Repurposing: You can cook double amount to have it in a few days. Use it under eggs, or add more veggies and have as a side dish.

Substituting: You can substitute quinoa for brown rice. You can substitute almonds for walnuts, pecans, pine nuts, or pistachios.

Adapted from LaaLoosh.com

LUNCH DAY 4:

Butternut Squash Soup with Chile Ancho

Butternut squash is a very satisfying and nutrient-rich soup. It feels like a cream soup but it does not have dairy. It is perfect for the kids too. When you take out the chiles, it is a sweet and creamy soup.

TOTAL TIME: 48 min.
Prep: 27 min.

Unattended: 21 min.

Storage Notes: This soup can stay in the refrigerator for up to 3 days.

Equipment Required: None

Gluten-Free, Dairy-Free, Sugar-Free, Soy-Free, Paleo
[2 Servings] [6 Servings]

INGREDIENTS

- Butternut squash [1 ¼ lbs.] [3 ¾ lbs.]
- Olive oil - Extra Virgin [1 Tbsp.] [3 Tbsp.]
- Sea salt [½ tsp.] [1 ½ tsp.]
- Ancho chile [1] [3]
- Onion [1 med.] [3 med.]
- Carrot [1 med.] [3 med.]
- Garlic cloves - peeled [1] [3]
- Olive oil - Extra Virgin - [1 Tbsp.] [3 Tbsp.]
- Chicken stock - organic - low sodium [1 Cup] [3 Cups]
- Water [½ Cup] [1 ½ Cups]
- Sea salt [to season] [to season]
- Pumpkin seeds- raw and unsalted [½ Cup] [1 ½ Cups]
- Cilantro - fresh [¼ Cup] [¾ Cup]

PROCEDURE

1. Preheat oven to 425 F.
2. Peel butternut squash and cut into smaller ½ inch cubes. Place butternut squash into medium-sized bowl.
3. Add the first olive oil and sea salt to the butternut squash.
4. Place the butternut squash into a deep baking sheet and spread it out evenly.
5. Cook the butternut squash for approximately 35 minutes, stirring occasionally so that it gets roasted all over.
6. Rinse the chiles. Remove the stem and seeds.
7. In a medium-sized pan, toast ancho chilies over high heat, turning once, until fragrant. When it cools down, break it down into pieces. Set aside.
8. Chop the onion, carrot and garlic.
9. Pre-heat a medium-sized pot on medium-high heat. When it is hot, add the second olive oil and the vegetables from step 8.

10. Cook until softened and just beginning to brown, about 5 minutes.
11. Add the chicken stock and water.
12. Add the Ancho chiles from step 7 and bring to a simmer. Monitor heat to maintain simmer.
13. Pour the ingredients from the pot into a blender.
14. Add the roasted butternut squash and blend on high speed until it is completely smooth.
15. Add salt as needed.
16. Serve the soup with pumpkin seeds and cilantro. Serving size if you are trying to lose weight is 1 Cup.

S.M.A.R.T. TIPS

Prep in Advance: You can prepare the soup the day before.

For Kids: Before you go to section 12, separate the kids' portion. Then add the Ancho chile to the rest and continue the process in two pots.

Repurposing: You can make extra servings to have as complements for other meals. Each meal should have a healthy fat and this recipe has very healthy fats.

Substituting: You can try it with different types of chiles and veggies.

Adapted from Seriouseats.com

Beef Adobo

Adobo is a marinade made from chili peppers, vinegar, herbs and spices that is frequently used in Mexican cuisine. It is not spicy. It just adds a lot of flavor and dimension to meat. The ingredients in the marinade are very powerful for weight loss, health and detoxification. You can use this adobo with anything: meat, eggs, chicken, fish, vegetables. It is up to you how you choose to enjoy it. Experiment. The chiles used are the dried versions. You can buy them online by going to www.spicesinc.com

TOTAL TIME: 55 min.
Prep: 10 min.

Unattended: 45 min.

Storage Notes: Adobo Sauce can be stored in the refrigerator for up to 1 week. Adobo and meat leftovers can be stored for 4 days.

Equipment Required: None

Gluten-Free, Dairy-Free, Sugar-Free, Soy-Free, Paleo
[2 Servings] [6 Servings]

INGREDIENTS

- Sea salt [¼ tsp.] [¾ tsp.]
- Black pepper [1 dash] [¼ tsp.]
- Beef - Grass-fed, organic, lean [10 oz.] [2 lb.]
- Mix of dry chiles (Pasilla, Guajillo and Ancho) [0.7 oz.] [2.1 oz.]
- Roma tomatoes- organic [6 oz.] [1.1 lb]
- Cumin powder [1 dash] [¼ tsp.]
- Oregano - dry [1 dash] [¼ tsp.]
- Black pepper [1 dash] [¼ tsp.]
- Clove - whole [1] [3]
- Garlic Clove - peeled [2] [6]
- Onion [0.7 oz.] [2.1 oz.]
- Olive oil - Extra Virgin [2 tsp.] [2 Tbsp.]
- Fruit vinegar (apple, berries, or wine) [1 tsp.] [1 Tbsp.]
- Beef Stock - organic [75 ml] [225 ml]

PROCEDURE

1. Cut the beef in 1-inch cubes and season with salt and pepper. Set aside.
2. Rinse chiles and remove the stems and seeds.
3. Place the chiles, tomatoes, spices, garlic, onion, olive oil and vinegar into a blender. Blend for 30 seconds on high speed.
4. Place blended ingredients in a medium or large sauce pan.
5. Add the beef stock to the sauce pan and bring to a boil. Once it is boiling, reduce heat to a simmer and let it cook for 15 minutes, stirring occasionally.
6. Add the seasoned meat cubes and return to a boil. Once it boils, reduce the temperature and simmer for 30 minutes.

S.M.A.R.T. TIPS

Prep in Advance: You can cook the beef marinade a few days in advance and store it in the fridge (steps 2-5). The day of you can do steps (1 and 6).

For Kids: You can blend all ingredients except the chiles and separate part of this sauce to cook the kids' meat in. Then add the chiles to the rest of the sauce and blend again.

Repurposing: You can cook double amount so you can have it in a few days without cooking again.

Substituting: You can substitute red meat for pork, chicken, fish, eggs. Follow the S.M.A.R.T. Protein guidelines to ensure quality protein.

Adapted from Thermomix

LUNCH DAY 5:

Vegetarian Butternut Squash Chili

This is a very powerful vegetarian recipe that is very easy to make and keep available to be repurposed for other days. One day you can eat it like it is here. The next day, try it with other roasted or cooked vegetables. This recipe tastes good hot or cold so you can take it with you to work. It is also good if you add chile. Try adding ½ to 1 Serrano or Jalapeño chile and see how you like it.

TOTAL TIME: 72 min.

Prep: 14 min.

Unattended: 58 min.

Storage Notes: Chili can be stored in the refrigerator for up to 5 days.

Equipment Required: None

Gluten-Free, Dairy-Free, Sugar-Free, Soy-Free, Paleo
[2 Servings] [6 Servings]

INGREDIENTS
- Butternut squash [0.5 lb.] [1.5 lb.]
- Red onion [½ med.] [1 ½ med.]
- Red bell pepper [1] [3]
- Garlic cloves - peeled [2] [6]
- Olive oil - Extra Virgin [1 tsp.] [3 Tbsp.]
- Sea salt [1 tsp.] [3 tsp.]
- Chili powder [1 ½ tsp.] [4½ tsp.]
- Cumin powder [½ tsp.] [1 ½ tsp.]
- Cinnamon powder [¼ tsp.] [¾ tsp.]
- Canned diced tomatoes - organic [7 oz.] [21 oz.]
- Black Beans - cooked [2 Cups] [6 Cups]
- Vegetable broth - organic [1 Cup] [3 Cups]
- Chipotle peppers - from a can [1] [3]
- Avocado [1] [3]
- Cilantro - fresh [¼ Cup] [¾ Cup]

PROCEDURE
1. Peel the butternut squash with a knife. Cut in small cubes.
2. Chop the red onion, bell pepper and garlic.
3. Heat a medium-size pan over medium heat. When hot, add the olive oil and immediately add the vegetables from steps 1 and 2. Cook for 3 minutes, stirring constantly so that the vegetables cook evenly.
4. Turn the heat down to medium-low.
5. Add olive oil, salt, chili powder, cumin, cinnamon, tomatoes, beans and vegetable broth. Stir well.
6. Chop the chipotle and add to the pot.
7. Stir all ingredients well. Cover the pot and let it cook for 60 minutes, stirring occasionally.
8. Dice the avocado and chop the cilantro.
9. Divide the chili in individual bowls. Top each bowl with the avocado and cilantro.

S.M.A.R.T. TIPS

Prep in Advance: You can cook the chili several days in advance.

For Kids: In step 6, separate some of the vegetables in a small pot to be used as the kids' meal, then continue with step 7 but now cooking 2 different pots.

Repurposing: You can use leftovers as a side dish to one of your S.M.A.R.T. Meals.

Substituting: You can substitute canned diced tomatoes for real tomatoes. However, I have found that good diced tomatoes give it better flavor. I have also found that home-cooked black beans make this recipe a lot better. So, cook this a night before. Look for the recipe in this book.

Adapted from CookandKate.com

LUNCH DAY 6:

Fish Ceviche

Mexican-style ceviche brings me very nice memories of my vacations on Mexican beaches. I love this recipe because once again, it is very quick and easy to make. The ingredients in this recipe are very strong detoxifiers and metabolism boosters. It is also a light meal that leaves you energized and not fatigued.

TOTAL TIME: 65 min.
Prep: 8 min.

Unattended: 57 min.

Storage Notes: Keeps for 2 days when refrigerated

Equipment Required: None

Gluten-Free, Dairy-Free, Sugar-Free, Soy-Free, Paleo
[2 Servings] [6 Servings]

INGREDIENTS

- Wild-caught white fish [8 oz.] [1.5 lbs.]
- Limes [5] [15]
- Sea salt [½ tsp.] [1 ½ tsp.]
- Roma tomatoes - organic [2] [6]
- Onion [¼ med.] [¾ med.]
- Serrano chile [1] [3]
- Avocado [1] [3]
- Cilantro -fresh [¼ Cup] [¾ Cup]

PROCEDURE

1. Cut the fish in cubes and place in a bowl.
2. Squeeze the limes and add the salt. Mix well and cover. Place in refrigerator for at least 1 hour to cook in the lime juice, but 4 hours would be better.
3. Dice the tomatoes and onion. Remove the seeds from the Serrano chile. Put aside in the fridge until ready to serve ceviche.
4. Take the fish out of the fridge and add the ingredients from section 3. Mix them altogether. Taste for seasoning and add more salt or lime juice if needed.
5. Just before serving, add the Serrano chile to the fish. Cut the avocado into small chunks and add to the ceviche.
6. Chop cilantro just before serving and mix into the ceviche.
7. Divide ceviche equally among servings.

S.M.A.R.T. TIPS

Prep in Advance: You can do steps 1-3 the day before and then continue with steps 4-8 when you are ready to serve.

For Kids: Before adding the chile in step 5, separate a portion of the other ingredients to be used for kids. Add the chile to the remainder. If you took out too much, then use less chile or try it.

Repurposing: You can do double amounts to eat again another day either as ceviche or as cooked fish..

Substituting: You can substitute white fish for different fish or another type of seafood if it is in the S.M.A.R.T. Proteins list.

Mexican-Style Brown Rice

Mexican rice is a staple for all Mexican families. However, in Mexico, it is frequently prepared with white rice and unhealthy oils. I have made this recipe healthy. I don't believe it has lost any of its charm. In fact, it may be your new favorite.

TOTAL TIME: 38 min.
Prep: 18 min.

Unattended: 20 min.

Storage Notes: Cooked rice can be stored in the refrigerator for 5 days.

Equipment Required: None

Gluten-Free, Dairy-Free, Sugar-Free, Soy-Free,
[2 Servings] [6 Servings]

INGREDIENTS

- Roma tomatoes - organic [6] [18]
- Onion [½ med.] [1 ½ med.]
- Garlic clove - peeled [1] [3]
- Carrot [½] [1 ½]
- Cilantro - fresh [¼ Cup] [¾ Cup]
- Chicken broth - organic, reduced sodium [½ Cup] [1 ½ Cups]
- Olive oil - Extra Virgin [1 Tbsp.] [3 Tbsp.]
- Brown rice [½ Cup] [1 ½ Cups]
- Frozen peas [1 Cup] [3 Cups]

PROCEDURE

1. Roast the tomatoes on a pan, turning them around so that they get fully roasted. Once roasted, put them into a blender and blend at high speed. Set aside.
2. Chop the onion, garlic, carrot and cilantro but keep them separate.
3. In a small pan, bring the chicken broth to a simmer and continue cooking.
4. Set a large pan over medium heat. When hot add the olive oil, brown rice and onion. Cook, stirring frequently, until both the rice and onion are light brown, approximately 7-10 minutes.
5. Mix in the garlic and cook for 2 more minutes.
6. Add the frozen peas and the carrot. Stir well.
7. Reduce heat to a medium low, cover and finish cooking- around 20 minutes.
8. Remove from heat and toss. Stir in cilantro.
9. Serving size for you is ½ of a cup of the cooked rice.

S.M.A.R.T. TIPS

Prep in Advance: You can cook the recipe in advance and store it in the refrigerator. You can also advance the recipe by doing steps 1 and 2 and then the day of, you can do the rest.

For Kids: All is kid friendly.

Repurposing: You can cook more than you need and use it over the next few days in the same way or in new ways. You could add other vegetables. It is a great side dish for lunch. You can also make it spicy by adding some Serrano Chiles on step 4.

Substituting: You can change carrots for cubed sweet potatoes.

LUNCH DAY 7:

Chicken with Chile Mulato and Prune Sauce

This sauce is very easy to make and combines a lot of interesting and contrasting flavors. It is very nutritious and satisfying.

TOTAL TIME: 38 min.
Prep: 8 min.

Unattended: 30 min.

Storage Notes: The sauce can be stored in the refrigerator for 5 days.

Equipment Required: Blender

Gluten-Free, Dairy-Free, Sugar-Free, Soy-Free, Paleo
[2 Servings] [6 Servings]

INGREDIENTS
- Mulato chile [1] [3]
- Onion [3 oz.] [9 oz.]
- Tomatoes - organic [10 oz.] [30 oz.]
- Garlic clove -peeled [1] [3]
- Prunes - without the seed [1 oz.] [3 oz.]
- Sea Salt [1 tsp.] [1 Tbsp.]
- Black Pepper [⅛ tsp.] [¼ tsp.]
- Chili powder [dash] [½ tsp.]
- Sesame seeds [0.4 oz.] [1.2 oz.]
- Olive oil - Extra Virgin [1 oz.] [3 oz.]
- Chicken thighs or chicken thighs with legs - organic - free range [8 oz.] [1 ½ lbs.]

PROCEDURE
1. Take the stem and seeds out of the chile.
2. Cut the chile, onion and tomato into medium-sized chunks and then place in the blender.
3. Add the garlic, prunes, sea salt, pepper and chile powder into the blender.
4. Blend on high speed for 10 seconds.
5. Pour mix from the blender into a medium-size pot.
6. Add the sesame seeds and olive oil into the pot. Cook the sauce over high heat and bring to a boil. Reduce heat to simmer and cook for 10 minutes stirring occasionally.
7. Add the chicken to the sauce and cook until desired level. Make sure you turn it around and keep it covered with the sauce.
8. Serve chicken covered in sauce.

S.M.A.R.T. TIPS

Prep in Advance: You can cook the sauce a few days in advance (steps 1-6).

For Kids: You can set aside chiles in step 1. Then do steps 2-4. Separate a part of the blend for the kids and then add the chile to the rest. Continue with two separate sauces.

Repurposing: You can use the sauce for any other type of S.M.A.R.T. protein.

Substituting: You can substitute chicken for red meat or pork. Follow the S.M.A.R.T. Protein guidelines to ensure quality protein.

Inspired by Thermomix

Mexican-Style Cauliflower Rice

This is a super healthy version of Mexican-style rice. You will be surprised how great cauliflower tastes in this recipe. It is very easy to make. You can add other vegetables typically used in Mexican-style rice, such as peas and carrots.

TOTAL TIME: 17 min.
Prep: 17 min.

Unattended: 0 min.

Storage Notes: The rice can be stored for up to 4 days in the refrigerator.

Equipment Required: Food processor or blender.

Gluten-Free, Dairy-Free, Sugar-Free, Soy-Free, Paleo
[2 Servings] [6 Servings]

INGREDIENTS
- Cauliflower [½ large] [1 ½ large]
- Serrano chile [1] [3]
- Onion [½ small] [1 ½ small]
- Garlic clove- peeled [2] [6]
- Cilantro - fresh [2 Tbsp.] [6 Tbsp.]
- Tomato - organic [1 large] [3 large]
- Sea Salt [¼ tsp.] [¾ tsp.]
- Black pepper [dash] [¼ tsp.]
- Cumin powder [¼ tsp.][¾ tsp.]
- Paprika [¼ tsp.] [¾ tsp.]
- Tomato paste - organic [2 oz.] [6 oz.]
- Cilantro - fresh [for garnish] [for garnish]

PROCEDURE
1. Chop the cauliflower into florets and put in the food processor or blender. Pulse until the pieces are the size and shape of rice. Set aside.
2. Take the seeds out of the chile, then chop and set aside.
3. Chop the Serrano, onion, garlic, cilantro and tomato, keeping them separate.
4. Heat a medium-sized pan over medium heat. When hot, add the olive oil and onion and chile from step 2-3. Sauté for 2 minutes.
5. Add the garlic from step 3 and sauté for 1 more minute.
6. Add the cauliflower and stir.
7. Add the salt, pepper, cumin and paprika. Stir and combine, cooking for 2-3 minutes.
8. Add the tomato paste and the cilantro and tomato from step 3.
9. Cook for 2-3 minutes. Taste for seasoning and adjust if necessary.
10. Garnish with cilantro.

S.M.A.R.T. TIPS

Prep in Advance: You can do the rice a day ahead, then reheat when you are ready to eat it.

For Kids: In step 4, start cooking in 2 separate pans, one without the chile and one with.

Repurposing: You can cook double amount so you can have it in a few days without cooking again. You can add peas, carrots or other vegetables.

Substituting: You can substitute Serrano chile for Jalapeño if you want it milder, although with the Serrano chile it is not hot at all.

Adapted from Paleo Cupboard.com

DINNER DAY 1:

Mexican-Style Chicken Soup

This is one of our family's favorite soups. It is also one of my favorites because it is super easy to make and delicious. I add rice or quinoa for the kids. I also love that you can cook it ahead of time and eat it over the next few days. You can add other vegetables too and more chiles if you need more. This uses canned diced tomatoes but you can also use real organic tomatoes. Try it with both and see what you like best.

TOTAL TIME: 60 min.
Prep: 30 min.

Unattended: 30 min.

Storage Notes: The soup and chicken can be stored in the fridge for 3 days. Soup can be frozen for up to 3 months without the chicken.

Equipment Required: None

Gluten-Free, Dairy-Free, Sugar-Free, Soy-Free, Paleo
[2 Servings] [6 Servings]

INGREDIENTS

- Chicken breasts - organic and free range [8-10 oz.] [1.5 lbs.]
- Olive oil - Extra Virgin [1 Tbsp.] [3 Tbsp.]
- Sea salt [season] [season]
- Chili powder [1 tsp.] [1 Tbsp.]
- Oregano - dried [¼ tsp.] [¾ tsp.]
- Cumin - ground [¼ tsp.] [¾ tsp.]
- Onion [⅓ large] [1 large]
- Jalapeño Chiles [½] [1 ½]
- Serrano Chiles [0.8 oz.] [2.4 oz.]
- Garlic Clove - peeled [1] [3]
- Olive oil- Extra Virgin [2 tsp.] [2 Tbsp.]
- Chicken broth - organic and low sodium [2/3 Cup] [2 Cups]
- Canned Diced Tomatoes - organic [7 oz.] [21 oz.]
- Sea Salt [½ tsp.] [1 ½ tsp.]
- Cilantro - fresh [½ Cup] [1 ½ Cups]
- Avocado [1] [3]

PROCEDURE

1. Turn the oven at 350 F.
2. Wash the chicken and place the pieces on a baking ban.
3. Brush the chicken with olive oil and then season with sea salt.
4. When the oven is warm, place the chicken in the oven and cook for 40 minutes. Cooking time will vary with each oven so check the chicken's internal temperature at 35 minutes. It should be 160-165 F. You can also cut a piece and make sure

there is no pink inside. While chicken is cooking, continue to make the soup.

5. Mix the chili powder, oregano and cumin and set aside to be used in step 8.

6. Remove the seeds from the hot peppers. Dice the onion, Jalapeño, Serrano and garlic.

7. Keep the garlic and the chiles separate.

8. Heat a large pot, over medium- high heat. As soon as it is hot, add the olive oil and all the ingredients from step 6. Cook for 3 minutes, stirring frequently.

9. Add the spices mix and cook 1 more minute.

10. Stir in the chicken broth, diced tomatoes, and salt. Bring to a boil, then immediately reduce heat and simmer for 20 minutes. While this is cooking, do the next steps.

11. Chop cilantro to be used on top of the soup.

12. Dice the avocado so you can serve it on each plate.

13. When the chicken is done, cut it in smaller pieces and set aside until soup is done.

14. When the soup is done, add the chicken so that it gets mixed in and let it simmer for 5 minutes to absorb flavors.

15. Divide soup into individual bowls.

16. Divide cilantro and avocado in equal parts according to the servings you are preparing. Add these to the soup.

S.M.A.R.T. TIPS

Prep in Advance: You can cook the chicken and the soup up to 3 days before (steps 1-10), keeping it in the refrigerator. When you are ready to serve, heat the soup first on medium-low heat, then add the chicken for a few minutes to warm and avoid overcooking it. Then follow the steps 11-15 to finish the dinner.

For Kids: In step 7, separate the chiles from the rest of the ingredients. Cook the appropriate portion of the other ingredients in a separate pot. Then keep following steps in parallel, one pot with chiles and one pot without. If the required portion without chile is larger, you will need to adjust the amount of chiles for the spicy one. I also like to add some quinoa or brown rice to the kids' plates.

Repurposing: You can cook double amount of everything so you can have it in a few days without cooking again. You can also cook double of the soup (steps 5-9) so that you can freeze it and use it when you require or desire.

Substituting: You can substitute chicken for any other S.M.A.R.T. Protein.

DINNER DAY 2:

Chicken with Tarasco Sauce

This recipe was a hit with my family and all my friends who have tried it. In fact, it may be the favorite in the book per my perception. When I cook this, I always have extra sauce to use over the next days for eggs, more chicken, or just for fun. Tomatillos are also known as Mexican husk tomatoes. They are small and green. They have a peel that is a papery husk that comes off easily. They are good source of vitamin C and K, fiber, niacin, potassium and manganese. They also have some amount of other important minerals. I have always loved all green sauces which are normally made with tomatillo.

TOTAL TIME: 40 min.
Prep: 10 min.

Unattended: 30 min.

Storage Notes: The sauce keeps well in the refrigerator for a week.

Equipment Required: Blender

Gluten-Free, Dairy-Free, Sugar-Free, Soy-Free, Paleo
[2 Servings] [6 Servings]

INGREDIENTS

- Chicken leg with thighs - organic, free-range [2] [6]
- Olive oil - Extra Virgin [1 Tbsp.] [3 Tbsp.]
- Tomatillos [1.1 lbs.] [3.3 lbs.]
- Onion [1.1 oz.] [3.3 oz.]
- Water [2 Cups] [6 Cups]
- Garlic [3] [9]
- Chipotle chile – canned [2] [6]
- Serrano chile [1] [3]
- Cilantro - fresh [1 oz.] [3 oz.]
- Sea Salt [1 tsp.] [1 Tbsp.]
- Olive oil -Extra Virgin [4 tsp.] [4 Tbsp.]

PROCEDURE

1. Turn the oven on to 350 F.
2. Wash the chicken and then brush it with olive oil. Sprinkle with garlic powder and sea salt.
3. Cook the chicken for 40 minutes or until there is no pink inside when cut in the middle.
4. Peel the tomatillos and wash, then place in a medium to large pot.
5. Cut the onion in large chunks, then add to the pot.
6. Add water to the pot. Bring to a boil and cook for 10 minutes.
7. When done, save ½ cup of water if you are doing 2 servings and 1½ cups if doing 6 servings, and discard the rest.
8. Place the garlic, chipotle, Serrano, cilantro and salt in a blender.

9. Add the cooked tomatillos, onion and ½ cup of the water saved for 2 servings and 1½ cups for 6 servings.
10. Blend on high speed for 15 seconds.
11. Heat a large pan on medium heat. When hot, add the olive oil and immediately add the blend. Bring to a boil and then reduce the heat to simmer. Cook for 10 minutes, stirring
12. Serve the cooked chicken covered with the sauce.

S.M.A.R.T. TIPS

Prep in Advance: You can cook the sauce a few days in advance and store it in the fridge (steps 4-11). The day of you can do steps (1-3) and reheat the sauce.

For Kids: On step 8, you can blend all ingredients except the chiles and separate part of this sauce to use for the kids. Then add the chiles to the rest of the sauce and blend again.

Repurposing: You can cook double amount so you can have it in a few days without cooking again. It is great on top of fried eggs. You can also use it with other S.M.A.R.T. proteins, as a dipping sauce or just a hot sauce.

Substituting: You can substitute chicken for red meat, pork, fish, eggs. Follow the S.M.A.R.T. Protein guidelines to ensure quality protein.

Inspired by Thermomix

Roasted Cauliflower with Pepitas

Cauliflower is an amazing veggie. Nutrient rich and very supportive of the body's detoxification process. It provides a large dose of vitamin C and good amounts of many other vitamins. Pumpkin seeds, known in Mexico as "pepitas" are an amazing source of protein and minerals, particularly manganese, phosphorus, magnesium and iron. They also provide a good source of iron, healthy fats, and some vitamins. In addition to their nutrition, they are a delicious snack or complement to many dishes. Just make sure you buy raw and unsalted.

TOTAL TIME: 32 min.
Prep: 15 min.

Unattended: 17 min.

Storage Notes: This recipe can be kept in the refrigerator for 5 days.

Equipment Required: None.

Gluten-Free, Dairy-Free, Sugar-Free, Soy-Free, Paleo
[2 Servings] [6 Servings]

INGREDIENTS
- Lime - fresh [1] [3]
- Cumin powder [1 tsp.] [1 Tbsp.]
- Chili Powder - Tajin [½ tsp.] [1 ½ tsp.]
- Sea salt [1 tsp.] [1 Tbsp.]
- Black pepper [¼ tsp.] [¾ tsp.]
- Cauliflower - large [½] [1 ½]
- Olive oil - Extra Virgin [2 Tbsp.] [6 Tbsp.]
- Garlic cloves - peeled [2] [6]
- Olive oil - Extra Virgin [1 tsp.] [1 Tbsp.]
- Pumpkin seeds [2 Tbsp.] [6 Tbsp.]
- Lime - fresh [½] [1 ½]

PROCEDURE
1. Preheat oven to 450 F.
2. Place a medium roasting pan in the oven while it is preheating.
3. Grate the peel of the lime and combine it with the juice in a small bowl.
4. Combine cumin, chili powder, salt and pepper in a small bowl.
5. Cut cauliflower in small pieces.
6. Remove the pan from the oven and pour the olive oil into it.
7. Add cauliflower pieces to pan and quickly toss with the hot oil.
8. Pour the lime juice and zest mixture over the cauliflower. Then sprinkle with the spices mix.
9. Toss cauliflower to combine, and then spread it out evenly in the pan. Place pan back into the oven. Roast for 15 minutes without stirring.
10. Slice garlic cloves in thin slices.
11. In a small bowl mix olive oil with the garlic slices.
12. When cauliflower is done, remove the pan and add the mixed oil and garlic slices from step 11.

13. Add the pumpkin seeds. Toss to combine, then place pan back into the oven to roast for another 5 minutes.
14. Remove from oven and sprinkle with fresh cilantro. Add more sea salt and black pepper, if needed.
15. Squeeze a little lime over each serving

S.M.A.R.T. TIPS

Prep in Advance: You can prep in advance steps 3-5, 10-11, and then do the rest close to the time of serving.

For Kids: You can keep some of the cauliflowers without spices from step 8.

Repurposing: You can use leftovers as topping for a salad, brown rice or quinoa. You can also add it to soups or just serve it alone to accompany any S.M.A.R.T. protein.

Substituting: You can substitute pumpkin seeds for almonds, sesame seeds or sunflower seeds.

Adapted from afarmgirlsdabbles.com

DINNER DAY 3:

Chayote Pasta with Turkey Meatballs

Chayote pasta is amazing. It carries the flavor of any sauce very well. The combination of this type of pasta with a spicy tomato sauce and turkey meatballs is amazing in flavor and nutrition. All the S.M.A.R.T. Players in perfect harmony.

TOTAL TIME: 35 min.
Prep: 22 min.

Unattended: 13 min.

Storage Notes: Sauce keeps well in the refrigerator for 5 days. Meatballs keep well for 3 days. Meatballs can be frozen and kept longer.

Equipment Required: Veggie Bullet or Spiralizer

Gluten-Free, Dairy-Free, Sugar-Free, Soy-Free, Paleo
[2 Servings] [6 Servings]

INGREDIENTS

- Mint - fresh [1 ½ Tbsp.] [4 ½ Tbsp.]
- Ground turkey - organic [0.5 lbs.] [1.5 lbs.]
- Yellow onion [2 Tbsp.] [6 Tbsp.]
- Garlic clove - fresh [1] [3]
- Oregano - dried [½ tsp.] [1 ½ tsp.]
- Sea Salt [½ tsp.] [1 ½ tsp.]
- Black Pepper [season] [season]
- Garlic clove - peeled [2] [6]
- Yellow onion [½ Cup] [1 ½ Cups]
- Serrano chiles [2] [6]
- Canned diced tomatoes - organic [14 oz.] [42 oz.]
- Sea Salt [½ tsp.] [1 ½ tsp.]
- Black Pepper [season] [season]
- Cilantro - fresh [2 Tbsp.] [6 Tbsp.]
- Chayote [1 ½] [4 ½]

PROCEDURE

1. Preheat the oven to 375 F.
2. Prepare a cooking sheet with parchment paper.
3. Chop the mint, onion and garlic.
4. Combine the mint, turkey, onion, garlic, oregano, salt and pepper in a large bowl.
5. Form small meatballs about 1 inch in diameter and space them evenly on the cooking sheet.
6. Bake meatballs for 10 minutes. While meatballs are cooking, begin the sauce in step 8.
7. Turn meatballs around and bake for 8-10 minutes more or until browned.
8. Heat a large pan or pot over medium heat. When hot, add the olive oil and immediately add the garlic. Cook for 30 seconds.

9. Add the onion and chile and cook for 2-3 minutes or until the onion is translucent.
10. Add the diced tomatoes and use a potato masher to squeeze them.
11. Season with salt and pepper.
12. Increase the heat to high and bring to a boil.
13. Add the cilantro and reduce the heat to low. Simmer for 10-15 minutes or until the sauce thickens, stirring occasionally.
14. Use the Veggie Bullet or the Spiralizer to make spaghetti-type noodles with the chayote. If you do not have the Veggie Bullet or the Spiralizer, you can use a julienne peeler.
15. Add the cooked meatballs to the sauce and continue to simmer, turning, to coat them, for 1-2 minutes. Take the meatballs out and set aside.
16. Add the chayote noodles to the tomato sauce. Toss to combine thoroughly and cook for 3 minutes.
17. Divide noodles among the plates and top with turkey meatballs and extra sauce.

S.M.A.R.T. TIPS

Prep in Advance: You can do many parts ahead of time but keep them separate until the day you use them. For turkey meatballs do steps 3-7 if you are refrigerating or 3-5 if you want to freeze them. For the sauce, do steps 8-13 and keep in refrigerator or freeze if you prefer. You can do the chayote noodles ahead of time or the day before (step 14).

For Kids: When preparing the sauce, in step 9, separate part of the onion/garlic for the kids' sauce and add the chiles to the rest. Keep cooking in two separate pans.

Repurposing: You can cook double amount so you can have it in a few days without cooking again. You can use the turkey meatballs alone, or with brown rice or another type of healthy pasta such as brown rice pasta or zucchini pasta. The sauce, you can use for other vegetables or for fish or meat.

Substituting: You can substitute the turkey for ground beef or chicken or any other S.M.A.R.T. protein that you like.

Adapted from Inspiralized

DINNER DAY 4:

Zucchini Pasta with Mexican Pesto

The inspiration of this recipe was one of my mom's cousins who prepared something similar but using real pasta and including cream (wheat and dairy not part of this diet). I love the way this recipe came out with all the adaptations made. I have cooked it several times for my family and friends and each time it is a winner. And, it takes very little time. Zucchini and the ingredients in the pesto make a powerful combination to support your health and weight. The pesto is also very filling and will satisfy hunger and help you fight cravings. It has lots of detoxifying power through the garlic, cilantro olive oil and lime juice.

TOTAL TIME: 18 min.
Prep: 18 min.

Unattended: 0 min.

Storage Notes: Pasta keeps well in refrigerator for 3 days. Pesto can be refrigerated for 1 week.

Equipment Required: Blender, Veggie Bullet

Gluten-Free, Dairy-Free, Sugar-Free, Soy-Free, Paleo
[2 Servings] [6 Servings]

INGREDIENTS

- Stevia [½ Cup] [1 ½ Cups]
- Water [1 oz.] [3 oz.]
- Chili powder - Tajin [4½ tsp.] [¼ Cup + 1 ½ tsp.]
- Olive oil - Extra Virgin [1 tsp.] [1 Tbsp.]
- Sriracha sauce [1 tsp.] [1 Tbsp.]
- Sea salt [1 tsp.] [1 Tbsp.]
- Pecans [1 ½ Cups] [4 ½ Cups]
- Garlic clove [3] [9]
- Shallot [1] [3]
- Cilantro [1 ½ Cups] [4 ½ Cups]
- Olive oil [3 Tbsp.] [½ Cup + 1 Tbsp.]
- Lime juice - fresh [1 oz.] [3 oz.]
- Pecans [½ Cup] [1 ½ Cups]
- Sea Salt [½ tsp.] [1 ½ tsp.]
- Black Pepper [season] [season]
- Zucchini [8 oz.] [1 ½ lb.]

PROCEDURE
Pecans

1. Heat the oven to 350 F.
2. Set up a cooking sheet with parchment paper.
3. In a small saucepan add the stevia and water and stir on low heat for 30 seconds. Turn the heat up to high and cook for 2 minutes. Remove from the heat.
4. Add the chili powder, olive oil, Sriracha sauce and salt to the pan and stir well.

273

5. Stir the first pecans into the blend until they are fully covered. Then spread them out flat in the sheet.
6. Place cooking sheet in the oven pan and bake for 8 to 9 minutes or until golden brown. Take out and let them cool. When cool, separate them into individual pieces.

Pesto
1. Add the garlic, shallot, cilantro, olive oil, lime juice and second pecans into a food processor or a blender. Blend all until smooth.
2. Season blend with salt and pepper.
3. If you have the Veggie Bullet or the Spiralizer, use it to make spaghetti-type noodles. There is no need to peel the zucchinis. If you don't have these equipments, then use a julienne peeler which will make a pappardelle-type pasta.
4. Heat a large-size pan on medium heat. When hot, add olive oil and immediately add the zucchini noodles. Cook for 2-3 minutes.
5. Serve each plate with a large portion of the zucchini noodles, add ¼ cup of the pesto on top and add a few of the pecans from step 6.

S.M.A.R.T. TIPS

Prep in Advance: You can do the pecans (steps 1-3) and the pesto (steps 1-2) in advance. The zucchini is better to do close to the time of serving.

For Kids: All ingredients are kid friendly. If they don't eat the pesto, then add another vegetable or a healthy spaghetti sauce.

Repurposing: You can cook extra pesto and use it as a snack for dipping vegetables, or a side dish for accompanying veggies.

Substituting: You can substitute pecans with almonds or walnuts.

Inspired by Monica Alba

Tomato Shrimps

This is a Mexican-style tomato sauce. It incorporates a variety of interesting flavors coming from the bell pepper and clove. Shrimps are a great source of protein, vitamin D and selenium. Selenium increases immunity so you don't get sick as often, helps in the antioxidant activity and is key for a healthy metabolism. Vitamin D is critical for healthy bones and teeth, heart health, hormone regulation, brain cell growth and a strong immune system.

TOTAL TIME: 30 min.
Prep: 15 min.

Unattended: 15 min.

Storage Notes: Sauce can be refrigerated for 5 days. Cooked shrimp can be kept for 3 days.

Equipment Required: Blender

Gluten-Free, Dairy-Free, Sugar-Free, Soy-Free, Paleo
[2 Servings] [6 Servings]

INGREDIENTS

- Red bell pepper [2 oz.] [6 oz.]
- Tomatoes - organic [1 lb.] [3 lbs.]
- Onion [10 oz.] [30 oz.]
- Clove - ground [¼ tsp.] [¾ tsp.]
- Olive oil - Extra Virgin [4 tsp.] [¼ Cup]
- Sea salt [1 tsp.] [1 Tbsp.]
- Black pepper [½ tsp.] [1½ tsp.]
- Shrimp - wild caught - peeled and deveined [8 oz.] [1½ lbs.]

PROCEDURE

1. Take the seeds out of the peppers.
2. Cut the tomatoes, pepper and onion in medium-sized chunks.
3. Add all the ingredients from step 2 into the blender.
4. Blend on medium-high speed for 30 seconds.
5. Heat a medium-sized pan over medium heat.
6. Pour blend on the pan. Bring to a boil, then lower heat to simmer for 15 minutes, stirring frequently.
7. Add the shrimp and cook over high heat for 2-3 minutes if smaller shrimp or 5-7 minutes for larger shrimp. Turn them halfway through the time.

S.M.A.R.T. TIPS

Prep in Advance: You can cook the sauce ahead of time, even a few days in advance, and store it in the fridge (steps 1-6). The day of you can reheat the sauce and do step 7. If you want the sauce to be fresher, then do steps 1-4 ahead of time and do steps 5-7 close to serving time.

For Kids: All ingredients are kid friendly.

Repurposing: You can cook double amount of the sauce to be used on other days to cook a fish.

Substituting: You can substitute shrimp for a white fish or try it with other types of S.M.A.R.T. protein.

Inspired from Thermomix

DINNER DAY 5:

Guajillo and Tomato Soup with Vegetables

Who doesn't like a warm vegetable soup? This one has the added benefit of spice, but not too spicy. You can do this base and vary the vegetables you use, or make it a full meal with a S.M.A.R.T. Protein and doubling the amount of avocado. Guajillo chile is a great source for vitamins A, B and C, as well as other minerals. It has Capsicum, an ingredient common in chiles, which has proven to be beneficial for a variety of health problems and for boosting metabolism. The hotness in chiles also raises the metabolism, contributing to your weight loss efforts.

TOTAL TIME: 24 min.
Prep: 18 min.

Unattended: 6 min.

Storage Notes: This soup keeps well in the refrigerator for 5 days. You can also freeze it.

Equipment Required: None

Gluten-Free, Dairy-Free, Sugar-Free, Soy-Free, Paleo
[2 Servings] [6 Servings]

INGREDIENTS

- Guajillo chiles [½] [1 ½]
- Tomatoes - organic [0.9 lbs.] [2.7 lbs.]
- Garlic cloves - peeled [2] [6]
- Onion [1] [3]
- Olive oil - Extra Virgin [1 oz.] [3 oz.]
- Sea Salt [1 tsp.] [1 Tbsp.]
- Chicken stock -organic -reduced sodium [7 oz.] [21 oz.]
- Zucchini [¾ Cup] [2 ¼ Cups]
- Carrot [¾ Cup] [2 ¼ Cups]
- Broccoli [¾ Cup [2 ¼ Cups]
- Cauliflower [¾ Cup] [2 ¼ Cups]
- Avocado [½] [1 ½]

PROCEDURE

1. Rinse Guajillo chile and then remove the seeds and veins.
2. Place Guajillo chiles, tomatoes, garlic, onion, olive oil and sea salt into a blender. Blend at medium-high speed for 30 seconds.
3. Pour blend on a medium-size pot and bring to a boil. Reduce heat to simmer and cook for 5 minutes stirring occasionally.
4. Add the chicken stock and bring it to a boil.
5. Reduce heat to simmer and cook for 13 minutes stirring occasionally.
6. Cut the zuchhini, carrot, broccoli and cauliflower into small pieces suitable for a soup. Set aside.

7. Add the vegetables to the soup and cook for another 5-7 minutes. Check vegetables and cook more if you like them softer.
8. Cut avocado in cubes and divide it among the servings.

S.M.A.R.T. TIPS

Prep in Advance: You can cook the soup in advance and reheat it when you are ready. Add the avocado and garnish at the time of serving.

For Kids: In step 2 you can blend all ingredients except the chiles and separate part of it for the kids' soup. Then add the chiles to the rest and blend again.

Repurposing: You can cook double amount so you can have it in a few days without cooking again. You can make it a full meal by adding double the amount of avocado and a S.M.A.R.T. Protein such as chicken, meat, pork.

Substituting: You can substitute the vegetables for other S.M.A.R.T. vegetables that you like.

Inspired from Thermomix

Cochinita Pibil

Cochinita pibil is a traditional Mexican pork dish from the Yucatán Peninsula on the south-eastern part of Mexico. The main ingredient in cochinita is the achiote in the marinade. Achiote gives the dish a characteristic color and adds flavor. The marinade also incorporates a variety of spices, orange and lemon juice. It is a very savory, fulfilling and true example of Healthy Eating that Feels Like Cheating™.

TOTAL TIME: 30 min.
Prep: 10 min.

Unattended: 20 min.

Storage Notes: The achiote and marinade can be refrigerated for 5 days.

Equipment Required: Food processor or blender, spice grinder or coffee grinder.

Gluten-Free, Dairy-Free, Sugar-Free, Soy-Free, Paleo
[2 Servings] [6 Servings]

INGREDIENTS
- Pork - lean - organic - pasture raised [8 oz.] [1 ½ lbs.]

ACHIOTE PASTE

- Annatto seeds [2 ½ Tbsp.] [7 ½ Tbsp.]
- Habanero chiles [1 ½][3 ¾]
- Orange juice [4 oz.] [12 oz.]
- Lemons [2 ½ lemons] [7 ½ lemons]
- Cumin - ground [½ tsp.] [1 ½ tsp.]
- Black pepper [1 ½ tsp.] [4 ½ tsp.]
- Allspice - ground [¾ tsp.] [2 ¼ tsp.]
- Clove - ground [1 dash] [¼ tsp. + dash]
- White vinegar [¼ Cup] [¾ Cup]
- Garlic cloves - peeled [4] [12]
- Sea salt [1 Tbsp.] [3 Tbsp.]
- Water [1 tsp.] [1 Tbsp.]

MARINADE

- Garlic cloves - fresh [3] [9]
- Oregano - dried [1 Tbsp.] [3 Tbsp.]
- Achiote paste (from this recipe) [0.5 oz.] [1.5 oz.]
- Black pepper [¼ tsp.] [¾ tsp.]
- Cumin - ground [¼ tsp.] [¾ tsp.]
- White vinegar [50 ml] [150 ml]
- Orange juice [75 ml] [225 ml]
- Red onion [2 oz.] [6 oz.]
- Sea salt [1 tsp.] [1 Tbsp.]
- Olive oil - Extra Virgin [2 ½ tsp.] [4 ½ tsp.]

SALSA

- Habanero chiles [½] [1 ½]
- Oregano - dried [1 ½ tsp.] [4 ½ tsp.]
- Garlic clove - peeled [1] [3]

- White vinegar [60 ml] [180 ml]
- Lime [1] [3]
- Red onion [3.5 oz.] [10.5 oz.]
- Sea salt [to taste] [to taste]

PROCEDURES
ACHIOTE

1. Cut the pork into small cubes of approximately ¾ of an inch. Set aside.
2. Using a spice grinder, grind annatto seeds. You can also use an inexpensive coffee grinder.
3. Remove the seeds from the habanero peppers.
4. Squeeze the oranges and the lemons.
5. Add to a blender or food processor the ingredients from steps 1-4. Add the cumin, pepper, allspice, clove, vinegar, garlic, salt and water. Blend all the ingredients on high speed. This will be the achiote paste that you will use below.

MARINADE

1. In a food processor or blender put all the following ingredients from the marinade list: garlic, oregano, achiote paste, black pepper, cumin, white vinegar, orange juice, red onion and salt. Blend on high speed for 30 seconds. Pour blend on a bowl that can hold this sauce and the pork.
2. Add the cubed pork and mix well with the marinade so all pork is covered. Cover the bowl and refrigerate for 3 hours.
3. When meat is done with the marinade, heat large saucepan on medium heat. When hot, add the olive oil and immediately add the meat with the marinade. Bring to a boil, then lower heat to simmer and cook covered for 40 minutes.
4. Mix the meat and the sauce and serve.

SALSA

1. It is customary to serve this dish with a special salsa.
2. To prepare the salsa, remove the seeds from Habaneros and cut into juliennes. Place them in a small mixing bowl.
3. Cut the red onion into julienne strips and add to bowl.
4. Add all the remaining ingredients from the salsa list.

S.M.A.R.T. TIPS

Prep in Advance: You can do the achiote paste (steps 1-5) up to a week in advance. The marinade you can do a few days before.

For Kids: You can do 2 types of achiote paste by blending all ingredients in step 4 except the habanero peppers, then separate a portion. Add the habaneros to the rest. Do 2 versions of the recipe after that.

Repurposing: You can cook double amount of marinade so you can have it in a few days without cooking again. Goes great with any type of S.M.A.R.T. protein.

Substituting: You can substitute pork with red meat, chicken, fish, eggs. Follow the S.M.A.R.T. Protein guidelines to ensure quality protein.

Inspired by Thermomix

DINNER DAY 6:

Zucchini, Cilantro and Poblano Soup

A very comforting smooth soup packed with nutrients. Uses three very powerful vegetables and makes a soup so smooth that it feels as if it has cream, but it does not. Zucchini is a good source of vitamins C and B6, Riboflavin, Manganese, Folate and Potassium. Poblano peppers are amazing sources of vitamin A, and good sources of Vitamin B6, Potassium, Iron and Fiber. Cilantro is a strong supporter of the detoxification process, and a good source of antioxidants, vitamins K, A and C.

TOTAL TIME: 44 min.
Prep: 9 min.

Unattended: 35 min.

Storage Notes: The soup can be kept refrigerated for 5 days and frozen for a few months.

Equipment Required: Blender.

Gluten-Free, Dairy-Free, Sugar-Free, Soy-Free, Paleo
[2 Servings] [6 Servings]

INGREDIENTS
- Poblano chile [7 oz.] [21 oz.]
- Zucchini [14 oz.] [42 oz.]
- Onion [2 oz.] [6 oz.]
- Garlic cloves - peeled [1] [3]
- Water [1 ½ Tbsp.] [4 ½ Tbsp.]
- Chicken stock -organic - reduced sodium [1 Cup] [3 Cups]
- Sea salt [½ tsp.] [1 ½ tsp.]
- Black pepper [dash] [¼ tsp.]
- Cilantro - fresh [1 oz.] [3 oz.]
- Cilantro - fresh [garnish] [garnish]

PROCEDURE
1. Remove the stem and seeds from the Poblano chile.
2. Cut the poblano, zucchini and onion into medium-sized chunks and place in a blender.
3. Add the garlic and water into the blender.
4. Blend on medium speed for 10 seconds.
5. Pour blend on a medium saucepan and bring to a boil. Reduce heat to simmer and cook for 10 minutes stirring occasionally.
6. Add the chicken stock, salt and pepper and bring to a boil again. Reduce heat to simmer and cook for another 25 minutes, stirring occasionally.
7. Pour soup on the blender and add cilantro. Blend on high speed for 1 minute.

S.M.A.R.T. TIPS

Prep in Advance: You can cook the soup ahead of time. If you just want to do part of it ahead, then do steps 1-4.

For Kids: You can blend all ingredients except the poblano and separate part of the blend for the kids' soup. Then add the poblanos to the rest of the blend and blend again. For the kids' soup, you will need to add a little more zucchini. Continue cooking in two versions.

Repurposing: You can cook double amount so you can have it in a few days without cooking again or to freeze and have for future meals.

Substituting: You can substitute chicken stock for organic vegetable stock.

Inspired by Thermomix

Tequila Salmon

There cannot be a Mexican food book without tequila. Tequila is Mexico and Mexico is tequila. I don't drink tequila often but when

I do, I like very fine tequila and as I have discovered, it can be as refined as the best wines in the world. Tequila is one of the few non-wine alcohols that I can drink (in moderation) and does not give me a headache. I did not know why so many liquors made me feel horrible. Well, tequila is one of the few gluten-free alcohols. Maybe that is one reason. This recipe does not have a lot of tequila and it is used for cooking and flavor so most of the alcohol is evaporated.

TOTAL TIME: 4 hr 18 min.
Prep: 18 min.

Unattended: 4 hr.

Storage Notes: The salmon can be stored for 3 days in the refrigerator.

Equipment Required: None.

Gluten-Free, Dairy-Free, Sugar-Free, Soy-Free, Paleo
[2 Servings] [6 Servings]

INGREDIENTS
- Jalapeño peppers [2] [6]
- Lime [3] [9]
- Tequila [⅓ Cup] [1 Cup]
- Olive oil - Extra Virgin [4 oz.] [12 oz.]
- Stevia [2 tsp.] [2 Tbsp.]
- Chili powder [2 tsp.] [2 Tbsp.]
- Sea salt [½ tsp.] [1 ½ tsp.]
- Wild Salmon Steaks [8 oz.] [1.5 lb.]

PROCEDURE
1. Remove the seeds from the Jalapeño and then chop.
2. Grate limes and place the zest in a small bowl.
3. Squeeze the juice from the grated limes and add it to the bowl.

4. Add tequila, olive oil, stevia, chili powder and salt to the bowl from step 2.

5. Add the chopped jalapeño peppers to the bowl and mix all well.

6. Place salmon into Ziploc plastic bag.

7. Pour marinade in the bowl over fish and close the bag. Place the bag in the refrigerator.

8. Let the salmon marinate for at least 4 hours.

9. Heat a grill pan on medium heat. When hot, lightly oil it and immediately place the salmon on the hot pan. Cook for about 4-5 minutes per side for an average thickness. Check for doneness and cook more if needed. Cook less or more for thin or thicker salmon.

10. Pour the remaining marinade into a small saucepan. Boil uncovered, stirring often, for 3 minutes. The marinade should be reduced by half.

11. When serving, use some of this sauce on top of the cooked salmon.

S.M.A.R.T. TIPS

Prep in Advance: You can prepare the marinade and leave the salmon marinating the night before.

For Kids: You need to separate the marinade in step 4, leaving a portion with no tequila or Jalapeños for the kids.

Repurposing: Any leftovers can be used for a salad the next day or to add flavor to scrambled eggs.

Substituting: Follow the S.M.A.R.T. Protein guidelines to ensure quality protein.

Adapted from CountryLady

DINNER DAY 7:

Chayotes with Spicy Tomato Sauce

Chayote is a type of squash very common in Mexico, so very present in my upbringing. It can be eaten raw or cooked. It can be made into healthy pasta by using the Veggie Bullet or the Spiralizer. It has a pear-like shape and a pale lime green coloring. It has a very high water content and offers a variety of vitamins and minerals, particularly vitamins C, B6 and K, folate, manganese, copper and zinc. When it is accompanied with other flavors, it does not overpower them, making it a perfect healthy carrying mechanism and a great substitute for wheat pastas.

TOTAL TIME: 40 min.
Prep: 25 min.

Unattended: 15 min.

Storage Notes: The cooked chayotes can be stored in the refrigerator for 5 days.

Equipment Required: None.

Gluten-Free, Dairy-Free, Sugar-Free, Soy-Free, Paleo
[2 Servings] [6 Servings]

INGREDIENTS

- Tomatoes - organic [4 oz.] [12 oz.]
- Garlic clove [1] [3]
- Chayotes [½ lbs.] [1 ½ lbs.]
- Anaheim chile [1] [3]
- Onions [1 Tbsp.] [3 Tbsp.]
- Cilantro - fresh [¼ Cup] [¾ Cup]
- Chile pepper flakes [¼ tsp.] [¾ tsp.]
- Water [1 oz.] [3 oz.]
- Salt [to taste] [to taste]

PROCEDURE

1. Roast tomatoes on a medium pan under high heat until skin begins to blacken. Turn them around so all sides are roasted and beginning to blacken.
2. Place the roasted tomatoes (with the skin) into a blender and add the garlic. Blend on high speed for 15 seconds. Set aside.
3. Peel the chayotes with a julienne peeler, then cut them into ¼-inch wide, 2-inch long julienne strips. Don't remove the core.
4. Remove the stems and seeds from the Anaheim chiles, then chop.
5. Chop the onions.
6. Chop cilantro.
7. Heat a large pan on medium heat. As soon as it is hot, add the onion and chiles. Cook on medium heat 3-4 minutes.
8. Add the tomato blend and red chile flakes, and continue to cook for 3 more minutes.

9. Add chayote, the chile pepper flakes, water and salt. Cover and cook for 15 more minutes, stirring occasionally.
10. Add cilantro, stirring well and cook for 5 minutes.

S.M.A.R.T. TIPS

Prep in Advance: You can cook it all ahead of time or do steps 1-5 ahead and the remaining at the time of need.

For Kids: In step 7 you can begin splitting the recipe. Use two different pans, don't add chile to the one for the kids. Continue cooking the two different versions.

Repurposing: You can use it as a side dish for your breakfast eggs. You can chop it finely and add it to your soups or scrambled eggs. You can serve it on top of arugula or quinoa.

Substituting: You can substitute the Anaheim chile with another chile. You can use another type of squash instead of the chayote.

Adapted from Simplyrecipes.com

Mexican-Style Fish

In Mexico, this recipe is known as "Pescado al Mojo de Ajo". I grew up eating this quite often. When I moved to the U.S. I did not have it. A few decades later, I was visiting my brother and his wife and she cooked it for us. It was at the early stages of my nutritional transformation. I loved it and realized how easy it is to make. Since then, I cook it all the time for our family. Both my daughters love it. Thank you, Dany, for teaching me how to do this recipe.

TOTAL TIME: 73 min.
Prep: 13 min.

Unattended: 60 min.

Storage Notes: Fish can be kept in the refrigerator marinated or cooked for 4 days.

Equipment Required: None.

Gluten-Free, Dairy-Free, Sugar-Free, Soy-Free, Paleo
[2 Servings] [6 Servings]

INGREDIENTS
- Garlic cloves [6] [18]
- Olive oil - Extra Virgin [2 Tbsp.] [6 Tbsp.]
- Red chili pepper flakes [¼ tsp.] [¾ tsp.]
- Sea salt [¼ tsp.] [¾ tsp.]
- Pepper [to taste]
- Wild-caught white fish [8 oz.] [1 ½lbs.]
- Lemon [2] [6]

PROCEDURE
1. Finely chop the garlic.
2. On a small bowl mix garlic, olive oil, pepper flakes, sea salt and black pepper.
3. Place the fish on a rectangular container and cover with the oil/garlic mix. Toss well so it is all covered.
4. Refrigerate fish with its marinade for at least 1 hour.
5. Heat a grill pan on medium heat. When hot put the fish and then squeeze 1 of the lemons, ½ for each side of the cooking. Cook the fish approximately 3 minutes on each side. Test for desired cooked level.

S.M.A.R.T TIPS

Prep in Advance: You can marinade the fish the day before or a few days early and cook it when you need it (steps 1-4).

For Kids: You can skip the pepper flakes or do 2 marinades on step 2.

Repurposing: You can serve this as part of fish fajitas or put it in a soup. It goes well with any type of veggie.

Substituting: You can do this recipe with other types of fish or with chicken.

SNACK DAY 1:

Guacamole de Spa

Guacamole is a very healthy and satisfying snack. It can also be a great side dish. Make sure you skip the tortilla chips. Healthier choices to have with guacamole are fresh vegetables, particularly celery, bell peppers, zucchini, cucumber, or jicama. This recipe is very special to me. It was adapted from one of my mom's recipes. My mom is a well-known chef in Mexico City whose touch in the kitchen is magical.

TOTAL TIME: 7 min.
Prep: 7 min.

Unattended: 0 min.

Storage Notes: Guacamole can be refrigerated for 3 to 4 days.

Equipment Required: None.

Gluten-Free, Dairy-Free, Sugar-Free, Soy-Free, Paleo
[2 Servings] [6 Servings]

INGREDIENTS

- Garlic cloves - peeled [1] [3]
- Roma tomato - organic [1] [3]
- Onion [1 Tbsp.] [3 Tbsp.]
- Cilantro - fresh [¼ Cup] [¾ Cup]
- Serrano chile [¼] [¾]
- Avocado [1] [3]
- Lime [2][6]
- Sea salt [¼ tsp.] [1 tsp.]
- Turmeric powder [dash] [¼ tsp.]
- Celery salt [dash] [¼ tsp.]
- Garlic powder [dash] [¼ tsp.]

PROCEDURE

1. In a small pan, roast garlic on both sides. When it is roasted, chop it and set aside.
2. Chop the garlic, tomatoes, onion, cilantro and Serrano.
3. Peel the avocado and place in a medium bowl. Use a potato smasher to smash the avocado.
4. Add lime, salt and spices to the smashed avocado.
5. Add ingredients on step 2.
6. Taste for season.
7. Serve with veggies (celery, zucchini, carrots, radishes, jicama, cucumbers).
8. Divide equally among plates.

S.M.A.R.T. TIPS

Prep in Advance: You can prepare in advance or the day before steps 1 and 2. When you are ready to serve, continue starting on step 3.

For Kids: On step 5, add all ingredients except the chile, then separate a portion for the kids. Add the chile to the other part. Continue recipe with the two different versions.

Repurposing: You can have guacamole as your healthy fat in other meals. It goes great with almost anything. Here are just a few ideas: hamburgers, fish, eggs.

Substituting: The only substituting I would recommend is to use Jalapeño pepper instead of Serrano pepper.

Adapted from Maru Pulido

SNACK DAY 2:

Cabbage, Jicama and Carrot Slaw

This is a great snack and side dish. It not only looks pretty; it also tastes delicious and is full of detoxifying power. The dressing is sweet and sour. If you don't like the sweet part, you can skip that. Or, if it is too sour then do less lime. Lime, jicama and cabbage are great sources of vitamin C which will boost your immune system. Both jicama and lime are on the top list of detoxifying elements. Jicama is also a great source of fiber. This snack is very satisfying and carries well for on the go situations.

TOTAL TIME: 20 min.
Prep: 10 min.

Unattended: 10 min.

Storage Notes: Keeps for 4 days when refrigerated

Equipment Required: None.

Gluten-Free, Dairy-Free, Sugar-Free, Soy-Free, Paleo
[2 Servings] [6 Servings]

INGREDIENTS
- Carrots [1] [3]
- Jicama [½ large] [1 ½ large]
- Red cabbage [¼] [¾]
- Lime [1 Tbsp.] [3 Tbsp.]
- Rice vinegar [1 Tbsp.] [3 Tbsp.]
- Chili powder [1 Tbsp.] [3 Tbsp.]
- Stevia [1 Tbsp.] [3 Tbsp.]
- Olive oil - Extra Virgin [½ Cup] [1 ½ Cup]
- Sea Salt [to taste] [to taste]

PROCEDURE
1. Peel and shred carrots and jicama using the Veggie Bullet or a shredder.
2. For the cabbage, use a sharp knife and cut it into thin smaller sizes appropriate for a slaw.
3. Mix all the shredded vegetables together in an appropriate-size bowl.
4. Mix together the lime, vinegar, chili powder, stevia, olive oil and sea salt.
5. Pour the dressing over the vegetables and toss to cover all.
6. Add the cilantro.
7. For maximum flavor, let it stand for at least 10 minutes for the dressing to penetrate the other ingredients.
8. Divide into equal sizes.

S.M.A.R.T. TIPS

Prep in Advance: You can prepare everything in advance. You can also shred everything (steps 1-3) and prepare the dressing (step 4). When you are ready, mix them together.

For Kids: All ingredients are kid friendly except the chili powder, so skip that part for the kids' dressing.

Repurposing: You can shred more vegetables than you need and then use them as side dish for other meals. You can also prepare more dressing and use if for another salad.

Substituting: You can add more chile if you are up for a spicy snack. Just chop a Serrano Chile.

Adapted from Bobby Flay

SNACK DAY 3:

Spicy Jicama Strings

This is an exciting snack. It is a healthy version of the horrible snacks I used to eat at school when I was younger. Those were made of flour and fried with unhealthy oils. This is made with the powerful jicama and with healthy oils. The spice stays the same. Jicama is loaded with vitamin C and fiber. A great boost to your immune system and a support for your digestion. Fiber will also allow you to stay full for longer.

TOTAL TIME: 35 min.
Prep: 10 min.

Unattended: 25 min.

Storage Notes: Jicama can be stored in the refrigerator for up to 3 days but it may lose its crunchiness.

Equipment Required: Veggie Bullet or Spiralizer.

Gluten-Free, Dairy-Free, Sugar-Free, Soy-Free, Paleo
[2 Servings] [6 Servings]

INGREDIENTS
- Jicama [½ large] [1 ½ large]
- Olive oil - Extra Virgin [1 Tbsp.] [3 Tbsp.]
- Sea salt [1 tsp.] [1 Tbsp.]
- Onion powder [2 tsp.] [2 Tbsp.]
- Cayenne pepper [1 tsp.] [3 Tbsp.]
- Chili powder [2 tsp.] [2 Tbsp.]

PROCEDURE
1. Preheat oven to 450 F.
2. Peel the jicama.
3. Make the jicama noodles using the Veggie Bullet or Spiralizer. Cut the noodles so that they are not too long.
4. Place the jicama on a large baking sheet.
5. Pour olive oil and toss around to cover well.
6. Sprinkle the salt, onion powder and cayenne pepper evenly.
7. Toss the jicama to get a full integration.
8. Spread the Jicama evenly on the cooking sheet.
9. Bake for 15 minutes. Flip the jicama and bake for 10 more minutes. Keep a close eye because they may start to burn earlier.

S.M.A.R.T. TIPS

Prep in Advance: You can do the jicama noodles the night before or have a stock of jicama noodles to use for this recipe or as side dish for other days.

For Kids: On step 6 you can separate the jicama into 2 cooking sheets. For the kids' portion skip the cayenne pepper and chili powder.

Repurposing: You can spiralize more jicama and keep it in the refrigerator. You can use this to add to any dish: salads, soups, snacks.

Substituting: If you don't have a spiralizer, you can use a sharp knife and cut very thin strips.

Adapted from Inspiralized

SNACK DAY 4:

Jalapeño Hummus

This is a flavorful and not very spicy hummus. It is a great snack that will keep you satisfied for a long time. If you eat with a variety of veggies, you will be getting a large dose of nutrients. Garbanzo beans, or chickpeas, will provide you with a large amount of fiber, iron, folate, protein, and a variety of important minerals such as phosphorus, copper and manganese.

TOTAL TIME: 6 min.
Prep: 6 min.

Unattended: 0 min.

Storage Notes: Hummus can be stored in the refrigerator for up to 5 days.

Equipment Required: Food processor or blender.

Gluten-Free, Dairy-Free, Sugar-Free, Soy-Free
[2 Servings] [6 Servings]

INGREDIENTS
- Garlic clove - peeled [4] [12]
- Jalapeño pepper [2] [6]
- Cilantro - fresh [¼ Cup] [¾ Cup]
- Garbanzo beans or chickpeas - canned [15 oz.] [45 oz.]
- Tahini paste [⅓ Cup] [1 Cup]
- Lime [¼ Cup] [¾ Cup]
- Olive oil - Extra Virgin [2 tsp.] [2 Tbsp.]
- Cumin powder [¾ tsp.] [2 ¼ tsp.]
- Sea salt [½ tsp.] [1 ½ tsp.]

PROCEDURE
1. Roast the garlic, then chop.
2. Remove the seeds from the Jalapeño, then chop.
3. Chop cilantro.
4. Place garbanzo beans or chickpeas, tahini paste, lime, olive oil, cumin and sea salt on a food processor or a blender. Add all the ingredients from steps 1-3. Process or blend until smooth. Taste and then you can add more chile, lemon or salt to taste.
5. Serve with a variety of vegetables such as carrots, jicama, cucumber, radish, zucchini.
6. Serving size if you want to lose weight is 1 cup.

S.M.A.R.T. TIPS

Prep in Advance: You can prepare the hummus in advance.

For Kids: In step 4, add all the ingredients except the Jalapeño. Process the ingredients, then separate a kids' portion. Add the Jalapeño to the remainder. Continue with two different versions.

Repurposing: You can use it as side dish for anything you desire, where extra fiber can be beneficial.

Substituting: You can substitute Jalapeño pepper for Serrano chile.

Adapted from Toriavey.com

SNACK DAY 5:

Black Bean Hummus

This snack is very quick and easy to prepare. Very nutritious and satisfying. Provides a good combination of protein, carbs and veggies. Great flavor and easy to take on-the-go.

TOTAL TIME: 30 min.
Prep: 10 min.

Unattended: 20 min.

Storage Notes: Hummus can be stored in the refrigerator for up to 5 days.

Equipment Required: Food processor or blender.

Gluten-Free, Dairy-Free, Sugar-Free, Soy-Free
[2 Servings] [6 Servings]

INGREDIENTS

- Black beans - cooked [15 oz.] [45 oz.]
- Cilantro - fresh [⅓ Cup] [1 Cup]
- Olive oil - Extra Virgin [1 Tbsp.] [3 Tbsp.]
- Lime juice [2 tsp.] [2 Tbsp.]
- Hot sauce - Tabasco [1 ½ tsp.] [4½ tsp.]
- Garlic clove - peeled [1] [3]
- Sea salt [½ tsp.] [1 ½ tsp.]
- Black pepper [¼ tsp.] [¾ tsp.]
- Cherry tomatoes - organic [7 oz.] [21 oz.]
- Cilantro - fresh [garnish] [garnish]
- Cherry tomatoes - organic [garnish] [garnish]
- Celery - organic [4 stalks] [12 stalks]

PROCEDURE

1. Drain the cooked beans.
2. Place cilantro, olive oil, lime juice, hot sauce, garlic, sea salt and black pepper into a food processor or blender and process until smooth. Leave ingredients in the processor or blender.
3. Cut the tomatoes into quarters.
4. Add tomatoes to the processor and process or blend in short intervals so that the tomatoes just get chopped.
5. Chop cilantro.
6. Cut the tomatoes into small slices to use as garnish.
7. Garnish with cilantro and tomatoes.
8. Cut the celery in small pieces to be used for dipping into the hummus.
9. Serving size if you are trying to lose weight is 1 cup.

S.M.A.R.T. TIPS

Prep in Advance: You can prepare the hummus in advance.

For Kids: In step 2 blend ingredients except the Tabasco sauce. Then separate a portion for kids and add Tabasco sauce to the rest. Continue with the remaining steps with two different sets.

Repurposing: You can cook double amount so you can have it in a few days without preparing again.

Substituting: You can substitute beans for chickpeas, also known as garbanzo beans. You can substitute Tabasco sauce with any other hot sauce. Instead of celery, you could do cucumbers, carrots, jicama, zucchini, radish or a mix of all.

Adapted from Twohealthykitchens.com

SNACK DAY 6:

Almond Butter with Apple

This is my favorite snack. When I discovered it in my first detox plan I became hooked on it. First it is very easy to prepare and take on the go. If you are going to be in meetings or on a plane and do not have access to healthy food, this is a great option to keep you until you do. Apples are full of nutrients and fiber and can satisfy your sweet tooth in a healthy way. The almond butter is very satisfying and filling. It will keep you full. This combination will provide you with a steady release of energy instead of blood sugar spikes followed by energy crashes.

TOTAL TIME: 2 min.
Prep: 2 min.

Unattended: 0 min.

Storage Notes: You can keep any remaining apple in the refrigerator for 5 days.

Equipment Required: None

Gluten-Free, Dairy-Free, Sugar-Free, Soy-Free, Paleo
[2 Servings] [6 Servings]

INGREDIENTS
*   Apple - organic [1] [3]
*   Almond butter - unsweetened and organic [2 Tbsp.] [6 Tbsp.]

PROCEDURE
1.   Wash the apple and slice it, dividing it into two plates.
2.   Add 1 Tablespoon of almond butter per plate.
3.   Enjoy dipping the apples in the almond butter or eating them separate.

S.M.A.R.T. TIPS

Prep in Advance: This recipe takes almost no time to prep.

For Kids: Great combination and flavor for kids' snacks.

Repurposing: You can use extra apple for your salads or breakfast grains. You can use almond butter alone or with anything. It is up to you.

Substituting: You can replace almond butter for pecan or walnut butter if you wish. There is also macadamia butter. Just pay attention if any of these makes your stomach upset.

SNACK DAY 7:

Blueberries with Nuts

The simplest yet most powerful snack. Blueberries are one of the best fruits you can eat. They have a very low impact on your blood sugar and are packed with fiber and nutrients such as potassium, folate, vitamin C, and Vitamin B6. Great for your health and a very satisfying early morning snack for those of you who wake up early to train. Together with the nuts, this snack provides you healthy fats, fiber and nutrients with little impact on your weight. This can be a great alternative to take with you if you are going to be on the go.

TOTAL TIME: 2 min.
Prep: 2 min.

Unattended: 0 min.

Storage Notes: Blueberries can be kept in the refrigerator for 1 week.

Equipment Required: None

Gluten-Free, Dairy-Free, Sugar-Free, Soy-Free, Paleo
[2 Servings] [6 Servings]

INGREDIENTS
- Blueberries – organic [½ Cup] [1 ½ Cups]
- Nuts - raw and unsalted almonds, walnuts, pecans or a mix [½ Cup] [1 ½ Cup]

PROCEDURE
1. Separate blueberries and nuts into individual servings and enjoy together.
2. If you are trying to lose weight, it is important to stick to the portions sizes.

S.M.A.R.T. TIPS

Prep in Advance: This recipe takes almost no time to prep.

For Kids: Great snack. Much better than the junk food many eat for snacks.

Repurposing: You can continue eating this every day if you want.

Substituting: You can substitute blueberries for strawberries, raspberries or blackberries. Strawberries need to be organic as they are part of the Dirty Dozen. You can use other nuts such as macadamia or any of the unsweetened butter nuts (almond, pecan or walnut). For the butter, the measure would be 1 Tablespoon per serving.

THE FAST TRACK FOR GETTING LEAN AND STAYING LEAN

MARU'S FAVORITE SHAKE RECIPES

Choco-Maca   Very Berry   Green Power   Piña Colada

Choco-Maca Shake

- 1 Flaca Stay Lean™ Chocolate or Flaca Detox™ Shake
- 10-12 oz. Unsweetened Almond Milk
- 1 Tablespoon Raw Cacao Powder
- 1 teaspoon Maca Powder
- 1 Tablespoon Chia Seeds
- 1 Tablespoon Unsweetened Almond Butter

Very-Berry Shake

- 1 Flaca Stay Lean™ Vanilla or Flaca Detox™ Shake
- 10-12 oz. Unsweetened Almond Milk or Unsweetened Coconut Milk
- 1 Tablespoon Acai Powder
- ¾ Cup of Fresh or frozen blueberries or strawberries or mixed berries

- 1 Tablespoon Chia Seeds
- 1 Tablespoon Unsweetened Almond Butter

Green Power Shake

- 1 Flaca Stay Lean™ Vanilla or Flaca Detox™ Shake
- 10-12 oz. Unsweetened Almond Milk
- 1 Cup Fresh Organic Spinach
- ¼ Avocado
- 1 Tablespoon Chia Seeds
- 1 Tablespoon Unsweetened Almond Butter

Piña Colada Shake

- 1 Flaca Stay Lean™ Vanilla or Flaca Detox™ Shake
- 8-10 oz. Unsweetened Almond Milk
- 1 Cup Frozen Pineapple
- ½ Frozen Banana
- 1 Tablespoon Coconut Butter
- 1 teaspoon Vanilla
- Unsweetened Coconut flakes for garnishing

INSTRUCTIONS:

1. Add all ingredients in the Nutribullet or blender and blend at high speed. You can also add ice cubes and blend again.

2. If you find that the shake is too thick, you can reduce the amount of chia seeds or not add them. Chia provides additional fiber which is great for you but it tends to make the shakes thicker, particularly when you let it stand for a while before drinking it. I don't mind this. In fact, I like it. The important thing is to find the right balance for you in terms of thickness and flavor.

NOTE: If you want to buy the Flaca Stay Lean™ or Flaca Detox™ Shakes, go to the shop at www.FlacaForever.com

PART 4

CONTINUE YOUR JOURNEY
WITH FLACA FOREVER®

FLACA DETOX™ THE FAST TRACK FOR GETTING LEAN AND STAYING LEAN

D uring the **7 days of the Mexican Food Diet**™, you have already begun detoxing and reducing the inflammation inside your body because I created the diet by choosing recipes that incorporate a lot of ingredients that are great for detoxing and reducing inflammation.

Detoxing and reducing inflammation is the number 1 thing you need to do if you want to be healthy, lose weight, and feel great in a major way. An effective detox will reset your health and your metabolism, setting you up for easier and faster weight loss. It is not hard at all.

Now I want you to try the fast track. Getting maximum results can be challenging and time-consuming because to have a major reduction in the toxins that your body has accumulated, you will need very high amounts of certain specific nutrients, vitamins, and minerals that your body needs to do the big job. It becomes difficult to do it through food alone. You would need to buy too many different things, lots of supplements, and be very religious about not missing any nutrient or having less than the necessary amounts. This is cumbersome and expensive.

Knowing how difficult and expensive it could be, I made it very simple. I created a product and program with the help of some of the most advanced physicians who conducted extensive research to develop an effective formula using all-natural, premium ingredients to maximize the elimination of toxins.

If you want to learn in greater depth the whys and hows of detoxification, I invite you to register for my **FREE Get Clean and Lean Detox Masterclass** that will make it very clear why you need to care about detoxing if you want to lose weight for good and stay healthy and happy.

REGISTER HERE FOR MY FREE GET CLEAN AND LEAN DETOX MASTERCLASS:

www.flacaforever.com/detox-tutorial

If you are knowledgeable and convinced that detox is the way to go, then check out the Flaca Detox™, 14-Day Reset and Renew program I am currently offering.

TO LEARN ABOUT THE FLACA DETOX RESET AND RENEW PROGRAM, COPY THIS ADDRESS INTO YOUR BROWSER:

www.flacadetox.com

If you already know you should do a detox and want to do one but don't have the time to plan for it, I can do everything for you. Contact me to apply for the VIP 1-on-1 Programs: info@flacaforever.com

GET CLEAN, GET LEAN, STAY LEAN™

laca is a Spanish word that means "thin" or "lean." To me, it means being at a healthy weight where you look and feel great. It is a mixture of Spanish and English reflecting my bicultural and bilingual life.

The Origin of Flaca Forever®

The 30 years of struggling with my weight and affecting my health made me obsessed with finding a permanent solution to reach a healthy weight and keep it that way. This led me to go back to school to get certified in integrative nutrition. I also found the top weight-loss and health experts to learn from them and their experiences.

The revolutionary program I developed is based on years of research by renowned doctors. It is also based on testing different alternatives on myself and my clients. And more important, It is based on decades of me doing everything that does not work and adversely affecting my physical, emotional, and mental health along the way. This has cost me a lot. But today I can use this experience and all my expertise to make it easy for you and help you avoid the pain and damage I went through.

The FLACA Forever® Programs

The focus is on helping you lose weight and keep it off, while getting you healthier and happier so you can be your best self ever: physically, mentally, and emotionally. Say goodbye to hunger, deprivations, or excessive exercising to reach your goals.

If you are tired of struggling to lose weight or keep it off, YOU are READY to BE FLACA Forever®!

THE FLACA FOREVER® PROGRAM: Get Clean, Get Lean, Stay Lean™ . . . *The fun, easy, and delicious way to get back on a healthy path so that you can look and feel better than ever!*

Foundations for Great Health. This is a discovery phase. We focus on doing a reset and renew of your health. We take you through a detox that is a mental, emotional, and physical. We use food and supplements to accelerate the removal of toxins, reduce inflammation, minimize cravings, and kick-start that initial weight loss, often overcoming years of no weight loss. We begin turning your body into what I call a "fat-burning machine." By going through this first part of the program only, most of my clients start to feel better than they have felt in years and many start losing weight again after years of not being able to lose weight.

Learning How to Fully Nourish Your Body. This phase is about learning about S.M.A.R.T. nutrition. This is where you really start to get Lean and what I call "fully nourished." You keep learning about foods and supplements but now at a deeper level. This is where we teach you how to control your cravings, optimize your metabolism, increase fat burning, preserve and build lean body mass or muscle, and get in the habit of healthy eating that feels like cheating. At this stage, you start to not only feel great, you start to really look great. You will be seeing the effects of getting in better shape, building muscle, losing fat, and feeling empowered, focused, and driven.

Adjusting Foods for What Your Body Needs. You will learn the importance of knowing what foods work for your body and those that don't. It is no different than putting the right type of gas in your vehicle. The right foods will keep you energized, lean, happy, and healthy. While the wrong foods will do the opposite. What is tricky is that wrong foods can be healthy for some but not for you. For example, I cannot eat apples, while apples are great for most people. I also cannot eat green beans, which are great veggies. So, it takes some work to figure out what you need to eliminate to look and feel your best.

Controlling Cravings for Sugar and Unhealthy Foods. Once you learn how to control your cravings, you will really start to crave wellness and a healthy lifestyle. You crave wellness more than you crave sugar, you crave wellness more than you crave all the things that are unhealthy to you. You start craving a healthy lifestyle, and maintaining that healthy lifestyle becomes one of your key priorities.

Achieving Finally the Freedom from Health and Weight Struggles and Becoming Your Best Self. This is where you really start to become a master of your own body. At this point, you start to truly take control in all areas of your life. This is where you know how to stay lean forever, stay nourished, and sustain your weight loss with little effort. By this time, you will have learned how to maintain that healthy lifestyle you adore and how to maintain a healthy metabolism. When you get to this point, you are feeling great, looking great, and living great. You have learned the secrets to living a great life where you can use your time and energy to pursue your dreams instead of using it to worry about your health and weight. And more importantly, you want and need to do it. It is no longer an obligation, it is your passion!

Our 3-step program is simple to follow. Start with the "Reset and Renew," then "Get Lean," and finally "Stay Lean."

The programs are offered privately, in small groups, or online. They all include access to live weekly training/support calls, access to a members-only area and a private group for support and accountability. We have fast-tracked programs that incorporate the most advanced nutritional foods and supplements developed by leading physicians in the US to make it even easier. Learn more about our products and programs at www.flacaforever.com.

VIP 1-on-1 private coaching and corporate programs are offered for those that qualify. If you are interested, contact us at info@flacaforever.com to apply.

STEP 1: **Flaca Detox™ RESET AND RENEW Program**: A 14-Day Reset and Renew program to kick-start your weight loss, reset your metabolism, clean up your body, and set strong foundations for permanent weight loss and optimal health. It is a plant-based, comprehensive, science-based nutritional program designed to support safe and effective detoxification.*

Everything you need is consolidated into packets to make the program portable and easy-to-follow to ensure that you don't miss any necessary nutrients. Replace any two of your daily meals with our delicious and nutritious shakes, take your all-natural supplements, then for your third meal have a S.M.A.R.T. meal using our guidelines. Your shakes, supplements and S.M.A.R.T. meal will provide you everything you need to stay satisfied, get rid of toxins and waste that have accumulated inside your body, reduce inflammation, burn fat, and feel happy.

Plant-based, gluten-free, dairy-free, soy-free, grain-free, sugar-free, non-GMO, no artificial ingredients or sweeteners, paleo meal

Benefits

- **Clean up your body** from accumulated toxins that prevent you from losing that stubborn weight and those trouble spots; or that can make you tired, sick, and sad.
- Get rid of those powerful **cravings** for sugar and unhealthy foods that are keeping you tired, moody, and fat.
- Establish lasting **healthy habits**.
- Recharge your **energy**.
- Improve **focus**, and feel a sense of **calm** and **happiness**.
- **LOOK** and **FEEL AMAZING**, so much that . . . others will notice!

Flavor: Berry-vanilla that mixes perfectly with all types of ingredients.

Flaca Detox™ is the simple, satisfying, and effective way to Detoxify your body! *

STEP 2: **Flaca Get Lean™**: An effective weight-loss program that is delicious and nutritious. It is a plant-based, comprehensive, science-based nutrition program designed to support fat loss and a healthy body composition.* Everything you need is consolidated into packets to make this program easy-to-follow to ensure that you do not miss any necessary nutrients. Replace any two of your daily meals with our delicious and nutritious shakes, take your all-natural supplements, then for your third meal have a S.M.A.R.T. meal using our guidelines. Your shakes, supplements, and S.M.A.R.T. meal will provide you everything you need to stay clean, satisfied, get rid of cravings, burn fat, and feel happy.

Plant-based, gluten-free, dairy-free, soy-free, grain-free, sugar-free, non-GMO, no artificial ingredients or sweeteners, paleo meal

Benefits

- **Boost your metabolism** to lose that extra weight, become a **fat-burning** machine, and preserve **lean body** mass.
- Keep your **hormones in balance** to control your appetite, increase fat burn, and improve your mood.
- Keep **blood sugar in balance** to burn fat instead of storing fat, prevent insulin resistance, and maintain steady levels of energy and a good, calm mood.
- Maintain **healthy cholesterol levels** to support your heart health.
- Keep your **body clean and nourished** to control those powerful cravings for sugar and unhealthy foods, strengthen your immune system and your gut health, and feel energized all day.
- **LOOK** and **FEEL AMAZING**, so much that . . . others will notice!

Flavors: Chocolate and vanilla that mix perfectly with all types of ingredients.

Flaca Get Lean™ is the simple, satisfying and effective way to GET LEAN and Fully Nourished!*

STEP 3: **Flaca Stay Lean**™: The healthy way to start every day! It's an all-in-one shake to stay lean, healthy, and happy. Great source of clean protein, nutrients, and fiber for everyone in the family, including kids. You can make shakes, add it to smoothies, or prepare delicious and nutritious snacks with it.

It is a truly superior plant-based functional food powder made with all-natural ingredients and designed to support healthy weight loss and weight management.* Promotes an optimal intake of protein, vitamins, minerals, and fiber to help you maintain muscle as you lose fat.

Plant-based, gluten-free, dairy-free, soy-free, grain-free, sugar-free, non-GMO, no artificial ingredients or sweeteners, Paleo Meal

Benefits

- Get an **optimal intake of protein, vitamins, minerals, and fiber**.
- **Maintain muscle** as you lose fat.
- **Excellent array of amino acids** including healthy levels of the important BCAAs (branched chain amino acids) that are especially helpful for maintaining lean muscle mass while losing weight.
- **Fiber and glucomannan** to help control appetite, keep weight under control, help improve lean body mass, and strengthen GI health.

Flavors: Chocolate and Vanilla that mix perfectly with all types of ingredients

Flaca Stay Lean™ **is the simple, delicious, and healthy way to start every day.***

SNACKS: Flaca Choco-coconut™ **Healthy Snack Bars** - with advanced prebiotic fibers and loaded with anti-oxidants. The

Healthy way to stay energized and nourished in-between meals or while on-the-go. Great alternative for the kids. They'll love it.

Plant-based, gluten-free, dairy-free, soy-free, grain-free, sugar-free, non-GMO, no artificial ingredients or sweeteners, paleo meal

Benefits

- **A sweet treat that is healthy** and does not impact your blood sugar (only 1 gram of sugar).
- **Stay energized the healthy way**. Its coconut oil can be easily converted to fuel for your body and brain.
- **Keep blood sugar stable** so you can stay energized throughout the day, keep your mood stable and happy, and prevent overproduction of insulin, which increases fat storage and eventually can lead to insulin resistance and diabetes.
- **Strengthens immune system and gut health** with the combination of prebiotic fibers and coconut that support digestive and immune systems, mineral absorption, and PH balance.
- Stay **satisfied** and in **control** of your **cravings** with the healthy fats from the creamy coconut filling and the prebiotic fiber.
- **Anti-oxidant** rich dark chocolate cover that boosts your mood and protects the body from the damage of free radicals.
- **Antibacterial and antivirus properties** from the coconut and coconut oil that help you stay healthy.

Flavor: Dark chocolate cover and smooth coconut filling. A delicious healthy bar that competes in taste with any chocolate bar.

Flaca Choco-Coconut™ is the healthy snack to stay energized and healthy in between meals or on-the-go.*

*These statements have not been evaluated by the Food and Drug Administration. These products are not intended to diagnose, treat, cure or prevent any diseases.

Are Flaca Forever® Programs Right for You?

I am committed to helping you get in the best shape of your life: physically, mentally, and emotionally. And to accomplish this I have created a program specifically for you where:

- You will get the tools to conquer the weight-loss battle for good without having to starve yourself, needing to exercise excessively, or needing to complicate your life.
- You will learn about the power of nutrition. It impacts every area of your life, not only the way you look, but also the way you think, the way you feel, and the way you live.
- You will live a happier, more satisfying life while getting empowered and inspired to reach your dreams and full potential.
- You will learn how to quickly get back on track when life takes you off your healthy path.

Here are some of the many things you will be able to leave in the past through the help of the Flaca Forever® program:

- No more worrying about not being ready to show up and look good and healthy at a moment's notice.
- No more 2-week restrictive diets to lose those 5 or 10+ pounds to be ready for the beach, the pool, or the tight dress.

- No more losing those 5 or 10 pounds, and then immediately gaining them back plus more.
- No more compromising your future wellness because you are eating for comfort or for weight loss.
- No more lacking knowledge on how to eat the S.M.A.R.T. and healthy way.
- No more being frequently sick and missing out on a lot of fun events and occasions.
- No more taking antibiotics and medicines for recurring physical or emotional health problems.

Flaca Forever® Programs Are Right for You If You Can Answer Yes to Any of the Following:

- You have been on two or more diets in the last 12 months, and you are still not at your ideal weight.
- You have been doing all the necessary things to lose weight but have not been successful in losing it or keeping it off.
- You get bored or very hungry with most of the diets you have tried.
- You want to learn how to eat healthier but don't know where to start.
- You frequently feel uncomfortable after eating: feeling bloated, gassy, or experiencing indigestion.
- You are tired of not having sufficient energy throughout the day, particularly in the early afternoons.
- You have been suffering from any of the following health symptoms: asthma, sinus infections, frequent colds and congestion, joint pain, difficulty concentrating, or unrestful or interrupted sleep.
- You are done with the struggle. You want to change.

- You don't want to follow this journey alone. You want to be part of a group of strong and like-minded women who will inspire and support each other to be their best.
- And more importantly, you want to avoid major diseases like the ones we discussed earlier in this book.

If you answered yes to any of the items above, then you are in the right place, and we want to invite you to consider joining our community. To learn more about our products and programs, please contact us at info@flacaforever.com or visit us at www.flacaforever.com.

I want to save you some time by also sharing with you what our programs and products are not about.

This Program Is NOT Right for You If:

- You are looking for a quick fix or magic pills and solutions.
- You prefer short-term versus long-term gains.
- You are not interested in your future health and wellness.
- You don't like to or want to invest in yourself.
- You believe that the future is the right time to start worrying about yourself, your weight, and your health.
- You are too busy with your life and responsibilities that you have NO time to take better care of yourself.
- You quit and give up easily, and do not respond well to motivation, encouragement, or inspiration to keep going. When you face a challenge or an obstacle, you just isolate yourself and stop responding to those that want to support you or help you.
- You want to get results but are not willing to follow the advice or use the tools given to you. When you don't advance, you blame others for your fate.

- You are not willing to consider new ways of eating and dealing with the stresses and challenges in your life.

If you answered yes to any of the points above, then our programs and products may not be right for you.

If you are not sure, we will be happy to help you figure it out. Contact us at info@flacaforever.com.

CONCLUSION-BEGIN THE BEST PART OF YOUR LIFE TODAY!

I hope that you have found this book to be a wealth of knowledge and an inspiration for you to begin the journey to transform your life and achieve absolute wellness. Through the satisfying and yummy recipes in this book and the perfect combination of S.M.A.R.T. foods, you will lose weight with "Healthy Eating That Feels Like Cheating™."

If you haven't made this change today, stop putting it off, telling yourself tomorrow is the day that you will make a change. Make today the day you commit to changing your life, losing weight, and achieving everything you have dreamed of!

Through the information on S.T.U.P.I.D. foods and details on the obesity bomb, you have enough knowledge to empower yourself to enter the best phase of your life and save your life. Start today on this wonderful journey towards absolute and true wellness, and see how you can feel better than you ever imagined.

Once you have lost the weight the S.M.A.R.T. way, you will notice that for the first time in your life, you are not struggling to keep it off. This will be the time to reward yourself with new clothes. You have a new-found confidence to shop now that you know that the excess weight that once held you back is gone. And it is not coming back! You will be feeling sexier and more confident than you ever have before. This happened to me and has happened to all my clients. It will make all your efforts totally worth it!

Now, even if you are committed to this change of lifestyle, there are times you may get tripped up and life gets in the way. I must be very watchful myself.

When You Fall Off Track . . . Get Back On!

There are many stresses in life that can cause you to leave the path of wellbeing. Perhaps you've been traveling a lot, had too many social events, a loved one is sick or has passed away, you lost your job or just hate it, or a relationship has failed. These things can make you want to give up and look to food as a comfort. It is important to remember that it is okay to get off track. Hopefully, over time, you will find that S.M.A.R.T. foods can be your best allies in these times of duress while S.T.U.P.I.D. foods will make everything much harder to overcome.

In the meantime, you should get back on track as quickly as possible. The best way to get back on track is to remember how much better you felt when you were living your healthy lifestyle, and do an effective detox to feel reset and renewed. And then continue your healthy path that you will get so in love with.

Get Clean and Lean Masterclass: Learn the SIMPLE WAY TO GET BACK TO YOUR BALANCED STATE

In part 4, you learned about all my amazing Flaca Forever® programs. Because you have already started detoxing in the 7 days on the Mexican Food Diet™, you are ready to take it to the next level. It is very simple, and I offer a FREE Get Clean and Lean Detox Masterclass to help you dive into this very important area of detoxification.

REGISTER HERE FOR MY FREE GET CLEAN AND LEAN DETOX MASTERCLASS:

www.flacaforever.com/detox-tutorial

Any time that there's a period where you feel like you have not eaten as healthy as you should, even if it is just for a week while on vacation, you should do a detox for at least three days to reset your body. A periodic detox will be beneficial to jump-start your weight loss again and reset your health. My Flaca Detox™ Reset and Renew Program is amazing for these purposes. You can learn more about it on www.FlacaDetox.com.

In the Flaca Forever® programs, we help you set new goals in all areas of your life and act on your long-held dreams. The S.M.A.R.T. eating you will learn will open new possibilities in every area of your life. Imagine a new career. Starting a new business. Learning how to play a new sport or instrument. Some of these ideas will open for you when you start looking, feeling, and thinking better than ever. I have seen it happen many times. I will be there behind you, inspiring you, supporting you, celebrating you, and most of all, being SUPER proud of how far you have come!

It is never too late to get in the best shape of your life: physically, mentally, and emotionally. I am committed to helping you achieve this goal.

I did it, and I know you can too!

I will see you in the kitchen!

My love,

Maru

REFERENCE SECTION

INDEX

1. OBESIITY-RELATED DISEASES

OBESITY and Inflammation

Your fat tissues consist of a lot of different cell types. One of these cell types (adipocytes) stores body fat and releases a type of chemical that is the most potent inflammatory chemical. The more fat there is, the more of these inflammatory chemicals there are too. Researchers have found that obese individuals secrete 50% more of these chemicals than normal weight individuals.

Once your body starts to secrete a lot of these chemicals, they begin to target your body tissues and are capable of also destroying your brain tissues, eventually leading to Alzheimer's. They can also damage the cells of your pancreas, leading to diabetes. Also importantly, increased inflammation compromises the integrity of certain cells that line your blood vessels. With these cells gone, your chances of having hypertension and a heart attack increase.

OBESITY and Autoimmunity

The story doesn't end here. Obesity is an "immune stimulating" condition too. The immune system is your body's first line of defense against invading viruses and bacteria. However, obesity makes your immune system function in an aberrant fashion. That's what researchers call "auto-immunity."

Autoimmunity is a process in which your body's defense systems backfire. Instead of protecting your body, they start to destroy your body's own systems. Researchers believe obesity plays a central role in the development of autoimmune diseases as well.

Your immune system has certain cells that can recognize any threat to your body and then destroy the threat. Fat tissues contain some other cell types that release another bad chemical. This chemical stimulates the immune system's specialized cells and makes them destroy your body's own tissues. Researchers have found that the amount of immune system cells is much higher in obese individuals, and together, with the other inflammatory chemicals, these destroy body structures like joints. No wonder joint diseases are so common among obese individuals.

As you can see, there are many things that when combined, leave you with a high level of internal inflammation and an overactive immune system. This unhealthy combination can eat up your body from within, and as a result, you can end up falling prey to countless diseases.

OBESITY and Infertility

Another hormonal complication of obesity is infertility, both in males and females. That, again, is due to the detrimental effects of obesity on your hormonal profile. Both male and female fertility is possible because of an intricate balance between many hormones. Researchers found that obese women are extremely prone to develop infertility due to decreased levels in certain hormones.

OBESITY and Type 2 Diabetes

Type 2 diabetes is a disease that is not hereditary. It is what is called a lifestyle disease, which implies that the choices of how you live your life are the main causes for this disease. One of the most important choices is unhealthy eating, in particular, a diet that is high in sugar and refined carbohydrates. What is sad is that this disease can be prevented in most cases, but once it is acquired, it is not easily cured.

Most people suffering from type 2 diabetes are often obese. Type 2 diabetes is a metabolic disorder characterized by insulin resistance. Simply put, insulin is produced by your pancreas to control glucose levels in your blood. When your blood sugar level rises, it starts a chain of events that sends signals to the pancreas to secrete insulin, which in turn, reduces your blood sugar levels and stops the secretion of more insulin through a feedback mechanism.

When insulin must be produced too frequently, your body cells become more resistant to it. As a result, your body cells are unable to use the secreted insulin properly and your blood sugar remains high.

One of the reasons that insulin resistance begins is that there is a certain protein that is released by fat cells that can desensitize liver cells to the effects of insulin. When liver cells become resistant to insulin, sugar levels stay high in your blood, which keeps sending signals to the pancreas to produce more insulin. Eventually, pancreatic cells exhaust and are unable to produce enough insulin. In the worst cases, insulin production stops altogether.

It should be clear by now to you that obesity leads to the production of toxic substances in your body that disrupt its metabolism and set a stage for the onset of type 2 diabetes as well as the other diseases.

OBESITY and Cancer

The rise in obesity has increased the incidence of cancer too. There are many reasons why this has happened. Among them:

- Obese people have a high level of oxidative stress in their body which means their body has a lot of toxins inside of it. These toxins affect cellular membranes, causing changes in cell function and resulting in cells becoming abnormal and dividing uncontrollably, which means they become cancerous.
- Obesity leads to insulin resistance, a condition that increases the levels of insulin-like growth factor-1 (IGF-1) in your body. Abundance of IGF-1 in blood also contributes to certain types of cancerous tumors.
- Fat cells are passionate about secreting some hormones called adipokines. Some of these hormones have strong cell proliferative abilities, which can promote abnormal cell growth in your body and cause cancers of different organs.

- Fat cells also impact tumor regulators in your body. These tumor regulators are responsible for keeping a check on your cell proliferation. Fat cells affect them negatively, and as a result, abnormal cell proliferation becomes a possibility.

- Obese women have high levels of the hormone estrogen, which contributes significantly to the formation of breast cancer. According to researchers, obese females are as much as 3 times more prone to develop breast cancer as compared to non-obese females. Researchers suspect that it is mainly due to an increased level of estrogen. Researchers found that levels of this hormone were as much as 4 times higher in obese females, which made them more prone to breast cancer.

OBESITY and Brain Health

Obesity can cause many other diseases including brain disorders. Believe it or not, obesity affects your brain health more than you may realize. By brain health, I don't mean lower self-confidence and depression only. I am also talking about diseases like Alzheimer's, Parkinson's, and dementia.

Research shows an increased risk of Alzheimer's with increased body weight. The underlying mechanism is still unclear, but a theory has been floating around recently. It explains that obesity increases the probability of the accumulation of certain types of proteins in the brain. This accumulation leads to an increased incidence of Alzheimer's.

Obesity is also related to lower brain volume. The more fat there is in abdominal areas, the smaller the brain volume is. This devastating finding has forced us to believe that obesity increases the risk of dementia significantly. It can reduce your brain power and impair your intellectual capabilities. Another study shows that obesity is also involved in declining cognitive function of the brain.

Parkinson's is another degenerative disease of the brain. In this disorder, your brain runs out of dopamine levels, an important brain chemical, which disrupts the ability of your brain to communicate with your body. Obesity has a strong relation to Parkinson's disease. Dopamine has been found to have significant declines in obese individuals, making them more prone to getting Parkinson's.

OBESITY and Heart Disease

If you think your abdominal fat has nothing to do with your heart, then you need to reconsider. Obesity plays a vital role in disrupting your cardiovascular system by causing metabolic and hormonal disturbances, as briefly mentioned before. There are many cardiovascular diseases that surface once you put on weight. One is hypertension.

Hypertension is an increase in your blood pressure, which also shows up when you gain weight. As your weight increases, the heart must work harder to deliver blood to your whole body. This puts extra pressure on the heart, impacting blood pressure greatly. Increased production of many hormones, common in overweight people, is another cause of hypertension. Obesity also disturbs the kidneys by making them work harder as your blood pressure continues to increase.

Coronary Artery Syndrome

Coronary artery syndrome is a crippling heart disease directly related to obesity. Obesity disturbs fat metabolism and leads to high levels of cholesterol in your body. This impacts your liver and damages your cardiovascular system. Cholesterol can accumulate in your blood vessels and form "plaque" that hinder the blood circulation and may not allow oxygen to reach the heart properly. If your heart gets starved without enough nutrition and oxygen, a heart attack emerges.

Angina

Angina, a painful condition, arises when there is reduced blood supply to your heart. The most important cause for it is obesity. Obesity leads to the formation of plaque in the arteries (atherosclerosis) followed by inflammation in some cases. Blood doesn't reach your heart muscles, and they get oxygen deficient, causing severe pain and deteriorating heart health.

Obese individuals are several times more likely to have angina than individuals who maintain a healthy weight.

2. THE TYPES OF SUGAR

There are three types of sugar.

- Glucose is what is commonly referred to as blood sugar. It comes from the foods you eat. It is the body's preferred source of energy. Most of the carbs and sugars you eat are converted into glucose soon after entering your digestive tract. Glucose is then used immediately for energy to support your activities or body functions. What is not used right away is stored in muscle cells or the liver for later use. When blood sugar levels get high, insulin is secreted to help maintain blood sugar at healthy levels and to facilitate the entry of glucose into cells. When there is no more need for glucose (fuel) or capacity to store the excess glucose, it gets stored as fat.

- Fructose is a sugar found naturally in fruits and vegetables. It is also added to various drinks, such as sodas and juice drinks. Fructose is very different from glucose in several ways. First, it is not the preferred source of energy for the muscles and brain, while glucose is. Second, fructose is only metabolized in the liver and is converted more often and more easily into fat than glucose. Third, fructose does not have any effect on the two key hormones that control the use and storage of energy (insulin and leptin). When glucose reaches a high level, it triggers insulin production to bring levels down. Conversely, when fructose reaches high levels, it is just converted into fat, particularly belly fat.
- Sucrose is what you normally refer to as table sugar. Fruits and vegetables also contain sucrose. Sucrose consists of equal parts of glucose and fructose. When you consume sucrose, the glucose part will be used first for energy. Any excess energy from fructose will be stored for energy reserves or fat.

3. UNHEALTHY CARBS

Here are some of the most common refined and processed carbs that you need to be aware of and avoid as much as possible:

- All refined and simple sugars (frequently called "added sugars")
- All desserts (except whole fruit)
- All types of dough
- Bagels
- Barbecue sauces
- Breaded or battered food

- Breads (all colors)
- Cakes
- Candies
- Caramel corn and kettle corn
- Coffee drinks
- Corn chips
- Crackers
- Croutons
- Dried fruit
- Flours
- Fried vegetable snacks
- Fruit juices and smoothies
- Honey mustard
- Honey-roasted nuts
- Ice cream, sherbets, sorbets, frozen yogurt
- Instant and refined grains: instant oatmeal, white rice, and instant rice
- Jellies, jams, and preserves
- Jello
- Ketchup
- Many salsas, sauces, dressings
- Most cereals
- Most granola bars, power bars, and energy bars
- Most pastas, noodles, and couscous
- Most rice cakes and corn cakes
- Muffins
- Pancakes
- Panko crumbs
- Pastries

- Pizza
- Pretzels
- Puddings and custards
- Refined starches: corn starch, potato starch, and modified food starch
- Rice wrappers
- Sweetened dairy products
- Sweetened drinks
- Sweetened sodas
- Tortillas

ACKNOWLEDGMENTS

This book began as a freebie download with a few recipes to be used to get my name out to the world. However, soon I began to see that too many people needed help in losing weight in a healthy way and transforming or optimizing their health. I realized that the clear majority of these people may not have the resources to pay for one of my programs or buy some of my amazing products. At that moment, I knew I had to write a book, which would make my message reachable to a larger audience.

Without even realizing it, this idea rapidly turned into a reality, and here I am, an international bestselling author and a frequent speaker and TV guest. As of today, my book has been featured on the news in TV stations around the country. As I am wrapping up this second version of this book, I am so happy that I did it. I must admit that it has been a LOT more work than I ever imagined. However, looking back, I can see that most of the times when I have taken a leap or done bigger things, I was never fully aware of the effort it was going to take. But because I had committed to the goal or project, and most of the times done so in an irreversible way (such as declaring my goal in public or paying money for a race), I ended up putting all the time and effort, and finding the necessary support and resources to do it.

Having said all that, this book is no exception: I declared my intention and found all the support and resources to do it. So, nothing would have been possible without all of you.

To my love, Andrew. You have always been supportive of me and all my dreams. You helped me fulfill the most important one: becoming a mom. Every day I thank you and God for this amazing gift. You helped me see how much unused potential I had and have always been been there for me, continuously looking for ways to support my dreams. I appreciate your patience and understanding during the "cooking up a storm" for several days to prepare for the photo shoot for the recipes of this book (yes, the kitchen was upside down), for allowing us to turn our living room into a photo studio for a week, and for understanding my lack of free time during the many months of very hard and uninterrupted work to finish this book or to travel around the country promoting it. And, very importantly, I want to thank you for being my expert meal tester (a.k.a. guinea pig) when I was selecting the recipes for this book. I love you!

To my adorable Charlotte. Your beautiful face, endless love, and perpetual smile remind me of why it is important to do everything that is in my control to stay healthy and to teach you how to do it too. You have brought so much happiness to my life. I am enjoying every second of seeing you grow. You inspire me to be the greatest role model possible. I love you!

To Avery and Isabel. You have been wonderful testers of the recipes as well and given me great feedback. I hope that my story inspires you to take great care of yourselves. Seeing the amazing opportunities you both have motivates me to spread my message of how powerful nutrition is in shaping your future. I love having you in my life. Love you!

To Rosy and Laura. You were my unconditional support team in preparing, cooking, and cleaning during endless weeks of recipe trials where there was food all over. You have also been my right and left hands in managing the house and my daughter while I have been writing, rewriting, or promoting this book. Thank you!

To my mom. You are an amazing chef, a very successful caterer, and the best mother I could wish for. Your endless love and generosity teach me every day how to be a better person all around. You exposed me to cooking from a very early age and allowed me to do all my crazy businesses selling cakes and then chocolate-based desserts. I look forward to co-writing a recipe book with you soon. And as you know, when I declare it, it happens. Thank you, and I love you!

To my dad. You always told me I could do whatever I set my mind to. You supported me in getting the best education so that I could be prepared for taking advantage of all of the opportunities that I have encountered. You also taught me how to be optimistic no matter what the circumstances were. Thank you! I love you!

To my brother. Your work ethic, focus, and discipline have already taken you very far. You make me very proud and inspire me to do the same. You have been the rock of our family. Thank you! I love you!

To JJ Virgin. This book would not have been possible without your incredible insights and knowledge of the health and wellness industry. When I shared my vision and my dreams with you, you had so much faith in me and tons of generous support. I can now say that this rocket has launched thanks to you, JJ. I am grateful for all that you have taught me and continue to teach me. I have enjoyed and benefited very much from being part of your Mastermind Program. You have also been a role model to me in many ways. Thank you, JJ!

To my YPO Forum. I still remember that retreat where we set our goals for the year. You all decided to adopt my goal of doing a triathlon for the first time, and this moment was my tipping point. I cannot thank you enough for that and the many times and hours we spent helping each other grow in every way. Love you all!

To Andi Neugarten. You are an amazing triathlete, friend, and businesswoman. You have been an amazing role model through your discipline and dedication as a triathlete, in your life, and in your business. You accepted me into your "A" Team for Alii Sport. This move was a critical part for me to overcome the depression I had been suffering from for a long time. You offered our team a detox program that helped me identify the impact that certain foods were having on my physical and emotional health. Your love and support during my tougher times were also fundamental. I will always be grateful to you!

To Tamara Renee. You introduced our racing team to the fabulous detox program that helped me begin to realize that my health issues were related to food intolerances. Had I not discovered this, my health would have continued to deteriorate. You opened my eyes to this fabulous world of nutrition, which has become my passion. I am lucky and grateful to have found you.

To Diane Halfman. Your professional organizing services and coaching have given me amazing tools for taking my home, office, life, and business to the next level. I look forward to continue learning from you. Thank you!

To Sandra Veum. You helped me get rid of all of the clothing from my past, and through your amazing personal shopper services, helped me get the new clothes I required for my new life. You gave me the courage to stop hiding and helped me feel more confident and beautiful. Your positive spirit and your permanent smile were very nurturing in difficult times. Thank you.

To Robin Stark. I met Andrew and now have Charlotte thanks to you. You have been very supportive, fun, and loving to me in many ways and through many years. You are an amazing aunt to Charlotte. I love your work ethic, unstoppable energy, and unlimited knowledge of wine. You gave me unlimited support during my dark period. Thank you!

To Adri. You have been the sunshine in my life already several times. I love your laughter, your optimism, your love for life, and how fun you are. You have helped me remember who I really am in those times when I have forgotten. Thank you for the many hours you have held my hand and lent me you ear. Love you!

To Jennifer. You are an amazing friend. You were right next to me in the most difficult time of my life. You and Gordon were critical and very generous to me. You gave me the right amount of love, support, and push to get me back on track and working towards my better self. I love seeing how dedicated and passionate you are in all that you do. It has inspired me in many ways. Love you!

To Charlie and Jen. The early discussions with you were instrumental to help me define how to start this journey. Your previous business successes have been very valuable and have inspired me. Thank you, and I love you guys!

To Jeremy Glazer, who has made amazing introductions that have made this book possible. You have also been very generous with your time and expert advice when I have needed it. Thank you!!!!!

To Mitch and Lynn. You have each been great role models for me and Charlotte, and a very strong source of love and support when I have needed it. Love you guys. Thank you!

To Elisa, Ilia, and Kyndra, who have always been there for me, particularly in the hardest times. I could not have survived or be where I am today without you. I love you all! Thank you!

To Pattie and Tricia. Thank you for being in my life, for inspiring me and supporting me, and for always being there for me while I go all out for my dreams. Love you!

To all my friends from JJ's Mastermind. You are all very generous in sharing your expertise and business learnings. I have been inspired by each of your successes. I have learned and keep learning every day from you. Thank you!

To Lisa Sasevich and my Sassy Mastermind friends. You all have been very supportive and inspiring in my journey. I have enjoyed sharing this ride with all of you. Thank you!

To Mike Koenings, Ed Rush, and the Publish and Profit community. I have learned a lot from you and all the people in the community. You pushed me to launch this book, and I will always be grateful!

To Alan De Herrera (photography), Cindy Epstein (Food Styling), and Betsy Haley (Food Styling). You were the best team I could have chosen. You helped me make my delicious recipes look even yummier. Each of you were so supportive, dedicated, and passionate about my dream. You made those long work days very fun. Thank you!

To John North. It has been an absolute pleasure to work with you on this second edition. You have gone out of your way to help me have a beautiful, high-quality book.

To my clients, readers, and viewers. You are my fuel to keep pursuing my dreams. To all of you who may benefit from my message, may you never forget that:

Success is failure turned inside out,

The silver tint of the clouds of doubt,

And you never can tell how close you are;

it may be near when it seems so far.

So, stick to the fight, when you're hardest hit,

It's when things seem worst that you must not quit.

ABOUT THE AUTHOR

Maru Dávila is a celebrity weight-loss expert and healthy chef. She is the creator of the Flaca Forever® brand to help people get in the best shape of their life: physically, mentally, and emotionally through the power of "Healthy Eating That Feels Like Cheating™."

Maru is a #1 international best-selling author, a certified Integrative Nutrition Health Coach, a graduate of Harvard Business School, a serial entrepreneur, a former competitive triathlete and marathon runner, and most importantly, a MOM of a 7-year-old girl and stepmom to two young adults.

Maru is determined to inspire and empower people to get healthy, lose weight, and improve their mood with delicious food. She is an expert in achieving big and difficult goals. She is fun and passionate, creative, disciplined, determined but patient, understanding, and daring. Her main guiding principle is "Don't Quit"!

Although she has achieved major goals, she has also had to overcome major challenges and setbacks. She suffered from eating disorders starting at age 15 and all through her 30s. She struggled with her weight for almost 30 years, always losing weight and gaining it back plus more. At one point she gained 60 pounds. She was also affected by depression for 20 years, went through multiple failed relationships, and got into major financial difficulties in her early 40s. After decades of permanent yo-yo dieting, self-neglect and ignorance of how much her unhealthy eating and other habits were affecting her health, she finally began to have multiple problems including the beginnings of an autoimmune disease, leaky gut, and chronic sinus infections among many others, all of which she has been able to overcome and control through her own products and programs. And finally, she was able to lose the weight and keep it off without hunger, deprivation or excessive exercising.

Today, Maru's passion is to empower and inspire people to get back in control of their weight, their health, and their life, so that they can stop the struggles in any of these areas.

Her programs are simple and fun, and do not include boring or restrictive diets that don't work for the long term. Instead, her passion is in finding Healthy Eating That Feels Like Cheating™.